Empire and Revolution

David Horowitz

E M P I R E

and Revolution:

A Radical Interpretation of Contemporary History

VINTAGE BOOKS

A DIVISION OF RANDOM HOUSE/NEW YORK

Acknowledgment is hereby made to the Council on
Foreign Relations for permission to quote from "Lenin
and Mussolini" by Harold J. Laski, which originally
appeared in *The Foreign Affairs Reader*, edited by
Hamilton Fish Armstrong, Harper & Row, New York,
publisher for the Council on Foreign Relations.
Copyright 1947 by Council on Foreign Relations, Inc.
The Clarendon Press for permission to quote from *The
New Economics*, by E. Preobrazhensky, translated by
Brian Pearce, The Clarendon Press, Oxford, 1965.

Library of Congress Catalog Card Number: 69-16446

Manufactured in the United States of America

VINTAGE BOOKS EDITION, SEPTEMBER 1970

Acknowledgments

I wish to express my debt to Ralph Miliband, who, besides offering useful criticism at several stages of composition, has been a constant source of encouragement and help to me in my labors. I would also like to thank Sam Coleman, Dieter Pevsner, Peter Wright, Alice Mayhew, John Spitzer, Bob Fitch and my parents for critical comments on the text, and Ralph Schoenman and Ernest Tate for critical discussion of the issues, all of which helped to make this a more balanced and coherent work than it otherwise would have been.

Finally, I wish to thank the Louis M. Rabinowitz Foundation, Bertrand Russell and The Bertrand Russell Peace Foundation for their material support during the period of preparation and writing.

London, October 1967

In memory of
ISAAC DEUTSCHER

The triumph of imperialism leads to the decay of culture—temporary decay during any modern war, or complete decay, if the era of world wars that has begun were to last and go on to its final conclusion.

Now therefore, . . . we stand . . . before this choice: either the triumph of imperialism and the devastation of all culture, as in ancient Rome—devastation, depopulation, degeneration, a huge cemetery; or the victory of socialism . . .

—Rosa Luxemburg, 1915

Contents

I

BOLSHEVIK MARXISM:

A PERSPECTIVE

Introduction

> The developing pressure of the proletariat, and especially its victories in individual countries, are strengthening the resistance of the exploiters and impelling them to new forms of international consolidation . . . which, organizing on a world scale the systematic exploitation of all the peoples of the earth, are directing their first efforts toward the immediate suppression of the revolutionary movements of the proletariat of all countries. All this inevitably leads to a combination of civil wars within the separate states with revolutionary wars, both of the proletarian countries defending themselves, and of the oppressed peoples against the yoke of the imperialist powers.
> —Bolshevik Party Program, 1919

Half a century after the Russian Revolution, and more than two decades since the inception of the cold war, the shape of contemporary history is beginning to look more and more like the classical conception of the early Bolsheviks: an epoch of revolutionary insurgencies and counterrevolutionary interventions, of civil wars within states and of international class wars between states, of global struggle between old capitalist powers and new revolutionary regimes. To be sure, the early Bolsheviks would probably not have recognized in some of these capitalist powers or revolutionary regimes the classical images of their own conceptions. Moreover, the very duration of the struggle—the survival of the

international capitalist system so long after the turning of
1917—they would not have expected. Nonetheless, the "class"
character of present-day conflicts accords more with the original Bolshevik perspective than with any other. It is not for
nothing that "Leninism" remains still the revolutionary watchword of the world.

No doubt international politics in the postwar period
have not always had such an emphatically "Bolshevik" character. Until very recently the international political scene
may well have seemed to be governed exclusively by the aims
and objectives of national power blocs and their ruling
groups, while class and class interests remained subsidiary to
the real conflicts and struggles. But as the high tide of cold
war in Europe receded—with the partial détente between
Russia and the United States and the breakup of the monolithic unity of the Communist camp—this view has become
increasingly difficult to maintain.

Recent interventions in Cuba and Santo Domingo, and
guerrilla struggles in Guatemala, Venezuela, the Congo and
South Vietnam, for example, can hardly be regarded as mere
epiphenomena of the rivalries between great continental nation-states. More and more clearly, these revolutionary antagonisms and the wars to which they give rise can be seen to
emanate directly from the local soils in which their roots take
hold. With this development, the cold war has begun to enter
what might be called the era of its authenticity: the international class war of the Bolshevik conception has at last begun
to come into its own.

Of course, it is not simply the Bolshevik schema. The
world has changed too profoundly in fifty years to be
understood through the unchanged concepts of so "distant"
a past. Moreover, the task of creating a contemporary revolutionary perspective must involve more than merely bringing
Bolshevik analyses "up to date." For the charge laid on Bolshevism by half a century of history includes far more than
the mere obsolescence of some of its concepts and intuitions.

Having made a revolution in Russia, Bolshevism is now laden with responsibility for the consequences of that revolution. Having been the guide to more than one subsequent seizure of power, it must account for the uses that have been made of that power, and for the state systems to which it has helped to give birth. Fifty years after the Russian October, an adequate perspective must analyze a world in which revolution not only challenges imperialism from the shadows but where it has already gained a foothold on the center stage, where "revolutionary" powers coexist with imperialist powers and confront them as part of an international status quo of nation-states.

To assess the failures and successes of the Bolshevik outlook and program is an enterprise fraught with difficulties. It is made infinitely more difficult, however, by the false and faulty representations of Bolshevism which have proliferated during decades of ideological conflict.

Thus, unlike its image as it is presented in the hostile West or as it is reflected in the present official Soviet mirror, Bolshevik Marxism was an extremely supple and analytically penetrating theoretical perspective. While "Marxism" is often reproached, for example, with not having anticipated the triumph of proletarian revolution in backward countries, like Czarist Russia, Bolshevik Marxists not only entertained this possibility beforehand but actively prepared themselves to achieve such a primitive socialist conquest of power.

Similarly, it is often suggested that the vital connection between socialist and nationalist revolutions which has been such a characteristic feature of the present historical period has no place in Marxist theory, lies outside its framework, and was completely unanticipated by its early adherents. Yet the Bolsheviks—with Lenin preeminent among them—were especially concerned with the relation between the national and the social revolutions in backward and oppressed countries, and were among the first to understand their interconnection.[1] In his "Last Testament," Lenin decried the Great Russian Chauvinism displayed by Stalin and Dzerzhinsky,[2] and expressed his apprehension that it would permeate the central state apparatus. For such chauvinism, Lenin maintained, would do infinite harm, "not only to us, but to the whole International, and to the hundreds of millions of the peoples of Asia, who are destined to come forward on the stage of history in the near future, following us."

Probing beneath the surface of nineteenth-century "peace" and "progress," the revolutionary Marxists, unlike their liberal antagonists, had seen capitalism as a basically predatory and expansionist social system. They were not disoriented, therefore, by the conflagration which civilized Europe unleashed on the world in 1914. While in the ensuing war hysteria the other parties[3] threw their support to the general slaughter in the sanctified names of "peace," "honor," "democracy," and "defense of the fatherland," the Bolsheviks had the integrity and fortitude to denounce the conflict, and to expose its basis in the clash of rival imperialisms. (This did not mean, as many of their later critics sought to imply, that the Bolsheviks thought the causes of the war could be reduced to rational profit-and-loss calculations. Chauvinistic nationalism, to mention but one "irrational" element, was for them an integral aspect of imperialist systems[4] and one of the factors that lay behind the great conflict.)

----

[1] Lenin's positive attitude toward national self-determination was, of course, one of the chief points of his theoretical conflict with Rosa Luxemburg. Some of his most important writings on the subject are collected in the booklet *Questions of National Policy and Proletarian Internationalism* (Moscow, n.d.). Cf. also E. H. Carr, *The Bolshevik Revolution 1917–1923*, Vol. I, Part 3, and Note B, "The Bolshevik Doctrine of Self-Determination," and also Vol. III, Chap. 26 ("Revolution Over Asia"). For Rosa Luxemburg on the national question, see J. P. Nettl, *Rosa Luxemburg*, (New York: Oxford University Press, 1966), Vol. II, Appendix 2.
[2] Ironically, a Georgian and a Pole.
[3] Including the orthodox Marxist labor parties.
[4] See below, pp. 43–44.

In Russia itself, the Bolsheviks proved themselves to be the only party able to assess the developing situation correctly—in particular, the relative strengths of internal social forces and the revolutionary mood and will of the brutally exploited and war-bled Russian masses. More important, they proved themselves to be the only party which possessed sufficient determination to express and to enforce that will in respect to the crucial questions of land and peace. On the strength principally of these virtues, but also as a result of their tactical brilliance, the Bolsheviks were swept into power in the course of 1917, proclaiming that their national triumph was but the beginning of an era of *world* revolution. Revealing at once the secret treaties of annexation that had been agreed to by the warring capitalist powers, the Bolshevik leaders called for a "democratic" peace (no annexations, no indemnities, and self-determination for the oppressed peoples), and incited war-ravaged Europe against its discredited rulers and their system, which had shown itself to be so prodigal with human life and treasure for such venal ends.

The hatred which the triumphant Bolshevik Revolution engendered in the capitalist states owed its origins not least to this exposure, which, as the London *Times* "informed" its readers, came from "a band of anarchists and fanatics," among whom "Lenin and several of his confederates are adventurers of German-Jewish blood and in German pay." [5] The hostility with which the capitalist powers, under the leadership of democratic England and France, set out to strangle the exhausted rebel regime exposed perhaps more than anything else the class character of their own national politics, and in so doing, confirmed the validity of the Bolshevik indictment.

At this juncture there were increasing rumbles of revolt in several of the war-ruined states of Europe,[6] and the Bol-

---

[5] Cited in Arno J. Mayer, *Wilson versus Lenin* (New York: Meridian Books, 1964), p. 277. Mayer describes the *Times*' editorial as "stinging," but "representative" of Allied newspaper reaction to the Bolshevik initiative.

[6] For analyses of these abortive revolutions, see Helmut Gruber,

shevik leaders felt that they were destined soon to be joined in other countries by fraternal revolutionary forces. But the anticipated course of events went awry. What happened now to thwart the Bolsheviks' long-term projection was first the failure of the West European revolutions and especially the revolution in Germany, and then, in consequence, the unforeseen development of both the preserved capitalist regimes and the first surviving "socialist" state.

Surveying the international scene in 1920,[7] Lenin had concluded that as a result of the war the contradictions of the capitalist system had become "immeasurably more acute." The division of the world into a handful of oppressor nations and a majority of dependent, colonial and generally exploited peoples was still the main fact of international life conditioning "all the basic contradictions of capitalism, [i.e.,] of imperialism, which [were] leading up to revolution."

Among those countries which had been relegated "to what is equivalent to colonial status" was Germany, one of the most technically advanced, enlightened and cultured nations. The war itself had been fought, Lenin maintained, to decide which of the small groups of the dominant capitalist states—the British (subsequently backed by the Americans) or the German—was to obtain hegemony in the system of imperialist exploitation of the world's riches. Defeated in this conflict, Germany was reduced by the Treaty of Versailles "to a state of colonial dependence, poverty, starvation, ruin, and loss of rights," being bound for many generations and placed "in conditions that no civilized nation has ever lived in."

Germany was not the only country ruined by the conflict and reduced to a condition of dependence, moreover; the

---

International Communism in the Era of Lenin, a documentary history (New York: Fawcett, 1967).

[7] "Report on the International Situation and the Fundamental Tasks of the Communist International," July 19, 1920, *Collected Works* (London: Lawrence and Wishart), Vol. XXXI.

debts of all the principal European states had increased seven
fold in the period between 1914 and 1920. Indeed, the United
States had emerged as "the only full beneficiary from the
war," having been previously a heavy debtor and having now,
in the course of the European destruction, become a general
creditor and in effect the dominant capitalist world power.

As a witness to the depths of ruin to which Europe had
been brought not only by the war but by the victors' self-
revealing terms of peace, Lenin invoked the newly prominent
figure of John Maynard Keynes. Keynes, who had supported
the conflict and attended the Versailles negotiations as a British diplomat, had come to the conclusion that as a result of
the terms of peace Europe and the whole world were heading
for bankruptcy. He had therefore resigned and written a
book, *The Economic Consequences of the Peace,* which, as
Lenin put it, he had "thrown in the government's face with
the words: 'What you are doing is madness.'" In Lenin's
view, the example of Keynes's belated understanding and
consequent condemnation of the victors' policy was an indication of what was taking place and would take place "in the
minds of thousands and hundreds of thousands of people
when they realize that all the speeches about a war for democracy, etc., were sheer deception," and that as a result of
the war "only a handful of people were enriched, while the
others were ruined and reduced to slavery." [8]

---

[8] "Incidentally, I do not think any communist manifesto . . .
could compare in forcefulness with those pages in Keynes's book
which depict Wilson and 'Wilsonism' in action. Wilson was the
idol of philistines and pacifists like Keynes . . . who exalted the
'Fourteen Points' . . . they hoped that Wilson would save 'social
peace,' reconcile exploiters and exploited and bring about social
reforms. Keynes showed vividly how Wilson was made a fool of,
and all these illusions were shattered at the first impact with the
practical, mercantile and huckster policy of capital as personified
by Clemenceau and Lloyd George. The masses of the workers
now see more clearly than ever, from their own experience—and
the learned pedants could see it just by reading Keynes's book—

In Lenin's eyes the predatory war and its self-revealing peace had intensified the "revolutionary crisis" of capitalism, exacerbating both the internal antagonisms between exploiting and exploited classes and the external antagonisms between oppressor and oppressed nations. "All Germany is seething; so is all of Asia. . . . In Germany there is . . . hatred of the *Entente* as can only be understood by those who have seen the hatred of the German workers for their own capitalists. As a result, they have made Russia the immediate representative of the entire mass of the oppressed population of the earth, i.e., both of the 'oppressed classes' and the 'oppressed peoples.' " [9]

Subsequently Lenin was to speculate on the probable issue of these crises: on possible conflicts between Japanese imperialism and the United States, between the Western imperialist powers and the East's rising revolutionary nationalism; on the plight of Germany and its consequences for the socialist revolution in Europe. Cautious in the short run, he was optimistic for the future. In the last analysis, the outcome of the struggle would be determined by "the fact that Russia, India, China, etc., account for the overwhelming majority of

---

that the 'roots' of Wilson's policy lay in sanctimonious piffle, petty-bourgeois phrase-mongering, and an utter inability to understand the class struggle."—*ibid*. Cf. C. Wright Mills's characterization of contemporary liberalism: "It is doubtful that liberalism is in a position to designate the conditions under which the ideals it proclaims might be realized. It has been detached from any tenable theory of society and from any means of effective action." Accordingly, however engaging as a set of ideals, even these ideals in their abstracted and formal conditions are no longer useful "as guide lines for those who would by the will of men consciously modify the course of historical events."—*The Marxists* (Baltimore, Md., Penguin Books), p. 29.

[9] "Speech at a Meeting of Activists," December 6, 1920, in *Collected Works*, XXXI, 453. In recognition of the importance of the national struggle, Lenin even sanctioned the modification of the Communist Manifesto's central exhortation, "Workers of all countries *and* all oppressed peoples, unite!"

the population of the globe." During the previous few years, this majority had been "drawn into the struggle for emancipation with extraordinary rapidity." This meant that there could not be the "slightest doubt" what the final outcome of the world struggle would be, that "the complete victory of socialism" was "fully and absolutely assured." [10] As for the short run, though he recognized the existence of formidable obstacles, and that there could be no certainty about the form of events, he had little inkling of the "detour" that was in store for the world socialist revolution. Thus, in advanced Europe, for example, the revolution was to be more than merely delayed. When the crisis of German and European capitalism did eventually mature, it was dominated not by revolutionary socialism on the left, but by fascist reaction and its coalition of anti-Communist forces on the right.

The triumph of Nazism amid the economic collapse of German capitalism and the ruins of the Weimar Republic represented a precipitous descent into barbarism that no one in the early twenties, including the Russian Bolsheviks, had foreseen. Trotsky, for example, who was subsequently to show such foresight about the probable consequences of a Nazi success, had written in 1923 (apropos of Italy) that if the bourgeoisie remained in power, it would soon dispense with fascism, "for the bourgeoisie could not coexist for long with a fascist regime, just as the proletariat could not live for years in a state of armed insurrection." [11] Only later did it become apparent that fascism in general and Nazism in particular could not be regarded merely as the "expedient" of a dominant bourgeoisie for crushing the revolutionary Left, but that, as a coalescence of atavistic social and cultural forces operating in a basically *non*-bourgeois (although capitalist) environment,[12] it possessed dynamics of its own. Hitler's anti-Communist crusade not only destroyed the Left in Germany

---

[10] Lenin, "Better Fewer, But Better," March 4, 1923, in *Collected Works*, Vol. XXXIII.

[11] *Through What Stage Are We Passing?* (pamphlet), p. 23.

[12] See below, pp. 48–49, pp. 174 ff.

and launched a *Drang nach Osten,* but by ruthlessly smashing
the containing framework of the Versailles system and assert-
ing against it the national destiny of the German Reich,
brought German power into total collision with the European
victors as well, and thereby forged an unexpected alliance between Soviet Russia and its Western capitalist foes.

An even more important influence that deflected the
world socialist revolution from its expected course was the
path that developments took in the infant Soviet state. Had
the first socialist revolution triumphed in one of the advanced
capitalist countries, with fully developed productive and cultural forces as in the classical Marxist prescription, then the
course of the revolution's development not only on its home
ground but elsewhere as well might have evolved more
according to form. However, isolated and harried in its
primitive and miserable setting, the socialist revolution in
Russia could not begin to fulfill the expectations with which,
everywhere, it had been so heavily, and so hopefully, laden.

"It is a terrible misfortune," Lenin observed more than
once in the first years of Soviet power, "that the honor of
beginning the first socialist revolution should have befallen
the most backward people in Europe." [13] The unexpected destiny of the revolution in the half century to follow—not only
in backward Russia, but internationally as well—is bitterly
foreshadowed in Lenin's recurrent remark. The task facing
the Russian Bolsheviks, he wrote in his last article, was to hold
power until "the next military conflict between the counterrevolutionary West and the revolutionary and nationalist
East, between the most civilised countries of the world and
the countries backward in an oriental way, but which com-
prise the majority." "This majority," he added, "must become civilised. *We, too, lack enough civilisation to enable us
to pass straight on to socialism* [emphasis added], although we
do have the political requisites of it." [14]

---

[13] Reported by Victor Serge in his *Memoirs of a Revolutionary*
(New York: Oxford University Press, 1963), pp. 113 f.
[14] "Better Fewer, But Better."

In the speculations of Lenin and the Bolsheviks, at this time, there was not the slightest inkling that the Soviet regime would survive for a long period, without aid from revolutions in the West. In 1905, Trotsky had predicted that if the Russian working class found itself in power "only as the result of a temporary conjuncture of circumstances in our bourgeois revolution," and if no supporting revolutions came to its aid, then "the working class of Russia will inevitably be crushed by the counter-revolution, the moment the peasantry turns its back on it." [15] A decade and a half later, in March 1918, Lenin declared to the party cadres: "Regarded from the world-historical point of view, there would doubtlessly be no hope of the ultimate victory of our revolution if it were to remain alone, if there were no revolutionary movements in other countries." And even more concretely: "At all events, under all conceivable circumstances, if the German revolution does not come, we are doomed." Nevertheless, he added, "this does not in the least shake our conviction that we must be able to bear the most difficult position without blustering." [16]

In his very last article, Lenin stressed the importance of displaying "extreme caution" in an effort to preserve the regime and lay the foundations of an industrial base until the progress of the international revolution would consolidate

---

[15] *Results and Prospects* (New York: Pioneer), p. 247. This formulation expressed accurately the prerevolutionary perspective of the Bolsheviks, which remained unchanged until Lenin's death. Even Stalin in April 1924 was still writing: "To overthrow the bourgeoisie the efforts of one country are sufficient: this is proved by the history of our revolution. For the final victory of Socialism, *for the organization of Socialist production, the efforts of one country, particularly of a peasant country like Russia, are insufficient* [emphasis added]; for that, the efforts of the proletarians of several advanced countries are required."—*Leninism* (London: Allen & Unwin, 1940), p. 153.

[16] "Political Report of the Central Committee" to the Extraordinary Seventh Congress of the Russian Communist Party (Bolsheviks), March 7, 1918, in *Collected Works*, XXVII, 95, 98.

and make possible a decisive advance of the Bolshevik enterprise. It was this general perspective, auguring defeat on the
one hand, or unbroken if at first delayed advance on the
other, that was most irremediably confounded by events. For
in the end, the revolution survived—but in isolation. The
peasantry did eventually "turn its back" on the regime—but
the regime was not crushed and a collectivized economy was
established. Not surprisingly, the resultant development, both
internally and internationally, proved to be as unexpected
and unforeseen as its premises.

Chief among the unforeseen effects of the revolution's
survival and development in backward Russia was the complicating factor it introduced into the projected confrontation
between a progressive international socialist revolution and a
retrograde, reactionary capitalist world system, which had
hitherto been such an essential feature of the Bolshevik and
Marxist programs. In 1920, Lenin had noted that "soon after
the victory of the proletarian revolution in at least one of the
advanced countries, a sharp change will probably come
about: Russia will cease to be the model and will once again
become a *backward* country (in the 'Soviet' and the socialist
sense)." [17] This revolution in an advanced capitalist country,
however, was not realized, and for several decades Russia remained the sole "model" of socialist progress, with its in-
extricable combination of progressive and backward elements.

Another factor which played a complicating role during the ensuing historical period, and particularly the first
two decades of the cold war, was the emergence of the
United States of America to a towering position in the international capitalist system. As, in many respects, the most democratic of the capitalist powers, and the one least encumbered
by colonial empire, the United States was able to cast itself in
the role of offering a liberal opposition to the older European

---

[17] " 'Left-wing' Communism—An Infantile Disorder," in *Collected
Works*, XXXI, 21. Emphasis added.

imperialisms, appearing still to advance those democratic values that had been associated with the classical bourgeois revolutions of the preceding era. It was able, therefore, to imbue the capitalist system with an aura of progressive possibility, which had the effect of restoring a considerable measure of confidence and resilience to the badly shaken system, and of further blurring the lines of the historic confrontation.

This restorative role of American liberalism was in a sense first evidenced in the Wilsonian response to the Bolshevik Peace Decree. For where the older European powers had initially shown reluctance to take cognizance of the Bolshevik challenge and to make a gesture of renouncing their annexationist designs and secret diplomacy,[18] Wilson came forward with a bold answer and counter-challenge in the form of his famous Fourteen Points.[19]

Wilson's "counter-manifesto" also rejected secret diplomacy and endorsed the principle of self-determination (although it did so equivocally with regard to colonial territories outside Europe) and went further than the Bolsheviks by setting out proposals for general disarmament. These lofty principles were broadly accepted by the other capitalist powers, under U.S. pressure,[20] but despite these verbal commitments,

---

[18] Before and during the war, Western socialists and liberals had advocated parliamentary control of foreign policy. The Bolshevik Peace Decree not only stated that the Soviet "Government [had] abolished secret diplomacy" but also expressed its "firm intention to conduct all negotiations absolutely openly before the entire people."—Mayer, op. cit., p. 264.

[19] While Lloyd George had made an address which seemed to anticipate Wilson's points some weeks earlier, he had done so partly under the general American pressure toward such an initiative and in a way that left crucial points, e.g., regarding the territorial integrity of Russia, totally ambiguous.

[20] "Wartime necessity eventually compelled the Allied war cabinets to declare publicly their verbal adherence to the New Diplomacy. As early as July 21, 1917, Wilson predicted that 'when the war is over we can force them to our way of thinking, because by

were disregarded and overridden in the actual settlement at Versailles. Indeed, the principle of self-determination, the crux of the international program of Wilsonian liberalism, was openly violated by Wilson himself in his intervention against the Bolshevik revolution shortly after his declaration.

The failure of Wilsonian liberalism to move beyond the realm of pious rhetoric was fairly typical of the progressivism which America was to display in the international setting over the next decades, and reflected the essential ambiguity of American history: a revolutionary Republic—with imperial ambitions; a "free" society—wedded to slavery.

But just as the "New Diplomacy" did seem to many to provide a prospect and hope of enlightenment within capitalism in the era following the First World War, so in the depression decade of the thirties, the American New Deal seemed to many liberals to offer a way forward within capitalism which would avoid the alternatives of German fascism and the Soviet system under Stalin. Again, in the postwar period of the Second World War, despite the equivocal nature of the "free world" coalition and the ambiguous character of America's support for national independence in the underdeveloped world, Washington's gestures toward a more liberal international framework carried enough conviction to contain, temporarily, the forces of anticapitalist revolt. It required a changed international and domestic balance—new developments on the Soviet side of the equation, an antirevolutionary war in Southeast Asia, and the emergence of the black rebellion in the United States—to strip the free-world colossus of its progressive aura, and to expose its imperial chauvinism and the class nature of its international conflicts. These developments, however, did not begin to come until the second cold war decade, when the historical drama entered a new revolutionary phase.

---

that time they will, among other things, be financially in our hands.' The collapse of Russia and the Caporetto disaster increased the dependence of the Allies on the United States."—Mayer, *op. cit.*, p. 332.

1. Marxism and Revolution

> Without revolutionary theory, there can be no revolutionary movement.
> —Lenin, 1902

To understand Bolshevism as a revolutionary perspective, it must be distinguished, first, from the image of Marxism that has been established during half a century by the orthodoxies of the Second and Third Internationals,[1] and their anti-Marxist critics. Thus, in the orthodox image, Marxism appears as a straightforward economic determinism for which revolutionary changes in the structure of society occur as the simple reflex of revolutionary changes in the economic "base." If this view of Marx's theoretical perspective were as balanced and accurate as it is familiar, however, one would be compelled to conclude that the Bolsheviks were not "Marxists" at all. For the Bolshevik stress on the need to *create* a revolutionary consciousness, and to forge a vanguard party (shaped specifically for the revolutionary struggle), and above all the Bolsheviks' actual decision to seize power by a planned revolutionary insurrection can hardly be made to fit the framework of a theory of historical inevitability.

There are, in fact, two distinct strains of determinism which can be discerned in Marx's writings: one, the familiar *causal* determinism; the other, a *conditional* determinism, a theory of social action in terms of the possible.

The essence of this "conditional" perspective, as absorbed by the Bolsheviks, was most lucidly expressed by Marx in his historical essay on the coup d'état of Louis Napoleon: "Men make their own history," he wrote, "but they do

---

[1] Several Communist writers have begun in recent years, however, to modify their own previous orthodoxy.

not make it just as they please; they do not make it under circumstances chosen by themselves, but under circumstances directly encountered, given and transmitted from the past." [2] In Lenin's writings, the same "conditional" perspective is evident, and if anything even more pronounced: "The idea of historical necessity," he observed in an early essay, "does not in the least undermine the role of the individual in history," for "all history is made up of the actions of individuals, who are undoubtedly active figures." But the "real question [that arises] in appraising the social activity of an individual is: *what conditions ensure the success of his actions, what guarantee is there that these actions will not remain an isolated act lost in a welter of contrary acts?*" [3]

Lenin's attitude toward the question of determinism was perhaps even more emphatically expressed in an interview which he gave in London in the year 1902: "The Mensheviks ['orthodox' Russian Marxists] think that history is the product of material forces acting through the processes of evolution. I think, with Marx, that man makes history, but within the conditions, and with the materials, given by the corresponding period of civilization. And man can be a tremendous social force!" [4]

If there were any doubt remaining, the "Marxist" character of Lenin's formulations would be unmistakably confirmed by the comments in Marx's generally ignored preface

---

[2] *The Eighteenth Brumaire of Louis Bonaparte* (1852). Cf. Sartre's treatment of a similar remark (by Engels) in his critique of "orthodox" Marxisms, *Search for a Method* (New York: Knopf, 1964), Part III.

[3] "What the 'Friends of the People Are' and How They Fight the Social Democrats" in *Collected Works* (London: Lawrence and Wishart, 1960–1968), Vol. I. Also printed as a pamphlet. Lenin's remarks appear in this edition on pages 32 and 33.

[4] M. Beer, *Fifty Years of International Socialism* (London: 1935), p. 158. This is also the underlying perspective behind Lenin's critique of the doctrine of "spontaneity" in the seminal pamphlet *What Is to Be Done?*

to the previously cited essay on Louis Napoleon.[5] For here Marx makes clear his view, that the conditioning circumstances which are external to the individual wills of historical agents determine only the *possibilities* of the historical situation, not the details of its future development.

In the Preface, Marx criticizes two contemporary studies of the coup d'état for falling into the twin pitfalls of "subjectivism" (or "voluntarism") on the one side, and "objectivism" on the other. In Victor Hugo's book *Napoleon the Little*, writes Marx, the coup d'état appears "like a bolt from the blue." Hugo sees in it "only the violent act of a single individual. He does not notice that he makes this individual great instead of little by ascribing to him a personal power of initiative such as would be without parallel in world history." Proudhon, on the other hand, "seeks to represent the coup d'état as the result of an antecedent historical development," i.e., as an inevitable outcome of preceding events. In the end, "his historical construction of the coup d'état becomes a historical apologia for its hero." (Precisely this charge was leveled at those Marxists who, by demonstrating what they took to be the necessity of the course pursued by the Stalin faction in Russia, also sought to absolve the historical agents of their responsibility for that course.) In this, observes Marx, Proudhon "falls into the error of our so-called *objective* historians." As for his own position, Marx writes: "I, on the contrary, demonstrate how the class struggle in France created the circumstances and relationships that made it *possible* for a grotesque mediocrity to play a hero's part."

In his writings on revolution, Marx includes, among the conditioning elements which determine a particular historical turning point, past tradition, ideology and even the historical situation of a strategically placed class (such as the Prussian bourgeoisie in 1848).[6] But for Marx the most critical deter-

---

[5] The preface was written by Marx for the second edition in 1869.
[6] See p. 24 below.

minants of the options available to a given social order are to be found in the economic framework of society and the position of the main social classes within that framework. Indeed, many of the ambiguities surrounding Marx's determinism disappear once it is recognized that the range of options in a historical situation is dependent to a large extent on the degree of development of the technological-economic framework. The more rigid and pervasive the economic framework, the more its parts are interlocking and interdependent through advances in technology, and the more subjected in their coordination and organization to the unplanned rule of a worldwide economic market, the fewer, naturally, the options available to the human agents within it,[7] while the material tendencies of its development assume a correspondingly greater role. Conversely, a more primitive technological and economic development, particularly if it exists within a generally more advanced international framework, would raise certain historical possibilities otherwise denied. It is not surprising, therefore, that Marx should have regarded backward Russia as possessing more than one historical option, among which was "the finest chance ever offered" to a people to pass directly from a feudal to a communist development.[8]

---

[7] "The capitalistic economy of the present day is an immense cosmos into which the individual is born, and which presents itself to him, at least as an individual, as an unalterable order of things in which he must live. It forces the individual insofar as he is involved in the system of market relationships, to conform to capitalistic rules of action. The manufacturer who in the long run acts counter to these norms will just as inevitably be eliminated from the economic scene as the worker who cannot or will not adapt himself to them will be thrown into the streets without a job."—Max Weber, *The Protestant Ethic and the Spirit of Capitalism* (New York: Scribner, 1948).

[8] Cf. Marx's letter to the editorial board of the *Otechestvenniye Zapiski*, in *Selected Correspondence*, pp. 376 ff., and the Preface to the Russian edition (1882) of the *Communist Manifesto*, in *Selected Works*, I, 24.

A second "orthodox" misrepresentation of Marxism identifies it with a theory of history in which social development is seen as proceeding inexorably through discrete stages, from primitive communism to feudalism, capitalism and socialism. It is extremely doubtful whether Marx, himself, adhered to any such supra-historical theory,[9] and it is certain that the Bolsheviks did not.[10] For acceptance of the doctrine of inevitable historical stages would not only have entailed the acceptance of an inexorable emergence and long-term growth of capitalism in Russia, but more important, it would have denied the possibility of an immediate proletarian conquest of power.

Such a historical theory was indeed held, however, by one school of Marxism in Russia at the time, which regarded Russia's semifeudal, absolutist society through the prism of what has since become virtually identified as *the* Marxian perspective. In this "orthodox" view, the next stage of the Russian Revolution was to be dominated by the nascent bourgeoisie, which would lead the struggle to overthrow Czarist absolutism, to establish democracy and to develop an industrial capitalist economy. Then and only then, as a consequence of the growing contradiction between the forces and

---

[9] Marx's explicit repudiation of any intent to formulate a general theory of historical development is expressed in the famous letter to the editorial board of *Otechestvenniye Zapiski* (see preceding note) on Mikhailovsky's review of *Capital*. The obvious incompatibility of such an abstract general theory with Marx's basic methodological outlook ought to have prevented confusion on this question. However, many writers, Marxist and otherwise, have insisted on treating Marx's comments in the Preface to *A Contribution to the Critique of Political Economy* as such a general theoretical statement, and so long as this is done, the confusion will persist.

[10] Cf. Lenin's reply to Mikhailovsky in "What the 'Friends of the People' Are." Lenin specifically attacks Mikhailovsky's suggestion that Marx laid claim to having formulated a general theory of history.

relations of production generated by capitalist development, would a new stage of revolution be ushered in—a *socialist* revolution, led by the industrial proletariat. This was the unwavering perspective at the time of the Menshevik Marxists, the true doctrinaires of the Russian Revolution.

Careful consideration of Marx's own writings shows that he himself had more than one scheme of social revolution.[11] The most famous of these, usually associated with "orthodox" Marxism and adopted by the Russian Mensheviks, was based on Marx's view of the historical tendencies of development in France and England, both of which had already entered the epoch of industrial capitalism. But Marx's attention had also been drawn to the class struggle in his native and more backward Germany, both during his "early" period and also at the time of the revolutionary defeats of 1848–49, and it was on this Marxian analysis and its lessons, rather than the other, that the Bolsheviks concentrated.

Thus, in an extremely important pamphlet assessing the 1905 Revolution in Russia, and drawing appropriate lessons for the future, Lenin cited Marx's analysis of the 1848 events and wrote: "With the proper allowances for concrete national peculiarities and with serfdom substituted for feudalism, all these propositions are fully applicable to the Russia of 1905." Moreover, "there is no doubt that by learning from the experience of Germany as elucidated by Marx," the Russian Bolsheviks could arrive at the correct revolutionary line.[12]

Like Czarist Russia, imperial Germany had experienced no bourgeois revolution, but within its feudal framework the new industrial technologies were already being introduced

---

[11] Cf. Oscar Berland, "Radical Chains: The Marxian Concept of Proletarian Mission," *Studies on the Left*, Vol. 6, No. 5 (1966). [12] "Two Tactics of Social-Democracy in the Democratic Revolution" (1905), in *Collected Works*, IX, 135-36. Cf. also "The Russian Revolution and the Tasks of the Proletariat" (1906), in *Collected Works*, Vol. X.

and a proletariat was in the process of formation. Moreover, because of the peculiar features of the *belated* bourgeois revolution developing in the womb of German society, Marx suggested a dramatically different course for Germany from that taken by her predecessors. "The Communists turn their attention chiefly to Germany," declared the *Communist Manifesto*, "because that country is on the eve of a bourgeois revolution that is bound to be carried out under the more advanced conditions of European civilization, and with a much more developed proletariat, than that of England was in the seventeenth, and of France in the eighteenth century, and because the bourgeois revolution in Germany will be but the prelude to an *immediately following* proletarian revolution." (Emphasis added.)

This prediction of a proletarian revolution following immediately on the heels of the bourgeois revolution, i.e., of an uninterrupted development of the capitalist "stage" toward its socialist completion—wrong as it turned out to be for Germany, where the bourgeois revolution was not only compromised but defeated, and prescient as it turned out to be for Russia in 1917—had been anticipated by Marx four years earlier. "Germany," he had written, "will not be able to emancipate itself from the Middle Ages, unless it emancipates itself at the same time from the partial[13] victories over the Middle Ages," i.e., from the bourgeois revolution as well. "Germany . . . can only make a revolution which upsets the whole order of things." [14]

For the Bolsheviks, the seminal analyses on the subject of belated bourgeois revolution were Marx's articles and addresses on the class struggles in Germany between 1848 and 1850. In these, Marx once again stressed the difference between the English and French revolutions of the seventeenth

---

[13] "Partial," because while establishing legal equality, the bourgeois revolution preserved economic servitude and inequality.
[14] "Introduction to the Critique of Hegel's Philosophy of Right" (1844), cited in Berland, *op. cit.*

and eighteenth centuries and the Prussian revolution of March 1848. In both the former, wrote Marx, "the bourgeoisie was the class that *really* formed the van of the movement," and "the victory of the bourgeoisie was . . . the victory of a new order of society." [15]

By contrast, the German bourgeoisie, as a result of the belated development of German society, was neither psychologically fitted, nor socially situated to play a truly revolutionary role: the German bourgeoisie had developed so "slothfully" and "cravenly" that "the moment when it menacingly faced feudalism and absolutism, it saw itself menacingly faced by the proletariat . . ." Unlike the French bourgeoisie which, as a class, represented the whole of modern society against the old, the Prussian bourgeoisie "saw inimically arrayed not only a class behind it, but all of Europe before it." In this situation, the Prussian bourgeoisie was not capable of becoming the vanguard, but played instead a vacillating role. It wanted change, but by bargain and compromise; its interests initially allied it with the proletariat and the peasantry against the feudal reaction, but it perpetually sought to come to terms with the conservative forces of the old order, the monarchy and the army, and to forestall the proletariat's own revolution against itself:

> Irresolute against each of its opponents . . . because it always saw both of them before or behind it; inclined from the very beginning to betray the people and compromise with the crowned representative of the old society because it itself already belonged to the old society; representing not the interests of a new society against an old but renewed interests within a superannuated society; at the steering wheel of the revolution not because the people stood behind it but because the people prodded it on before it; . . . revolutionary in relation to the conservatives and conservative in relation to the revolutionists; . . . dickering with its own desires, without initiative, without faith in itself, without faith in the people, without a world-historical calling; . . . such was the Prussian bourgeoisie that

---

[15] "The Bourgeoisie and the Counter-Revolution," *Selected Works*, I, 67–68.

found itself at the helm of the Prussian state after the March Revolution.

This Prussian class, far from being unique, was to become the archetype of the bourgeoisie of belated capitalist development. For in all post-1789 bourgeois revolutions the moderate liberals were to pull back, or transfer into the conservative camp at an early stage.[16] It was a peculiarity of the French Revolution that a section of the middle class had been "prepared to remain revolutionary up to and indeed beyond the brink of anti-bourgeois revolution." For the French bourgeoisie had not yet, like subsequent liberals, the instructive memory of the French Revolution itself to take to heart. After 1794, it was clear to moderates that "the Jacobin regime had driven the Revolution too far for bourgeois comfort and prospects, just as it [was] clear to revolutionaries that 'the sun of 1793,' if it were to rise again, would have to shine on a non-bourgeois society." [17]

So vivid and terrifying was the prospect of the "next" revolution to the propertied classes that the theoretical attack on liberalism itself more and more came to be based on the proposition that democratic ideology and reform would pave the way to this new upheaval. Thus, in 1862, the conservative German legal historian Sohm denounced liberal doctrine in the following vein: "From the third estate itself there have arisen the ideas which now . . . incite the masses of the fourth estate against the third. . . . The education that dominates our society is the one that preaches its destruction. Like the education of the eighteenth century, the present-day education carries the revolution beneath its heart. When it gives birth, the child it has nourished with its blood will kill its own mother." [18]

---

[16] The exception is the American Civil War. See below, p. 96.*n.*
[17] E. J. Hobsbawm, *The Age of Revolution 1789–1848* (New York: Mentor Books, 1962), p. 85.
[18] Cited in Franz L. Neumann, *Behemoth* (London: Gollancz, 1942).

Marx's portrait of the stunted, wavering and compromising bourgeoisie of belated German development—so unlike its Jacobin forebears and so typical of its successors—reappears at the center of Lenin's analysis of class forces in Russia. In Lenin's view the bourgeoisie in Russia is not consistently revolutionary, and like its Prussian counterpart cannot be trusted to carry through the bourgeois-democratic revolution, but to ally itself, in crisis, with the feudal reaction. On the basis of this subsequently confirmed analysis, Lenin evolved the Bolshevik program: a conquest of power by the proletariat and the peasantry "to crush by force the opposition of the autocracy and to paralyze the instability of the bourgeoisie." Then having seized the initiative and the power from the bourgeoisie *within the bourgeois revolution* (a feat made possible by the failure of the bourgeoisie to carry through its revolution, by its betrayal of its own democratic program and of its allies, especially the peasants) the proletariat would be well placed for its struggle for socialism, against the remaining property-owning classes.[19]

Not only was Lenin's appraisal of the role of the bourgoisie and its relation to the peasantry based squarely on Marx's analysis of the revolution of 1848,[20] but his general strategy for the proletariat was drawn from it as well. With the victory of the new bourgeois government, Marx had written, the workers must simultaneously establish their own "revolutionary workers" governments, in the form of councils (such councils or soviets had already appeared in Russia spontaneously in 1905). They must organize *independently* and *centralize* their organization, and "from the moment of victory, mistrust must be directed no longer against the conquered reactionary party, but against the workers' previous allies, against the party that wishes to exploit the common

[19] "Two Tactics," *Collected Works*, IX, 100.
[20] Understood, of course, in the light of the Russian events of 1905. *Ibid.*

victory for itself alone." [21] (For no sooner had the liberal bourgeoisie made its peace with feudal-military power in Prussia, than the whole weight of that power had been used to force the workers "into their former oppressed position.")[22]

None of the bourgeois parties, in fact, had any desire to revolutionize all of society, observed Marx, but only wanted to make their own position in society more comfortable, and to consolidate the conditions of bourgeois rule. Such "revolutionary" demands as they put forward, therefore, could in no way suffice for the party of the proletariat. In characterizing the demands which *were* to embody the proletarian program to be advanced against the bourgeoisie during its aborted revolution, Marx employed a concept which was to reverberate throughout the history of the later Russian development:

"While the democratic petty bourgeois wish to bring the revolution to a conclusion as quickly as possible, and with the achievement, at most, of [their own demands], it is our interest and our task to make the revolution permanent, until all more or less possessing classes have been forced out of their position of dominance, until the proletariat has conquered state power, and the association of proletarians, not only in one country but in all the dominant countries of the world, has advanced so far that competition among the proletarians of these countries has ceased and that at least the decisive productive forces are concentrated in the hands of the proletarians. For us the issue cannot be the alteration of private property but only its annihilation, not the smoothing over of class antagonisms but the abolition of classes, not the improvement of existing society but the foundation of a new one." [23]

In the concept of "permanent revolution," even as expressed by Marx in this rudimentary form, are adumbrated all

---

[21] "Address of the Central Committee to the Communist League," *Selected Works*, Vol. I.

[22] *Ibid.*

[23] "Address . . . ," *Selected Works*, I, 110.

of the major elements of Bolshevik theory[24]—the uninterrupted progress of the revolutionary development; the program of completing the merely partial emancipation of the
bourgeois stage, and making "permanent" its reforms; the
recognition of the international scope of the revolutionary
process. This last element, in particular, was to be developed
by later Marxists, and especially the Bolsheviks, in conjunction with the theory of imperialism, the interaction of uneven
levels of capitalist development and the interdependence of
revolutionary and counterrevolutionary dynamics on a trans-
national scale.

Just as Marx had recognized the interconnectedness of
revolutionary developments in France and Germany, and had
speculated on the one providing a spark for the other, or on
the intervention of the Holy Alliance itself igniting a revolutionary explosion, so Lenin regarded the Russian Revolution
as a catalyst for the European Revolution. So, too, Trotsky
very early had anticipated international intervention against
the domestic upheaval and Russia's own reciprocal international impact. Even as Marx, however, had been more confident of an initial triumph of the proletariat in advanced Paris
accelerating the then retarded German development, so the
Bolsheviks had counted on the triumph of revolution in industrial Germany to consolidate and carry forward the "premature" Russian gains.

---

[24] Lenin referred to "uninterrupted" or "continuous" revolution
rather than "permanent revolution," which had been revived as
a term by Parvus and Trotsky. But as E. H. Carr, *The Bolshevik
Revolution 1917–1923* (Baltimore, Md.: Pelican Books), I, 56n,
and others have pointed out, there is no substantive difference between the two concepts.

2. Imperialism and Revolution

> The imperialist war is ushering in the era of social revolution.
>
> —Lenin, 1915

The unfulfilled expectation of revolution in Europe, on which the Bolsheviks had counted so heavily and whose failure to materialize was to cost them so much, was not merely an ad hoc formulation by Bolshevik theorists, designed to justify the attempt to introduce socialism into backward Russia. It stemmed, rather, from a global revolutionary perspective, which was itself a logical extension of Marx's original analysis of capitalism to the epoch of imperialist expansion. Based on the experience of capitalism in Western Europe, this Bolshevik analysis focused on the development of the economic framework of society and in particular on the way the rapid growth of the forces of production, under increasingly monopolistic conditions, impinged in a revolutionary fashion on the structure of social and international relationships.

Inserted originally into the stable framework of feudal society, the capitalist mode of production rapidly revealed itself to be a destabilizing and disintegrating force. "Constant revolutionizing of production, and the uninterrupted disturbance of all social conditions," distinguished the capitalist epoch from all earlier ones.[1]

---

[1] "The bourgeoisie cannot exist without constantly revolutionizing the instruments of production, and thereby the relations of production, and with them the whole relations of society. Conservation of the old modes of production in unaltered form, was, on the contrary, the first condition of existence for all earlier industrial classes."—*The Communist Manifesto*.

Alongside its disintegrating, revolutionizing thrust, however, the new capitalist mode of production also exerted an
integrating force. The same process that broke down the par-
ticularism and traditionalism of feudal productive and social
forms, to replace them with the rationalized relationships of
the capitalist market, also ended the local seclusion of feudal
society by opening up new channels of communication and
unprecedented forms of commercial and technological interdependence. Capitalism unified the nation-state[2] only to her-
ald the transcendence of the nation-state and the emergence
of *international* relations on a truly global scale.

For capitalism establishes a world market which calls
forth immense developments in transportation and communication and these in turn prompt the extension of industry, the
further increase of capital and demand. "The need of a constantly expanding market for its products chases the bourgeoisie over the whole surface of the globe"; the cheap prices
of its commodities are "the heavy artillery with which it bat-
ters down all Chinese walls," and . . . compels all nations,
"on pain of extinction," to adopt its own system of production and distribution. "It compels them to introduce what it
calls civilisation into their midst, i.e., to become bourgeois
themselves. In one word, it creates a world after its image." [3]

Ultimately the profound dynamism and expansionist
tendency of capitalism derive from its mode of production:
the private accumulation of capital on an expanding technological basis.[4] For individual capitals, the law of such a mode

---

[2] Capitalist production according to Marx and Engels had centralized population and industry and concentrated property in a
few hands. The "necessary consequence" of this was political centralization. "Independent, or but loosely connected provinces, with
separate interests, laws, governments and systems of taxation, became lumped together into one nation, with one government, one
code of laws, one national class-interest, one frontier and one cus-
toms-tariff."—*ibid.*

[3] *Ibid.*

[4] Such a mode historically requires the existence of a market for

of production is inevitably: increase (accumulate) or die. The individual capitalist or corporation is compelled to seek out and conquer new markets, ceaselessly develop new technologies, and increase its revenues, on pain of being eliminated by rivals. This is the iron rule of its existence, which can only be changed by a revolution of the system itself: the socialization of the accumulation process and its organization according to a general social plan.

With the continuing expansion of the forces of production and the progress of capitalist competition, the related phenomena of *monopoly* and *imperialism* eventually come to predominate within the national and world economies of the capitalist system. It is in focusing on these, as *characteristic* phenomena of the conservative epoch of capitalist development, that the Bolshevik perspective differs from that of Marx.

In analyzing this perspective, it should be noted at the outset—particularly since so much error has arisen from a failure to understand the point—that the colonization movement, the "partition of the world" characteristic of the end of the nineteenth century (and hence the subject of most Bolshevik theorizing) represents but a single phase of both capitalist *and* imperialist development. In other words, the particular political forms associated with "classical" imperialism neither wholly originate in the conservative epoch of capitalist development nor necessarily exhaust its possibilities.

As Marx recognized, monopoly and imperialism, i.e., the concentration of power within the domestic political economy, and the expansion of capital (and its forms of domination) beyond national frontiers are inherent in the very process of capitalist development: the constantly required revolutionizing of the forces of production, the continual expansion of their base, the constant extension and international-

---

free wage-labor, and the "mode of production" is defined *sensu stricto* by Marx in terms of this capital-labor relationship.

ization of commerce, and above all, the inexorable struggle between capitalist economic units for domination and control of the expanding markets of the capitalist world.

Just as domestically capital is and must be not only an expansionist but a dominating force, so also must it be internationally. For capital does not seek merely to enter markets, but to conquer them. It is compelled to do so by the whip of the competitive struggle which has driven its accumulation and expansion from the beginning: "In order that monopoly may be complete, competitors must be eliminated not only from the home market (the market of the given country) but also from the foreign mɔrket, from the whole world . . . the means to this end are—financial dependence, the cornering of sources of raw materials and the buying out of all the competitors' enterprises." [5] The same process by which the bourgeoisie subordinates the country to the industrial town with its superior labor productivity and cheap goods, it employs to make "barbarian and semi-barbarian countries dependent on the civilised ones, nations of peasants on nations of bourgeois, East on West." [6]

Correctly viewed, therefore, imperialism is simply the phenomenon of capitalist relationships reproduced on an international or rather a trans-national scale, with the struggle for domination between nations replacing, overlapping and intersecting the struggle between economic classes. In different historical periods and contexts, reflecting different balances of international forces, the battle for control of international markets (in *both* the developed and underdeveloped world)[7] is fought with different means and can be accom-

---

[5] Lenin, "A Caricature of Marxism and Imperialist Economism," cited in E. Preobrazhensky, *The New Economics* (New York: Oxford University Press, 1965), p. 154.

[6] *The Communist Manifesto*. The effects of this economic subordination are discussed below. See pp. 107 ff.; see also the following note.

[7] This is an important point. Kautsky, for example, defined im-

plished either with predominantly economic or a combination of economic, political and/or military methods.

The unchallenged supremacy of a single capitalist power such as England enjoyed from 1815 to 1870 is naturally conducive to solving the problems of control by relatively peaceful means. But where the armed power of the nation-state is required to secure international markets the history of capitalism shows that armed power will be generally forthcoming. The national bourgeoisie is able to enlist the state to secure its domestic market by tariff restrictions and the like; so it is even more able to invoke state power to underwrite its expansion and quest for dominion overseas. It can do this firstly because of its preponderant power within the domestic political economy, and secondly because as long as the national economic framework remains capitalist, domestic prosperity will be dictated by the nation's place in the hierarchy of the international market;[8] therefore imperial and national interest will appear to coincide.[9] Thus the history of monopolistic capitalism is at the same time the history of the strengthening of the state and the expansion of its military arm.

While spokesmen of the most advanced and most expansionist capitalist nations have often been forthright in the past about this basic coincidence of interests, and have well understood the inherent relation between the logic of capitalist commerce and the necessity of overseas economic dominion,

---

perialism purely in terms of the domination of agrarian by industrial countries, thereby ignoring the struggle for market hegemony *between* industrial powers, and was criticized, accordingly, by Lenin. On the other hand, many of Lenin's own critics have erroneously attributed a Kautskyan view to him, and assumed that the mere fact of imperialist investment in relatively advanced areas undermines his theory of imperialism.

[8] On the notion of a hierarchy, cf. Paul Baran and Paul Sweezy, *Monopoly Capital* (New York: Monthly Review Press, 1962), pp. 178 ff.

[9] Cf. Charles A. Beard, *The Idea of National Interest* (Chicago: Quadrangle Books, 1966).

few have expressd it more clearly than the "idealistic" American statesman Woodrow Wilson. "Since trade ignores national boundaries and the manufacturer insists on having the world as a market," he told an audience in 1907, "the flag of his nation must follow him, and the doors of the nations which are closed must be battered down." [10]

In the period when the Bolshevik analysis of imperialism was formulated, the principal feature of international relations was undoubtedly the rapid colonial partition of the underdeveloped world. This vast movement to acquire new colonies represented a reversal of the previous trend of policy by the dominant capitalist powers, and by England in particular.[11] That it *was* a reversal indicated the fact already mentioned but often overlooked, namely that overt political control, however characteristic of a particular phase of imperialist development, is not an indispensable instrument for metropolitan capitalist powers seeking to maintain their economic dom-

---

[10] Wilson went on to explain: "Concessions obtained by financiers must be safeguarded by ministers of state, even if the sovereignty of unwilling nations be outraged in the process." Cited in William A. Williams, *The Tragedy of American Diplomacy* (New York: Delta Books, 1962), p. 66. Despite the rhetoric of the Fourteen Points, Wilson remained committed to this outlook throughout his presidency and it was without hypocrisy or sense of impropriety that his Secretary of State, the reformer William Jennings Bryan, was able to tell a gathering of top businessmen, "I can say, not merely in courtesy—but as a fact—my Department is your department; the ambassadors, the ministers, and the consuls are all yours. It is their business to look after your interests and to guard your rights."—*ibid*, pp. 78–79. Defense of overseas corporate interests against the claims of foreign governments, however legitimate these claims may be in terms of international law (or latterly, U.N. principle), has invariably been the practice of U.S. administrations.
[11] Thus, in 1852 Disraeli made his famous and fairly representative remark: "These wretched colonies will be independent in a few years and are millstones around our necks," while twenty years later he announced his conversion to a policy of imperial consolidation and expansion.

ination of dependent markets and raw material supplies. Lenin, himself, recognized this and as early as 1916 suggested that a change in the strategic relations of the major capitalist powers might, for example, make feasible the formation of an independent India in the future. As he put it, "The domination of finance capital and of capital in general is not to be abolished by any reforms in the sphere of political democracy." [12]

The actual sources of this dramatic conversion to overt political colonialism in the late nineteenth century are manifold, and the complex historical question presented by the phenomenon cannot be resolved merely by reference to the economic "bases" of social action. On the other hand, there can be no doubt that the economic framework of international relations at the time played a very significant role in shaping those developments. Without entering into the complicated details of its influence (the growth of international monopoly forms, economic stagnation in national markets, etc.), it is possible to isolate one major change in the international picture that provided the ground upon which all other influences may be seen to have operated. Hitherto, and at least since 1815, Britain had been the world's supreme indus-

---

[12] "The Socialist Revolution and the Right of Nations to Self-Determination" (in *Collected Works* Vol. XXII), reprinted in *Questions of National Policy and Proletarian Internationalism* (Moscow, n.d.), p. 126. Cf. Huberman and Sweezy, "Imperialism and National Independence," *Monthly Review*, December 1963: "As long as it remains enmeshed in the capitalist world market an underdeveloped country is *ipso facto* a subject of imperialist exploitation (manipulated prices for its exports and monopoly prices for its imports) and *at best* in constant danger of falling into renewed political subjugation." For studies of "neo-colonial," i.e., non-overtly political means of control, cf. Michael Kidron, *Foreign Investments in India* (New York: Oxford University Press, 1965), A. Gunder Frank, *Capitalism and Underdevelopment in Latin America* (New York: Monthly Review Press, 1967), K. Nkrumah, *Neo-Colonialism* (New York: Nelson, 1965), and Hamza Alavi, "Imperialism Old and New," in Miliband and Saville, eds., *The Socialist Register 1964*.

trial and naval power, and had increasingly advocated principles of open competition in international markets, a natural position for a competitor of such unchallengeable supremacy to take. With the rise of two new industrial giants, the United States and Germany, however, Britain's position became suddenly open to economic challenge.

Against the background of this challenge it is possible to understand the universal rush[13] after colonies at the time. Given a world of increasingly competitive and internationally oriented rivals, a movement by any one of them to secure markets or raw material sources by political means (whether or not the drive for such empire was economically motivated to begin with), would inevitably tend to provoke a general *preemptive* scramble for colonial preserves to prevent the loss of presently held or potentially valuable markets.[14] In retrospect this appears to have been a very great—even determinant—factor in producing the phenomenon.

Another important feature of the particular and transient phase of capitalist-imperialist development which dominated international relations at the turn of the century was the role played by surplus capital export in the drive for overseas markets. This, too, has been wrongly and confusingly associated with the general Bolshevik theory of imperialism. The notion that excess savings or a deficiency of investment demand in domestic markets (in classical Marxist terms—the difficulty

---

[13] In 1875 only 10 percent of Africa was partitioned. By the end of the century only 10 percent of the continent remained independent.

[14] In fact, the scramble appears to have been spurred by a weaker rival, France. Precisely because the scramble was largely preventive in nature, moreover, many of the colonial territories secured were not worth the cost, when measured in immediate returns— a fact often erroneously used to discount the importance of the economic framework for understanding the phenomenon. The preventive and anticipatory character of much of this expansion is discussed in Sweezy, *op. cit.*, p. 303, and Lenin, *Imperialism*, 11th impress. (Moscow), p. 156.

of "realizing surplus value") is *the* mechanism that drives capitalists abroad and makes imperialist expansion indispensable to capitalism *generally* is one properly associated with Rosa Luxemburg and the liberal J. A. Hobson,[15] but explicitly repudiated by Lenin and other Bolshevik theorists.[16]

This is a fundamental point, for the Hobsonian thesis, as a theory of the general phenomenon of imperialist expansion, can be faulted on empirical grounds and then used, as it has been, to discredit the economic theory of imperialism as such. It is not possible to argue, of course, that the insufficiency of domestic markets and the problem of disposing of surplus capital play no role or even an insignificant one in producing the phenomenon of imperialist expansion. Indeed, in the events of the turn of the century, it is recognized even by critics to have been a very important factor, while its place in the ideological perspective of the imperialists themselves often gives it a greater weight and significance than its objective reality may warrant.[17] But to identify it as *the* fundamental cause of the *general* expansionist drive of capitalism is both empirically unjustified and theoretically wrong-headed. For the basis of capitalist expansionism is, as we have already seen, the fact that capitalism develops a commodity market which "transcends the limits of the state" [18] and that it extends capitalist relations with their monopolistic and dominative tend-

---

[15] According to Hobson, "Imperialism is the endeavour of the great controllers of industry to broaden the channel for the flow of their surplus wealth by seeking foreign markets and foreign investments to take off the goods and capital they cannot sell at home."

[16] For example, cf. Bukharin, *Imperialism and World Economy*, p. 84; Lenin, *The Development of Capitalism in Russia*, Chap. I, Sec. viii ("Why Does the Capitalist Nation Need a Foreign Market?").

[17] Cf. the discussion of the ideology of U.S. imperialism below, pp. 54 ff.

[18] Lenin, *Development of Capitalism in Russia*. See the discussion of Marx, pp. 30–32 above.

encies into the inter-state sphere. At the most basic level, therefore, *imperialism is capitalism which has burst the boundaries of the nation-state* even as it first overcame the seclusion of the village community of the feudal epoch. It follows from this that the two phenomena are inseparable: there can be no end to imperialism without an end to capitalism, and capitalist relations of production.

A basic source of the confusion over these questions, which is in effect a confusion between one phase of imperialist development and the phenomenon of capitalist imperialism as such, lies undoubtedly in the Marxist theories themselves, and the theories of the Bolsheviks in particular. For the Bolsheviks regarded the period of the domination of finance capital and political colonialism as a final, "highest" stage of capitalist and imperialist development,[19] and the particular phase of imperialist social relations as *the* form of the transition to an international socialist order. They therefore unduly emphasized the importance of the phase and its features in their writings, and tended to rule out any possible evolution of its forms within the capitalist framework.[20] This, in turn, led subsequent Marxists to identify the particular with the general: imperialism, the highest stage of capitalist development, itself had no stages. This erroneous view was, of course, compounded by the Stalinist cult of Lenin which subsequently bestowed on a pamphlet which originally had no pretensions to setting forth a formal theory of imperialism virtually canonical authority.[21] Among the consequences of this

[19] For a Marxist view of the inapplicability of aspects of the "Leninist" schema to the contemporary stage of imperialist development, cf. Michael Kidron, "Imperialism, Highest Stage But One," *International Socialism* (London), Summer 1962.

[20] Although Lenin, as we have seen, was aware of such possibilities (see p. 35 above).

[21] Lenin's pamphlet *Imperialism, the Highest Stage of Capitalism* did not even pretend to be original, but as Lenin acknowledged, was derived from the works of the liberal Hobson and the Marxist Hilferding. Comparison of Lenin's work with Bukharin's com-

quasi-religious regard for Lenin's writings was not only that his errors were repeated, but many of his correct insights were falsified by being applied in changed circumstances. Moreover, it became impossible to develop a perspective on Leninist or Bolshevik theory itself, whereas such a perspective is essential both for evaluating the Bolshevik success and failure, and for analyzing the path of subsequent historical development.

The idea of a "final" phase of capitalist development may have been a source of theoretical confusion for subsequent generations, but for the Bolsheviks it framed a perspective on the prospects of international revolution; this was extremely important for the outcome of their own struggle in Russia. In formulating the analysis behind this general revolutionary perspective, the Bolsheviks laid particular stress on the increasing concentration and centralization of the "internationalized" means of production, and in doing so, consciously linked their analysis with Marx's previous description of how revolutionary contradictions matured within the isolated national capitalist economy:[22]

Originally—so Marx's analysis went—capitalism had battled its way into the world in the name of freedom, against the protectionist monopolies of the feudal economy.[23] However, monopoly, or the concentration and centralization of economic power—the very negation of capitalist competition —appeared also as its inevitable outcome.[24] Having abolished

---

parably short book immediately reveals the difference between a theoretical analysis of imperialism and a political essay on the subject.

[22] Cf. "The Historical Tendency of Capitalist Accumulation," in *Capital*, Vol. I.

[23] This formulation also needs to be qualified in the cases of Germany and Japan.

[24] Cf. Engels' brilliant early essay "Outlines of a Critique of Political Economy," in Marx and Engels, *Economic and Philosophical Manuscripts of 1844* (Moscow, 1961).

feudal control, therefore, capitalism, by the very logic of its development, proceeded to abolish capitalist freedom and even, in a sense, capitalist property itself, as the centralization and concentration of economic power increasingly divorced legal ownership from control.[25] But the new monopolism was no mere reproduction of the old. Taking place on an incomparably higher technical basis, this monopolism prepared the way for a "higher," more rational social framework. This was Marx's revolutionary perspective: the centralization of production is also the socialization of production, the development of an increasingly interdependent and cooperative basis of social labor. But capitalist monopolism, while abolishing the private, independent character of production, maintains its restricted corporate organization. This contradiction between the social character of production and its "private" basis manifests itself in increasing crisis and social poverty, amid increasing productive capacity and potential plenty,[26] and provides the revolutionary ground for its transformation into a fully social and rational industrial system.[27]

This process, which had seemed to the Bolsheviks to have matured by the end of the nineteenth century, despite the rise in living standards,[28] was not, of course, restricted to the level

---

[25] Cf. Capital, Vol. III, Part V, Chap. 27. Of course, stock ownership is still the basis of control. See Lewis Corey, The Decline of American Capitalism (New York: Covici-Friede, 1934), p. 337, and Don Villarejo, Stock Ownership and the Control of Corporations (The Radical Education Project, Ann Arbor, Mich.) for correct interpretations of this phenomenon which has been so grossly misunderstood and even misrepresented in the literature of the so-called managerial revolution.

[26] For a post-Keynesian revision and re-formulation of this perspective, cf. Baran and Sweezy, op. cit. For a Marxist critique of the doctrine of increasing misery, cf. R. L. Meek, Economics and Ideology (London: Chapman & Hill, 1967).

[27] Cf. Capital, Vol. I.

[28] The Bolsheviks recognized an improvement in the lot of the Western working classes and attributed it to imperialist exploitation. The objective conditions of the transformation had matured, the subjective conditions of revolution were still lacking.

of the national economy. Increasing combinations and con-
centrations of international capital recapitulated the domestic
phenomenon. Moreover, even as the ideals of bourgeois order
and the "harmonizing" rule of the market had been subverted
at home, so on the international level the reign of bourgeois
peace abroad was destroyed and the old evils of feudal mercantilism were resurrected: protectionist trade, political empire and imperialist war.[29] The source of this transformation,
according to the Bolsheviks, lay in the basic contradiction of
the international capitalist system, the incompatibility of the
trans-national expansion of the productive forces, and the restricted "national" appropriation of international wealth.
Moreover, just as the internal contradiction between the socialization of the forces of production and their restricted and
increasingly concentrated "private" control appeared to be
providing the ground for deeper and deeper domestic economic crises (and hence increasing foreign expansion), so the
contradiction between the internationalization of production
and its restricted national framework was leading inexorably
to inter-imperialist war.[30]

---

[29] Cf. R. Hilferding, *Das Finanzkapital* (1910): "The demand for
a policy of expansion revolutionizes the entire *Weltanschauung* of
the bourgeoisie. . . . The old freetraders believed in free trade not
only as the best economic policy but also as the beginning of an
era of peace. Finance capital has long since abandoned any such
notions. It does not believe in the harmony of capitalist interests,
but knows that the competitive struggle approaches ever closer
to a political battle for power. The ideal of peace dies out; in place
of the ideal of humanity steps that of the might and power of the
state." This passage is taken from a translated excerpt included as
Appendix B, "The Ideology of Imperialism," in Paul Sweezy, *The
Theory of Capitalist Development*, 2nd ed. (New York: Monthly
Review Press, 1962). Cf. Bertrand Russell, *Freedom versus Organization* (New York: Norton, 1962), Introduction.

[30] This perspective seems to have originated with Parvus, but
the theme runs throughout Bolshevik writing. The following passage on page 106 in Bukharin's book is typical: "Production is of a
social nature; international division of labour turns the private 'national' economies into parts of a gigantic all-embracing process,

By the end of the nineteenth century this process had matured in several striking ways. The political partition of the world by a few great powers was approaching its completion, and already it was evident that this partition could not be final but was only the prelude to a military struggle for redivision. For within the framework of international capitalism the basis of any such "sharing out" of spheres could be no more than an estimate of the comparative current strengths of the powers involved. Strength, however, "changes with the course of economic development," and already the profound *unevenness* of capitalist development had worked to undermine the existing balance. For Germany, a "nonentity" compared with England fifty years previously, was now emerging as the dominant power in Europe, without enjoying any comparable share in the previously established international division. In this situation lay obvious seeds of conflict.[31]

Another expression of the maturing revolutionary contradictions of international capitalism was the unprecedented growth of *militarism* in the period. In part this was a consequence of the accumulation problems of the mature and monopolized capitalist economies. War industries not only provided profitable investment outlets for one group of increasingly jingoistic capital interests but also a means for

---

which extends over almost the whole of humanity. Acquisition, however, assumes the character of 'national' (state) acquisition where the beneficiaries are huge state companies of the bourgeoisie of finance capital. The development of productive forces moves within the narrow limits of state boundaries while it has already outgrown those limits. Under such conditions there inevitably arises a conflict, which, given the existence of capitalism is settled through extending the state frontiers in bloody struggles, a settlement which holds the prospect of new and more grandiose conflicts."

[31] Lenin, "Socialism and War," in *Collected Works*, XXI, 341; also *Imperialism, the Highest Stage of Capitalism*, Chaps. VI, VII. See also Russell, *op. cit.*, pp. 210–11.

raising demand in the economy as a whole.[32] In countries like Germany and Japan the growth of militarism was also profoundly related to the "lateness" of capitalist and industrial development.[33] Yet another source of the phenomenon during this period was the need for military power itself—to subject colonial dependencies, to provide the means to support the diplomatic struggle between the great powers over these dependencies and the control of international markets, and to prepare for the increasingly inevitable militarization of this conflict.

Closely related to the ominous growth of militarist tendencies in the era of monopoly capitalism and imperialist expansion were the resurgence and transformation of *nationalism*. In the early phases of capitalist development in the West, nationalism had been a basically progressive force. The bourgeois revolution in France had established the conception of the *national* sovereignty (the sovereignty of the people in and through the nation), abolishing thereby the conception of the state as the monarch's personal domain. The liberation of the serf from the tyranny of the lord, of the people from the tyranny of the sovereign and of the nation itself from the tyranny of empire—all these movements had been summoned to one extent or another under the banner of nationalist self-determination.

With the advent of monopoly capitalism and the colonial expansion of the late nineteenth century, however, the content of Western nationalism underwent a dramatic change. Ceasing to embody the goals of self-determination and the liberation of oppressed peoples, nationalism became, instead,

---

[32] Cf. Rosa Luxemburg, *The Accumulation of Capital*, Chap. 32, and Sweezy, *op. cit.*, p. 309.

[33] On the relation between militarism and the combination of feudal structures and modern technology, see Veblen, *Imperial Germany and the Industrial Revolution*. Cf. also O. Tanin and E. Yohan, *Militarism and Fascism in Japan* (New York: International Publishers, 1934).

the ideology of expansion and domination, hence the bearer of those chauvinistic and racist sentiments with which it has been ever since so catastrophically connected.[34] The social roots of this transformation in the developments of the imperialist epoch were analyzed at the beginning of the twentieth century by the German Marxist Hilferding. "The economic advantage of monopoly," he wrote, "is mirrored in the favored place which must be ascribed to one's own nation. The latter appears as chosen above all others. Since the subordination of foreign nations proceeds by force, . . . it appears to the dominant nation that it owes its mastery to its special natural qualities, in other words to its racial characteristics." In racial ideology, therefore, "there emerges a scientifically cloaked foundation for the power lust of finance capital, which in this way demonstrates the cause and necessity of its operations." The democratic ideal of equality, which hitherto formed the basic content of nationalism, is thus replaced, in the imperialist epoch, by an oligarchical ideal of mastery.[35]

In the case of Germany, where chauvinistic nationalism appears and reappears in particularly virulent form, we may add to the factors in Hilferding's analysis the various legacies of belated development. Industrial technology and capitalist economic relations with their powerful unifying impetus were introduced in Germany into a framework of feudal

---

[34] Cf. Bertrand Russell, op. cit., p. 235. On an internal level, too, nationalism becomes a reactionary force in the era of capitalist consolidation, providing a source of conservative cohesion for the ruling bourgeoisie against the permanent revolution implied in its program and actively advanced by the lower classes.

[35] Thus a recent student of imperialist doctrine, in comparing the British Empire with the Third Reich asks, "Although their manners were distinctive were the ideologies really so? Did not imperialism supply their motive force and their continuing purpose? Did they not both take for granted the doctrine of a master-race, a superior order, a greater efficiency, a truer reading of the map of life?"— A. P. Thornton, Doctrines of Imperialism (New York: Wiley, 1965). However, compare the remarks of Neumann, p. 178n below.

structures and relationships. Without the purging and liberating effects of a successful bourgeois revolution, the backward forms of feudal servility and allegiance were directly transferred, during unification, from local principalities to the "dynastic" nation-state.[36] The proximity of the period of unification to that of imperial expansion in Germany also intensified the atavistic forces of German chauvinism, as did her late emergence as a world power, which gave her a permanent national "grievance" against the already dominant capitalist powers. (A similar set of factors can be seen to have operated in the development of modern Japan.)

The tendencies toward expansionism, militarism and chauvinistic nationalism, rooted in the very structure of international capitalist relationships and operating on the uneven ground of capitalist development, prepared the way at the turn of the century for imperialist world war. In 1907 and 1912, the Second International of socialist parties and organizations formally recognized the approaching war as a crisis of capitalism and called upon socialists to organize against its preparation; or in the event of its outbreak, to use the crisis to overthrow the system itself. When the war came, however, only the Bolsheviks honored the commitment, while the other parties flocked to support their national governments.

Even though the European socialist movement had betrayed the international working class,[37] Lenin believed that when people saw the ruin and destruction that their predatory rulers had brought on them—not for "peace" or "self-determination" and "democracy," as their governments claimed, but for a redivision of imperialist spoils[38]—they

---

[36] Cf. Veblen, *op. cit.*

[37] "The proletariat was congratulated by military commanders, and the bourgeois press warmly praised the resurrection of what it called 'the soul of the nation.' This resurrection has cost us three million corpses."—Paul Golay, cited in Lenin, *Collected Works,* XXI, 350.

[38] Not merely territories, but the surplus that accrues to dominant positions in the international capitalist market.

would learn the revolutionary lesson that "only the social revolution of the proletariat opens the way towards peace and freedom." [39] This revolution was a real possibility in Lenin's perspective because the war had *"linked up* the Russian revolutionary crisis, which stems from a bourgeois-democratic revolution, with the growing crisis of the proletarian socialist revolution in the West." (Emphasis in the original.) The Russian revolution was, therefore, "not only a prologue to, but an indivisible and integral part of," the general European revolution.[40]

This expectation went unfulfilled. The successful revolutions in the West which followed the war were not socialist—the socialist revolutions were crushed. These failures, which isolated the Bolsheviks, had enormous unforeseen consequences for their attempt to build a new social order in the ruins of the old empire of the Czars. It did not, however, invalidate their general perspective on capitalism and revolution. For this perspective did not postulate the inevitability of revolution in the crisis of this particular imperialist world war, but only its imperative necessity. "My duty as a representative of the revolutionary proletariat," as Lenin put it, "is to prepare for the world proletarian revolution as the only escape from the horrors of a world war." [41] These horrors, he thought, would themselves serve to open the eyes of the masses and to steel them for the absolutely essential revolutionary struggle against their own ruling classes; this struggle would take place "if not today, then tomorrow, if not during the war, then after it, if not in this war then in the next one." [42]

---

[39] *Ibid.*, p. 355.
[40] *Ibid.*, p. 379.
[41] *The Proletarian Revolution and the Renegade Kautsky* (1918).
[42] "The Position and Tasks of the Socialist International," November, 1914, in *Collected Works*, Vol. XXI. "Imperialism sets at hazard the fate of European culture: this war will soon be followed by others, unless there are a series of successful revolutions.

As for the short-term future, even though the postwar reestablishment of capitalist equilibrium (through economic recovery and political reform) was considered possible and even likely by the Bolsheviks, it was bound to be, in their view, as impermanent as the equilibrium that had preceded the war itself. For neither "conjunctural" economic booms, nor reformist political changes would eliminate the unevenness of capitalist development, the ruthlessness of the competitive capitalist struggle, or "the basic incompatibility between the productive forces and the state frontiers within which they are exploited," i.e., the fundamental causes of the war's outbreak. "The productive forces," declared Trotsky in 1924, "are now still more cramped than before the war, in the state frontiers established by the Versailles peace and the new relationship of world forces. From this results a profound, protracted chronic crisis of capitalism." [43]

In retrospect, this perspective seems to have been well borne out by the concatenation of economic and political crises which shook the capitalist world and shattered its peace in the inter-war period, leading finally to yet another military conflict. In the period after the Second World War the structure of international politics became more complicated. An impressive equilibrium was achieved in the advanced capitalist countries of the West, while disequilibrium intensified in the underdeveloped world. At the same time the tension between the noncapitalist Soviet Union and the capitalist powers in the West grew to warlike proportions.

The key to an understanding of these developments lay in a set of phenomena for which the classical Marxist and Bol-

---

The story about this being the 'last war' is a hollow and dangerous fabrication, a piece of philistine 'mythology.' "—*ibid.*

[43] *Through What Stage Are We Passing?* p. 27. Compare also Trotsky's extremely interesting "Report on the World Economic Crisis and the New Tasks of the Communist International" to the Second Session of the Comintern, June 23, 1921, in *The First Five Years of the Communist International* (New York: Pioneer, 1945), Vol. I.

shevik schemes often provided no more than a point of departure for analysis. Most important among these phenomena
were the development of the socialist revolution in backward
Russia and the emergence of the Soviet state as a world power
in 1945. For the Soviet development affected not only the policies of the capitalist states themselves, but also the balance of
internal class forces and hence the prospects of other socialist
revolutions, which were not affected everywhere in a parallel
way.

A second, related phenomenon was the complex fate of
the bourgeois revolution after its initial successes in England
and France. As already noted, the original course of revolution, particularly in France, profoundly affected its development elsewhere, as did the expansion of its economic forms
and institutions and the subsequent penetration of more backward societies by developed capitalist states. The Leninist
program of revolution was based on an acute recognition of
the significance of retarded capitalist development and particularly the debilitating effect of this delay on the strength and
revolutionary resolve of the nascent bourgeoisie. As a result
of the imperialist expansion of the late nineteenth century,
vast regions of the underdeveloped world were enmeshed in
social and economic relations which, in important respects
and despite important differences, paralleled those of prerevolutionary Russia. It is for this reason that in understanding
these regions and their revolutionary dynamics, which play
such a formidable role in the cold war, classical Bolshevism
remains an extremely relevant and even fundamental perspective.[44]

However, in the case of certain belated developments,
most notably those of Germany and Japan, which escaped
colonization and domination, and hence where real industrialization was able to take place, we find a third path,[45] about

---

[44] See below, pp. 95 ff.
[45] These three paths to industrial development are defined and discussed from a somewhat different viewpoint in Barrington Moore,

which classical Marxism and Bolshevism have less concretely
to say while the "orthodox" Marxist base-superstructure model
virtually breaks down. For while capitalist economic development proceeds at a furious pace in both these countries,
in neither does the bourgeois-democratic revolution succeed,[46] except as an externally imposed reform in military defeat and occupation (to some extent in 1918 in Germany, and
to a greater extent in 1945 in Germany and Japan).[47] Thus,
for a crucial historical period, two of the most important
world powers develop on a capitalist economic basis, but with
a fundamentally non-bourgeois, non-democratic political and
social "superstructure." [48] This quasi-feudal, quasi-capitalist
development gives rise to an intensely militaristic expansionism, which is integrally related to the emergence of fascism in

---

Jr., *Social Origins of Dictatorship and Democracy* (Boston: Beacon, 1966).

[46] In Japan it is difficult to speak even of an attempt at social
revolution by the bourgeoisie in terms of the dethronement of a
ruling class. The Japanese revolution, spearheaded by an alliance
between feudal-military and merchant forces was carried out
under the banner of an imperial restoration. Its revolutionary direction was determined by the threat of Western penetration and
the resolve of a wing of the Japanese ruling class to resist this subjugation by introducing Western techniques and economic forms,
and inducing an industrial development through the agency of the
imperial state. For a first-rate Marxist analysis of Japanese development, cf. E. H. Norman, *Japan's Emergence as a Modern State*
(New York: Institute of Pacific Relations, 1940).

[47] See below, pp. 186 ff.

[48] Many rationalizing and centralizing reforms essential to capitalist and industrial development were naturally carried out even
in the course of the Japanese revolution from above (cf. Moore,
op. cit., p. 248) as part of the conscious effort of the Japanese ruling class to acquire the power base of a modern state. Power within
the state, however, remained vested ultimately in the absolute
monarch, as a result of the absence of any bourgeois-democratic
revolution. Indicative of the attitude with which the question of
a "modern" constitution was approached was the advice of
Iwakura, one of the leaders of the Restoration, "to form a cabinet
with no regard for parliament, on the model of *Prussia*."

these countries in the inter-war period, and to the conflicts of the Second World War and its aftermath.[49]

A third major factor in shaping the structure of postwar relations was the United States's assumption of undisputed supremacy in the capitalist world system. For though a late-emerging power the United States did not experience a belated development in the manner of Germany and Japan. Geographically isolated and protected from Europe, possessing a vast internal frontier with its damping effect on internal class struggle and lacking an initially dominant feudal aristocracy, the United States evolved as a more classically bourgeois-democratic state than any of its European predecessors. The resultant progressiveness of character and outlook manifested at least superficially in U.S. policies, and certainly in contrast to its European competitors, was, as previously suggested, a factor of no small consequence in restoring equilibrium to the badly shaken postwar capitalist system.

In the analysis that follows, we begin with the world course charted by the United States, not only because the very "purity" of its bourgeois development makes it most intelligible in terms of the preceding theoretical framework, but also because in terms of the actual historical experience, the United States and the global system which it has come to dominate play such determinant roles. Thus, the infant revolution in Russia was already faced in 1917 with a set of difficult options posed for it not only by the backwardness of its own national environment but also by the hostile forces of the surrounding capitalist world system. Similarly, in 1945, when the Soviet Union finally emerged as a truly international power, it was confronted by a United States now dominant in the global economy and so vastly stronger as to be able to exert a decisive influence on Soviet relations with the rest of the world, and thus on the range of policy options available to the Soviet leaders.

---

[40] See Chapter 9.

II

CONTAINMENT AND

REVOLUTION

3. Open Door Empire

> . . . our Cold War foreign policy of
> containment is most basically a re-
> sponse to the fact that non-Western
> political cultures are for the first time
> threatening to contain *us*, to resist or
> restrict that long-term expansionary on-
> slaught of the West upon the East
> which is the overarching theme of mod-
> ern history.
>
> —Carl Oglesby

The global scope and counterrevolutionary bias of U.S.
foreign policy in the cold war[1] are presented in orthodox
analyses (when they are presented at all) as paradoxes to be explained, rather than the self-evident consequences of preceding developments. For the United States' own revolutionary
origins, the enshrinement of the principle of self-determination in its most central national heritage, and the alleged lack
of any firm tradition of imperial dominion are all held to
point in a direction opposite to the overseas expansion and
counterrevolutionary intervention which have characterized
U.S. policy in the postwar years.[2]

---

[1] The proposition that U.S. cold war containment policies can
only be understood as policies of containing social revolution
rather than national expansion is a central thesis of my book *The
Free World Colossus* (New York: Hill & Wang, 1965), and, therefore, no attempt is made to prove it in any detail in the present
work.

[2] Thus, it is a signal but expressive irony of the American intervention in Vietnam that the 1946 declaration of independence

If the United States' postwar foreign policy is set in its historical framework and analyzed in terms of the Marxist theory of imperialism, however, these developments hardly appear obsure and unintelligible, or even of recent origin. Far from proceeding along such lines of analysis, orthodox historians tend to assume the United States to be an *anti*-imperialist power, and at worst, as occasionally manifesting an imperialist bias "in spite of itself." This result is achieved by identifying imperialism with political colonialism, so that it is only necessary to note one "exceptional" period of American history when the United States embarked on an overt imperialist course, in connection with the Spanish-American War and the conquest of the Philippines. However, colonialism, as has already been stressed, is not the only form that imperialist domination can take, and the mere fact that the United States may have found a noncolonial form more congenial to its purposes is no reason for failing to analyze the phenomenon at all.

Yet, the orthodox failure to see the United States as an imperialist power reflects more than a mere inability to come to terms with the facts of U.S. relations with dependent and exploited countries within its orbit. On the positive side, it represents a recognition of the anti-imperialist idealism which does inform at least the rhetoric of U.S. policy and which expresses the historical fact of a real clash of interests between the United States as an emerging world force and the older imperial (and colonial) powers.

It is only recently, as the United States has attained the pinnacle of the international capitalist hierarchy and become its guardian force, that Washington has begun openly to adopt the vocabulary of a ruling power and to speak officially of its "counter-insurgency" programs. Previously, Washington had presented its policies as primarily, if not solely,

---

issued by the Democratic Republic of Vietnam was explicitly modeled on the American Declaration of Independence of 1776.

geared to the defense of smaller nations against the imperialist expansion of other great and more backward states. Yet historical analysis shows that this "transformation" is much less of a departure than it appears, and that the current expansionist and counterrevolutionary directions of American foreign policy are deeply rooted in the American past.

An examination of that past reveals that the lack of an imperial tradition, in a European sense, was the direct result of geography and late industrial development, rather than any unique characteristic of American capitalism promoting self-containment. Thus, as one extremely influential student of the American past observed more than seventy years ago: "For nearly three centuries, the dominant fact of American life has been expansion." [3] This expansion continued until the end of the nineteenth century within the natural geographical frontiers of the North American continent. The indigenous Indian nations were destroyed, their populations virtually exterminated, and the newly acquired territories were all fully integrated into the national and constitutional frameworks. The repercussions and effects of the expansion in the annexed regions were of a different character, therefore, than those resulting from the expansion of the old European powers which entailed the continuing subjection of the colonized peoples and the exploitation of their labor.

Still, the "dominant fact" of expansion made a profound impression on the consciousness of the leaders of the revolutionary republic (who actually conceived their new nation as a "rising empire")[4] and has determined the outlook of Amer-

---

[3] The observation appears in an article by Frederick Jackson Turner, first published in the *Atlantic Monthly* in 1896 and excerpted in Lloyd C. Gardner, *A Different Frontier*, Selected Readings in the Foundations of American Economic Expansion (Chicago: Quadrangle Books, 1966).

[4] The term is George Washington's. On this subject, see R. W. van Alstyne, *The Rising American Empire* (Chicago: Quadrangle

ican policy makers ever since.[5] This outlook is based on a commonly shared assumption (first formalized in Frederick Jackson Turner's famous thesis) that America's prosperity and democracy had been unique products of her continuously expanding geographical frontier. Such expansion, it was argued, served to provide vital new markets for American industry, to promote individualism, and to stifle dangerous factional strife at home. This last benefit was not the least important, moreover. Thus in *The Federalist Papers*, No. 10, Madison stressed the role of expansion in making possible a pluralistic republic. In fact, the very basis of the compromise of 1787 between the Northern mercantile interests and the Southern slavocrats was the expectation of both parties that their respective spheres would expand more in the future, insuring their own dominion in the republic.[6] The closing of the slave frontier in the election of 1860 not only heightened internal tensions to a dangerous level but actually precipitated a civil war.

It was but one logical step from the basic propositions of the frontier thesis to the even more momentous conclusion that *continuing* expansion, in one form or another, was necessary for the very *preservation* of domestic "freedom" and economic prosperity. This conclusion was reached very early in American history, but was first widely and dramatically articulated during the crisis of the 1890's.

Behind this crisis lay several decades of far-reaching domestic economic change and dislocation in the United States

---

Books, 1960), and William A. Williams, *The Contours of American History* (Chicago: Quadrangle Books, 1966), especially pp. 114–17.

[5] Cf. William A. Williams, *The Tragedy of American Diplomacy* (New York: Delta Books, 1962); also "The Frontier Thesis and American Foreign Policy," *The Pacific Historical Review*, Vol. XXIV No. 4 (November 1955), and "The Large Corporation and American Foreign Policy," in *The Corporations and the Cold War*.

[6] Staughton Lynd, *Class Conflict, Slavery and The United States Constitution* (Indianapolis, Ind.: Bobbs-Merrill, 1967).

which seemed to carry ominous portents for the future. The completion of the railroads, the merger movements in industry and agriculture, the tremendous expansion of production accompanied by the panics and depressions of 1873 and 1893, the piling up of surpluses in the warehouses and growing labor unrest in the cities were climaxed in this decade by the final closing of the geographical frontier—a sequence of events which appeared to many to augur an era of profound economic stagnation and dangerous social turmoil. The solution projected for this multifaceted and unprecedented crisis (which was exacerbated in the international sphere by the scramble of the European powers to close the remaining free markets of the world) was a policy of overseas *economic* expansion, under the strategy of the "Open Door."

This strategy, which was hailed as a triumph of anti-imperialism, in fact merely eschewed formal for informal empire.[7] The Open Door Notes, which were circulated at the turn of the century by the U.S. Secretary of State, sought ostensibly to prevent the partition of China by the older imperial powers, but basically to establish the principle of free access for all to the Chinese market. This open door, as Woodrow Wilson candidly disclosed, was "not the open door to the rights of China, but the open door to the goods of America."[8] As a strategy, it both reflected and attempted to resolve the contradiction between America's democratic shibboleths and the role of overseas expansion and domination on which she had embarked. It was also dictated, of course, by the late arrival of the United States on the international scene. For this rendered the attempt to secure formal territories a difficult enterprise—one rife with the dangers of military conflict (as the war with Spain already served to illustrate).

---

[7] The term originates with the historians of British non-colonial (or neo-colonial) imperialism in countries like Argentina.

[8] Cited in John Gittings, "The Origins of China's Foreign Policy," in David Horowitz (ed.), *Containment and Revolution* (Boston: Beacon Press, 1967), p. 186. On the preceding point see *ibid.*, p. 185.

But most importantly, Open Door expansion represented the natural policy of a newly great economic power, recognizing (as England in her supremacy had recognized before) that competition in foreign as in domestic markets was merely the most efficient way of ensuring victory, and subsequent privilege, to the strongest. As the London *Times* reported when the policy was announced: "Even protectionist organs [in the United States] are for free trade in China, where freedom is for the benefit of American manufacturers." [9] And as the industrialist Andrew Carnegie had argued in 1898: "The United States does not know the destiny that is lying immediately at her feet, provided she turns from . . . phantom schemes of annexation of barbarous peoples in distant lands and just looks down . . . and sees what the gods have placed within her grasp—the industrial dominion of the world." [10]

Both President McKinley and Secretary of State Hay, author of the Open Door Notes, assured Carnegie that there was no difference between them on the issue of colonial versus economic empire, and after the annexation of the Philippines,[11] which seemed temporarily to contradict the position, U.S. leaders showed in a clearly consistent manner that they understood well "what the gods [had] placed within [their] grasp."

However uncharacteristic it may have appeared in other respects, the war with Spain over Cuba and the Philippines

---

[9] Cited in Williams, *The Tragedy of American Diplomacy*, p. 18.
[10] Cited in John W. Rollins, "The Anti-Imperialists and Twentieth Century American Foreign Policy," *Studies on the Left,* Vol. III, No. 1 (1963).
[11] In fact, the annexation of the Philippines was both anticipatory and preventive in nature. (See p. 36 above.) Manila was seen as a gateway to the markets of China, and in the context of the global colonial scramble, the only guarantee of U.S. access to the port seemed to be political annexation of the country. Cf. "Documents, The Spanish American War: Business Recovery, and the China Market," *Studies on the Left*, Vol. I, No. 2 (1960).

brought to the surface a set of responses which were to remain permanent features of subsequent U.S. diplomacy. One of these was the inherent tendency of an expansionist ideology to externalize good and evil, to project the possibilities for domestic prosperity and advance onto foreign frontiers and at the same time to blame the presence of domestic ills on the activities of foreign movements and powers. Thus Spain's inability to control revolutionary unrest in Cuba, where U.S. corporations had substantial interests, was regarded by President McKinley as a condition which "causes disturbance in the social and political condition of our own peoples . . . and tends to delay the condition of prosperity to which this country is entitled." [12]

The Spanish-American War revealed yet another important facet of the expansionist ideology of U.S. foreign policy. For when it became clear that the Spanish government could not control the rebellions in its empire, the United States entered the fray under the guise of *containing* Spain's external threat to the Cuban and Philippine peoples, only to dominate them and their destinies afterward in their "own" interests.[13] Thus, having entered the Philippines under the banner of sav-

---

[12] Cf. Williams, *The Tragedy of American Diplomacy*, p. 34, and *The Contours of American History*, pp. 365 ff., and Walter La-Feber, *The New Empire, An Interpretation of American Expansion 1860–1898* (Ithaca: Cornell University Press, 1963), pp. 335 f.

[13] "The Philippines have developed economically in a typically colonial fashion. Money crops for which there was a duty-free market with protected price levels in the United States have been stimulated by the use of American capital; foodstuffs for domestic consumption have been crowded out; domestic industries have not been much encouraged."—Jenkins, *American Economic Policy Towards the Philippines* (Stanford, Calif.: Stanford University Press, 1954). "In 1945 just prior to independence, U.S. capital owned 30% of the islands' sugar *centrales*, 70% of the electric power sources, and 40% of the mining industry, while over 70% of the Philippines trade was with the United States."—Lloyd C. Gardner, *Economic Aspects of New Deal Diplomacy* (Madison: University of Wisconsin Press, 1964), p. 179.

ing the Filipinos from the oppression of Spanish empire, Washington turned its forces on the Philippine rebels themselves. After two years of bloody suppression of the indigenous rebel movement by more than 100,000 U.S. troops, President McKinley declared, in by now familiar tones: "The Philippines are ours not to exploit, but to develop, to civilize, to educate, to train in the science of self-government." In fact, like Cuba,[14] which remained nominally independent, the Philippines belonged to the United States to be drained of its natural wealth and manufactured surplus, and to be bound in permanent penury, backwardness and national subjection, even after formal political control was relinquished nearly half a century later.

Economic expansion and domination under the banner of containing political expansion and domination was, in fact, to become a general pattern of U.S. foreign policy in the twentieth century, whether one looked to the East or the West, whether to the Pacific region, dominated under the policy of the Open Door, or to the countries of the Western hemisphere, "protected" and secured for exploitation by U.S. interests under the formula of the Monroe Doctrine.

In the decades following the war with Spain, the United States was to face two major threats to its growing informal empire. One of these was posed by the Axis powers in the 1930's, and especially by Japan's attempt to close the open door in Asia. The other, far more serious because more permanent and pervasive, was that posed by the rising tide of *revolutions* of both nationalist and communist description. Between 1900 and 1917 alone, for example, Washington was to intervene militarily on more than twenty occasions in foreign countries, from Colombia to China, to contain threats to U.S. property during revolutionary outbreaks and to help

---

[14] Documentation of Cuba's poverty-stricken and stunted development under U.S. dominaton is available in numerous sources. Cf. Lowry Nelson, *Rural Cuba* (Minneapolis: University of Minnesota Press, 1950).

establish regimes ready to favor and protect these interests.[15]

By far the most momentous instance of counterrevolutionary containment in this period, however, occurred when the United States joined the allied Entente in its intervention in Russia following the Bolshevik triumph in October 1917.

Woodrow Wilson, who was responsible for the decision to intervene, was in full accord with the expansionist outlook of his predecessors. Like them, he stressed the dependence of national prosperity on the availability of international markets ("Our industries have expanded to such a point that they will burst their jackets if they cannot find a free outlet to the markets of the world"); like them, he regarded economics and politics interdependent phenomena ("If America is not to have free enterprise, then she can have freedom of no sort whatever"); and like them, he projected the crusade to preserve "free" institutions at home onto the international plane ("The world must be made safe for democracy").

The main moral and political dilemma which Wilson's intervention in Russia posed—the conflict between the commitment of the New Diplomacy to self-determination and the violation of that principle in the intervention itself—was also solved by the President in a traditional manner. Thus Wilson and his advisers, despite their knowledge to the contrary,

---

[15] Cf. "Instances of the Use of United States Armed Forces Abroad, 1798–1945," a list compiled by the U.S. State Department and reprinted in *Studies on the Left*, Vol. 3, No. 2 (1963). These military interventions were, of course, merely the continuation of standing policies by other means. Thus, in the early twenties, upon conducting an extensive investigation of U.S. loan operations in Latin American countries, Senator Hiram S. Johnson concluded that U.S. money was used to "maintain dictators in power," and that it was "party to the suppression of every natural right of citizens of South American Republics" (Williams, *op. cit.*, p. 119). Naturally these dictators were more than hospitable to North American capital. For an account of U.S. political, economic and military intervention in Latin America during this period, cf. Scott Nearing and Joseph Freeman, *Dollar Diplomacy* (New York: Monthly Review Press, 1966).

justified their action by invoking the claim that the Bolshevik leaders were *German* agents, and therefore, that the U.S. and Western aggression was not counterrevolutionary intervention, but a necessary measure for containing imperial German expansion.[16]

The actual intervention, however, swiftly revealed its true character as an attempt to crush the revolutionary forces in Russia. Containment now took on a profoundly new dimension. To be sure, the traditional motives for "restoring law and order" were not absent, as forty percent of all the stock capital of Czarist Russia was owned by foreign interests (principally of the British, French and Belgian intervening powers, but also American and German).[17] But the threat represented by the Bolshevik insurrection was different *in kind* from all previous threats to specific U.S. property interests.

In contrast to the threats posed previously by sundry nationalist revolutions and disturbances in exploited regions, the menace posed to property interests by the Bolshevik Revolution was open-ended and general. Both by nature and by design, the victory of Bolshevism was nothing less than an incitement to oppressed classes and nations everywhere to rise up against their rulers and oppressors. As the U.S. Secretary of State himself described the challenge at the time, the Bolsheviks sought "to make the ignorant and incapable mass of humanity dominant in the earth"; they were appealing "to a [particular] class and not to all classes of society, a class which does not have property but hopes to obtain a share by process of government rather than by individual enterprise. *This is of course a direct threat at existing social order in all countries.*"[18] (Emphasis added.)

---

[16] Cf. William A. Williams, "American Intervention in Russia, 1917–1920," in Horowitz (ed.), *Containment and Revolution*.

[17] Trotsky, *The History of the Russian Revolution*, I, 32.

[18] Cited in Williams, "American Intervention in Russia." These sentiments were, of course, expressed by Secretary of State Lansing only in private letters to Wilson. In public he was careful to frame his objections to Bolshevism in more ideologically acceptable terms.

Given a conception of the threat in these terms, it is not surprising that, despite initial hesitations, U.S. leaders should have decided to join the other capitalist powers of the Entente in taking a course of military intervention against the revolutionary regime. Nor is it surprising that they should have thrown their support in the civil war behind General Kaledin who shortly became "the main hope of the propertied and military classes of Russia." [19]

The intervention in Russia failed in its ultimate purpose of destroying the Bolshevik revolution. Elsewhere, however, the counterrevolutionary program of the Western powers was more successful. In famine-ridden Hungary, for example, the United States was able, by manipulating food supplies through the American Food Relief Mission, to help the British and the French defeat the revolutionary regime of Bela Kun and to ensure victory to the conservative forces. Similarly, in Poland, Hoover and Wilson were able to use U.S. control of food supplies to help bring conservatives to power, who were then given money and arms and encouraged to extend Poland's boundaries eastward into Russia and the Baltic states. [20]

One of the principal reasons for the intervention's failure in Russia was the rivalry between the intervening powers;[21] another, the internal opposition—particularly among labor groups—in the Western countries themselves. But despite its failure in terms of ultimate objectives, the action of the Western powers was successful in helping to destroy whatever foundations might have existed for a healthy and progressive development of the revolution in its backward and impoverished environment. [22]

---

[19] William H. Chamberlin, *The Russian Revolution* (New York: Universal Library, 1965), I, 348.

[20] Williams, *The Tragedy of American Diplomacy*, p. 113.

[21] Cf. Lenin, *Collected Works*, XXXI, 318 ff., for his analysis of the rivalry.

[22] "The West European capitalist powers, partly deliberately and partly unconsciously, did everything they could to throw us back,

The Bolshevik insurrection of October 7 in Petrograd, according to the most hostile eyewitness accounts, had resulted in the loss of not more than ten lives. This was because of the tactics of its leadership, the discipline of its rank and file and its overwhelming popular mandate.[23] The Russian General Staff, and the Bolsheviks' opponents, generally, were acutely aware of their own lack of support and consequently were demoralized and inclined to accept defeat. It was then, however, that the official representatives of the Entente began arming, inciting and mobilizing the opposition and in general fanning the fires of civil war. The promise of intervention did, in fact, put courage into the hearts of the defeated parties. "It was only after the promise had been made," writes Isaac Deutscher, "after British, French, and American liaison officers had appeared at the headquarters of the White generals and the first foreign cargoes of guns and munitions had reached Russian shores that the ranks of the White Guards began to swell and the civil war flared up in earnest." [24]

---

to utilize the elements of Civil War in Russia in order to spread as much ruin in the country as possible. . . . They argued somewhat as follows: 'If we fail to overthrow the revolutionary system in Russia, we shall, at all events, hinder her progress towards socialism.' And from their point of view they could argue in no other way. In the end . . . they failed to overthrow the new system created by the revolution, but they did prevent it from at once taking the step forward that would have justified the forecasts of the socialists. . . ."—Lenin, "Better Fewer, But Better." This strategy has been a constant element of U.S. policy toward revolutions generally (see p. 78 below) and, in particular, explains much of the seemingly "irrational" element in the long blockades of Cuba and China.

[23] E. H. Carr, *The Bolshevik Revolution 1917–1923* (New York: Macmillan, 1965), I, 151–52; Chamberlin, *The Russian Revolution*, I, 313; Isaac Deutscher, Introduction to *The Age of Permanent Revolution* (New York: Dell, 1964).

[24] Isaac Deutscher, *The Prophet Armed* (New York: Vintage Books, 1965), p. 448.

Unlike the Bolshevik insurrection, the civil war and the famine which followed it did not take a mere handful of lives, but several *million*. This unbelievably savage conflict, instigated and sustained by the capitalist democracies of the West, had profound and dire consequences for the long-term development of the revolution in Russia. For the civil war and its violence not only ruined the already damaged economy; it brutalized and demoralized the population, destroyed the party system, institutionalized the terror as an instrument of state,[25] and generally prepared the way for the emergence of the Stalinist regime and its rule.

With the waning of the military intervention and the failure of the counterrevolutionary forces, the antagonism of the capitalist powers abated but did not cease. The end of open hostility witnessed, naturally, a more complex and ambiguous form of relation between the new regime and the capitalist states. The intentions behind the diplomatic recognition, trade and even aid, which followed the peace, represented complex motives,[26] and often conflicting domestic pressures. For some domestic factions, for example, trade was seen as an avenue of real cooperation; for others, as an instrument of Western anti-Bolshevik influence at a time when the Bolshevik regime was beset by enormous internal difficulties. The fact remained, however, that all these fairly limited exchanges took place within a larger context of basic hostility, which was far more significant than the details of any particular act of cooperation.

---

[25] Carr, *op. cit.*, Vol. I, Chap. 7.

[26] Of course, such complex motives may lie behind policy at any time. Thus, in the period when the original decision to intervene was being considered, U.S. Secretary of State Lansing proposed that Herbert Hoover take charge of an economic commission that could be used as a cover for the intervention. For, as Lansing noted, "Armed intervention to protect the humanitarian work done by the Commission, would be much preferable to armed intervention before this work had begun."—cited in Williams, "American Intervention in Russia."

One of the most important structures of this hostility had emerged out of the peace settlement with Germany as part of a scheme devised by the European victors to quarantine the Bolshevik regime and contain the Bolshevik revolution. This counterrevolutionary containment scheme was subsequently to play a key role in the origins of the cold war in the period after the Second World War.

In 1919, in conjunction with the Versailles Treaty, five new states were created out of parts of the former Russian empire: Finland, Estonia, Latvia, Lithuania and Poland. These, together with other countries in the belt from Finland to Rumania (and including Czechoslovakia and Yugoslavia), were then regarded by the Western powers as forming a cordon sanitaire to prevent the expansion of Bolshevism, i.e., of Bolshevik ideology and revolution. The fact that the majority of these states had, or soon came to have, reactionary authoritarian regimes (Rumania and Hungary later providing a million troops for Hitler's Eastern Front) only served to recommend them to the leaders of the Western democracies who took this to be a sign of their durability as bulwarks of the existing order.

In fact, however, the existing social order not only in Eastern Europe but throughout the capitalist world could not be stabilized by the measures adopted at Versailles. For the Versailles system was designed to ratify and strengthen the new postwar status quo as seen from the vantage point of the victorious and now dominant capitalist powers. But the very fact that this status quo denied an appropriate place to the potentially most powerful industrial nations in both Europe and Asia, namely Germany and Japan, made it an unstable arrangement. Moreover, the international capitalist system, over which the Versailles settlement was built, itself lacked internal equilibrium. The war had not only not solved the contradictions of the prewar system, but in many ways had actually intensified them, and thus prepared the ground for renewed international conflict.

To be sure, a measure of prosperity returned to Europe, albeit sporadically and temporarily, and the formal institutions of political democracy were introduced in many countries. But these phenomena took place on the surface of society. Underneath, the fundamental contradictions—between productive capacity and available markets, between economic nationalism and economic interdependence, between the increasing socialization and internationalization of production and its "private," nationalistic basis—grew progressively sharper, producing intermittent shocks at first, until by 1929 they gathered a cumulative force which shattered the economic foundations and shook the political structure of the entire postwar capitalist world.[27]

This economic and social crisis, with its attendant political developments, served in part to weaken the hostile front of the major capitalist powers toward Soviet Russia. Domestic alliances between leftist and liberal forces against the economic conservatism and political fascism of the right inevitably moved some of the capitalist powers to adopt a less hostile posture toward the Communist state. Economic pressures to open potential new markets in Russia, which was the only country not touched by the Depression, acted in a similar direction. In 1933 the United States finally recognized the sixteen-year-old regime (the last major power to do so), with President Roosevelt emphasizing in his explanation of the action Russia's importance as an export market.[28]

---

[27] In the weaker states, economic and social disequilibrium had already led, by 1928, to the breakdown of parliamentary systems in Italy, Spain, Portugal, Hungary, Austria, Yugoslavia, Poland and Rumania.

[28] Williams, *op. cit.*, p. 165 f.; Gardner, *op. cit.*, pp. 33–35. Despite its nonrecognition of the Bolshevik regime, the United States was at this time, of all the major capitalist powers, least hostile to Russia and most receptive to the idea of coexistence. Among the reasons for this contrast with America's postwar position, the most important was the fact that the leadership of the international capitalist system and the main responsibility for defending its status quo still belonged to England (and, to a lesser extent, France) in

(Whatever the full reasons for the step, the belated recognition certainly underlines the inadequacy of those explanations of U.S. policy toward the Soviet Union which stress the moral issue as a determinant factor. For U.S. recognition and the general accommodation of the capitalist democracies to Stalinist Russia came only *after* the great violence and massacres of the collectivization of 1929–1931 and on the eve of the purges, while they had greeted the infant revolution— popular, democratic and virtually innocent of blood—with bullets and with bared bayonets.)

If the economic and political crisis helped to weaken the front against Russia, the progressive breakdown of European capitalism, with its inevitable polarization of political forces, also renewed the threat to the Soviet regime. In Germany the general crisis served to unhinge the already unstable social equilibrium that lay at the basis of the Weimar Republic. Under the banner of triumphant Nazism, the forces of the German counterrevolution smashed the organizations and parties of the German working class and attempted to resume the course of Germany's imperialist expansion, which had been momentarily thwarted by the Versailles powers. In 1936 Hitler forged an international "anti-Comintern" axis with the other fascist powers, Italy and Japan, menacing Russia on two fronts. Throughout the next period, therefore, Stalin attempted to secure his defenses by collective security agreements with the capitalist West, but his maneuverings toward this end came to nothing.

On the one hand, elements of the ruling groups in the capitalist democracies actually welcomed the advent of Hitler (as they had Mussolini earlier),[29] in whom they saw a rigorous

---

the inter-war period, while conversely it was against the British Empire rather than the American that the weight of Comintern agitation was directed.

[29] "The historian of the next generation cannot fail to be impressed by the different reception accorded to the changes of which Lenin and Mussolini have been the chief authors. Where Lenin's system has won for itself international ostracism and armed intervention,

defender of the increasingly threatened capitalist order against the rising (internal) Bolshevik menace.[30] Churchill and Lloyd George were among these, as was Lord Halifax, one of the principal Munich appeasers, who told Hitler in November 1937 that "he and other members of the British Government were fully aware that the Fuehrer had not only achieved a great deal inside Germany herself, but that, by destroying Communism in his country, he had barred its road to Western Europe, and that Germany could rightly be regarded as a bulwark of the West against Bolshevism." [31]

On the other hand, there were those who sincerely hoped that by appeasing Hitler's "legitimate" demands peace could be bought in Europe without having to pay the price of an alliance with Soviet Russia. Finally, there was a minority who rightly feared the threat of German expansionism to the West itself, and who saw that the impending catastrophe could only be averted by a collective security arrangement such as Stalin had been promoting. However, precisely because the basic orientation of the governing classes of the capitalist states was anti-Bolshevik rather than antifascist, this minority, which included the later Churchill, was able to gain a decisive voice only after the war had already begun.

In August 1939, frustrated by the appeasement policies

---

that of Mussolini has been the subject of widespread enthusiasm. He himself has been decorated by the governments of foreign powers; ambassadors have exhausted the language of eulogy at official banquets; and great men of business have not hesitated to say that only the emulation of his methods can reduce the working classes to a proper state of mind. Yet, save in intensity, there has been no difference in the method pursued by the two men; and it is difficult to avoid the conclusion that the different reception of their effort is the outcome of their antithetic attitudes to property." —Harold Laski, "Lenin and Mussolini," *Foreign Affairs* (September 1923), reprinted in H. A. Armstrong, *The Foreign Affairs Reader* (New York: Harper, 1947), p. 54.

[30] A. J. P. Taylor, *The Origins of the Second World War* (London, 1961), pp. 111 f.

[31] *Documents and Materials Relating to the Eve of the Second World War* (New York: International Publishers, 1938), I, 19–20.

of the great European powers and menaced by the refusal of
Poland, Finland and the Baltic states to cooperate in securing
the defenses of the region against the imminent Nazi invasion, Stalin came to terms with Hitler and marched for the
first—but not the last—time into the cordon sanitaire. (In doing so, however, he went considerably further than the mere
dictates of realpolitik would have taken him. He proclaimed
his pact to be not merely necessary but desirable as well, and
agreed to a secret partition of Eastern Europe north of Hungary.)

When Stalin sent his troops into Finland, the Western
powers, who had previously been so reluctant to oppose Hitler's expansion, promptly announced their readiness to go to
the aid of the Finns. However, when Russia herself was attacked in 1941, after the fall of France and the Battle of
Britain, an alliance of convenience was forged between the
former antagonists, and Russia was temporarily enabled to re-
enter the entente which she had left in 1917.

During the war against Nazi Germany and despite
Churchill's persistent efforts to prevent it (but also, in an
ironic sense, because of them),[32] a change occurred in the European situation, already heralded in Stalin's advance into the
Baltic states and the eastern marches of Poland, which dramatically affected the old arrangement for containing the
Bolshevik Revolution. Throughout the entire backward and
extremely anti-Russian (not to say anti-Communist) region
which hitherto constituted the cordon sanitaire, Stalin's Red
Army emerged first as the liberating, and then occupying,
force.

---

[32] Churchill's delaying of the Second Front caused the Russians to
shoulder the main burden of the war, facing 185 German divisions
in 1943, compared to the allies' 6. By the same token, however,
these delaying tactics resulted in the eventual liberation of Eastern
Europe by the Red Army, which would not have occurred had
the Second Front been opened in 1942, when it was first promised.
Cf. J. Bagguley, "The World War and the Cold War," in Horowitz (ed.), *Containment and Revolution*.

4. Capitalism and the Cold War

> Every time the Soviet Union extends its power over another area or state, the United States and Great Britain lose another normal market.
> —Former U.S. Ambassador to the Soviet Union, William C. Bullitt, 1946

As the war drew to a close, the Soviet Union found itself dealing with the Western capitalist powers for the first time as a state with a sphere of influence beyond its geographical borders. The cold war, which developed out of the Western challenge to this sphere, has been portrayed by orthodox historians as the inevitable consequence of the expansionist policies of the Russian state, to which the West, because of its lack of preparedness, was condemned to give initially only a weak and essentially helpless response. This orthodox picture does not correspond to the realities of power in 1945, nor to the sequence of actual events. In fact, the initial "offensive" was conducted not by the war-ruined, semi-underdeveloped and isolated Russian state but by its unscarred and immensely powerful antagonist in the West. Moreover, the cold war crusade, under whose banner this offensive was eventually mobilized, did not arise solely out of the "crisis" created by the Soviet Union's national hegemony in Eastern Europe, but was also a calculated response to the *global* crisis in the capitalist system itself.

The collapse of the cordon sanitaire had been accepted in principle (however ambiguously) by Churchill and Roosevelt during the last year of the European war. In order to secure the defeat of Germany and to gain a free hand for containing the very real prospect of revolution in Western Europe (where armed Communist parties were among the driving forces of the resistance, while the parties of the Right had been generally compromised by their collaboration with Nazism), Churchill and Roosevelt came to terms with Stalin and recognized the de facto division of the continent into spheres of influence. The recognition of Stalin's sphere, in Red Army-occupied Eastern Europe, was registered in the series of agreements culminating in the accords at Yalta in February 1945 and including the armistice agreements for the Nazi satellites Hungary, Bulgaria and Rumania and the Churchill-Stalin pact of the preceding October.[1]

Whatever the full *intentions* of the parties to these agreements (and there was confusion as well as deliberate ambiguity at several levels and on both sides in their drafting),[2] in effect the accords provided room for the Soviet Union to organize the governments of the region in a manner consonant with Soviet national interests, as well as in accord with the previous and current practice of the United States and Britain in Italy, Greece,[3] and Western Europe generally (and later in the Pacific region).[4] The Russians agreed to establish "demo-

---

[1] Under this pact, which is described in Churchill's *Triumph and Tragedy*, the two men, at Churchill's suggestion, divided the Balkans into areas of respective predominance, with Yugoslavia acting as a buffer between the Soviet and Western spheres.

[2] Cf. Isaac Deutscher, *Stalin* (Baltimore, Md.: Penguin Books, 1966), Chap. 13.

[3] On the U.S. precedent in Italy for the unilateral imposition of unpopular regimes by "liberating" military powers, see J. Bagguley, *op. cit.*

[4] The further obvious parallel between the security sphere granted to Russia and the U.S. sphere in Latin America was recognized at the time by as important a figure as U.S. Secretary of War Henry L. Stimson, who cast a critical eye at Truman's initial East European diplomacy, observing to an aide: "Some Americans are anx-

cratic" as well as "friendly" governments, but they did so
with the implicit understanding that the democratic process
would be allowed scope only insofar as it was compatible
with their own security interests. Accordingly it was agreed
that democratic rights were not to be extended to "fascist"
parties, while the West deliberately reserved for itself no
means for implementing its own interpretation of the clauses
on democratic procedures.[5]

With the military defeat of Germany in May 1945 and
the successful test of the atomic bomb in July, the Anglo-
American attitude to Russia's sphere in Eastern Europe
underwent a change. Believing themselves to possess "powers
which were irresistible" (Churchill) and to be in a position
"to dictate our own terms" (U.S. Secretary of State Byrnes),[6]
the Western allies increasingly turned their backs on those
aspects of the Allied agreements which had acknowledged
Russia's prerogatives. They embarked on a campaign to prevent Russia from consolidating her sphere and to compel her

---

ious to hang on to exaggerated views of the Monroe Doctrine and
at the same time butt into every question that comes up in Central
Europe."—cited in Lloyd C. Gardner, *Economic Aspects of New
Deal Diplomacy*, (Madison: University of Wisconsin Press, 1964),
p. 308. As the cold war developed, the Yalta agreements were attacked by conservatives in the United States and elsewhere in the
West (actually, the initial attack was delivered by Goebbels) precisely on the grounds that they yielded a sphere of influence to
Stalin. The liberal defense of Roosevelt was that he conceded no
prerogatives to the Russians that they could not have obtained any-
way as the occupying military power in the area. This "domestic"
dispute did not prevent both liberals and conservatives in the West
from uniting, however, to denounce Stalin when he attempted to
exercise those same prerogatives.

[5] Cf. Gar Alperovitz, *Atomic Diplomacy: Hiroshima and Potsdam*
(New York: Simon and Schuster, 1965), p. 135.

[6] Alperovitz, *op. cit.*, p. 13. Cf. also pp. 25, 86, 87n, and William A.
Williams, *The Tragedy of American Diplomacy* (New York:
Delta Books, 1962), Chap. 6, for the prevalence of this view in
Washington at the time.

to contract it,[7] and thus to reopen the door to Western predominance in the East European area. As DeGaulle accurately and disparagingly described the campaign later: "The Americans and British hoped to recover in application what they had conceded in principle [at Yalta]." [8]

Within weeks of the Potsdam Conference, and in the immediate wake of Hiroshima and Nagasaki, this Western offensive in Eastern Europe moved into the open with Secretary of State Byrnes's attack on the governments of Bulgaria and Rumania as not adequately representing "the important democratic elements." This attack, coupled with previous American refusal to grant diplomatic recognition to the two regimes, had serious implications for the internal stability of the Soviet sphere, since opposition political leaders throughout the Balkans had already approached American representatives for support.[9] It also cast a revealing light on the nature of the new American policy.

Soviet-occupied Rumania, for example, had been a Nazi satellite and had sent 26 divisions to participate in the Nazi devastation of the Soviet Union. In his Moscow meeting with Stalin in October 1944, Churchill had agreed to a 90 percent Soviet influence in Rumania, paralleling his own 90 percent influence in Greece. Washington had issued no protest over Britain's recent military intervention in Greece (indeed it had provided troop planes and pilots to support it) and did not challenge the resultant protégé regime for its undemocratic character; it had granted immediate recognition to the equally undemocratically composed (but dependably right-wing) Badoglio regime[10] in Italy the year before. Yet, it now

---

[7] Walter Lippmann, *The Cold War.*

[8] De Gaulle, *Salvation 1944–1946* (London, 1960), p. 199. Cf. also De Gaulle's discussion of Yalta, on pp. 87–89, which recognizes that whatever their intentions, Britain and America had made an agreement which "in practice . . . meant leaving the Soviets to their own devices."

[9] Alperovitz, *op. cit.*, p. 142.

[10] Marshal Badoglio, the conqueror of Abyssinia, had succeeded Mussolini after a palace coup.

refused recognition to the Soviet-sponsored government in Rumania, and it did so in the name of *principle*, i.e., the defense of freedom and self-determination. This was to prove an increasingly effective rallying cry for the cold war program in the West, but its consequences for the countries of Eastern Europe, which lay on the Soviet side of the armistice line in the Soviet Union's most sensitive security zone, were the reverse of what the program promised. For as the Western challenge to its influence intensified, Moscow was inevitably compelled to meet it by tightening the reins of control. (It is instructive to contrast the liberal character of Soviet policy toward Finland, which was not in a strategic position, militarily speaking, and where the Western powers did not make a concerted effort to undermine Soviet influence.) This was certainly understood by U.S. leaders who were not primarily concerned with fostering freedom *within* the Soviet sphere, but with *expelling* Soviet influence from the sphere altogether and reasserting Western dominance.[11]

Washington's Balkan initiative was also revealing in terms of the role played in its development by open door expansionism. This policy was, at the time, receiving a vigorous reemphasis by U.S. leaders who, on the basis of widely held fears of a postwar slump, asserted the necessity of reopening old outlets and finding new ones "for our surplus production" (Secretary of State Hull).[12] Thus, while Washington publicly

---

[11] As Paul Nitze, a member of the Policy Planning Staff of the State Department and later its director, explained: "In 1948 it was our purpose that the . . . area would come to be governed by regimes responsive to the will of the peoples of Eastern Europe—in other words, *that it would be in the power zone of the free world*. . . ."—cited in Klaus Knorr, ed., *NATO and American Security* (Princeton, N.J. University of Princeton Press, 1959). (Emphasis added.)

[12] Already in 1933, Hull was formulating the alternatives in pretty stark terms: "Every country can get along in some sort of fashion by depending almost entirely on its domestic market. . . . Such a process, however, means a reconstruction of the country's whole domestic economy. To agriculture it implies the cutting of

stressed the importance of free elections for the formation of
an adequately representative Rumanian government, in private the State Department advised Truman not to grant recognition until it was possible to "obtain equality of opportunity for U.S. business interests in these areas, and an
agreement protecting the rights of U.S. property owners." [13]
(Prior to the war, U.S. companies had owned, for example,
more than 85 percent of Rumanian oil.) This was not a
minor point of conflict, moreover, for the Russians were by
no means ready to open the door to an unlimited influx of
American capital and influence in Eastern Europe, which was
for them a primary security zone.[14]

---

acreage; to industry, the curtailment of production. . . ."—cited
in Charles A. Beard, *op. cit.*, p. 537. On the consensus in Washington over the issue, cf. Williams, *op. cit.*, Chap. 6.

[13] State Department memorandum cited in Gardner, *op. cit.*,
p. 310. In this context, it is interesting to note that W. A. Harriman, Ambassador to Russia and one of the chief architects of
Washington's postwar hard-line policy in Eastern Europe, is the
Harriman of Brown Brothers, Harriman & Co., one of the largest
financial groups in the United States, with extensive interests in
the raw materials of prewar Eastern Europe. While hardly incon-
sequential, the role of even so key a figure as Harriman should not
be overdrawn. In the first place, the most important policy makers
were generally from the investment banking or raw material exploiting sections of the ruling class. In the second place, the ideology of Open Door Expansion was shared by members of the political directorate generally. Progressives like Henry Wallace thought
it possible to get Russia to cooperate in the extension of America's
Open Door empire; conservatives thought not.

[14] Compare the following remarks by Soviet Foreign Minister,
V. M. Molotov: "The principle of so-called 'equal opportunity'
has become a favorite topic of late. What, it is argued, could be
better than this principle, which would establish equal opportunity
for all states without discrimination? . . . let us discuss the principle of equality seriously and honestly. . . . [Take] Rumania, enfeebled by the war, or Yugoslavia, ruined by the German and
Italian fascists, and the United States of America, whose wealth
has grown immensely during the war, and you will clearly see

In the end, Washington's attempt to restore the prewar status quo in the ruptured cordon failed because the power balance which the Yalta agreements had recognized had not, in fact, changed significantly enough to force a unilateral Soviet withdrawal from the armistice line. Washington was able to mobilize its diplomatic, economic and infant nuclear power to back the planned political showdown in 1945, but the crucial factor—conventional manpower—was missing. To be sure, Truman attempted to secure an armed force sufficient to back his diplomacy, and even announced his intention (three days after the Japanese surrender) to press for universal military training and peacetime conscription unprecedented in U.S. history, but these initiatives proved abortive.[15]

Behind this failure lay several factors which Western leaders were able to overcome only four years later, at which time a counter-buildup in the East had become possible. In particular, because of the wartime role of the Soviet Union (and the pro-Soviet, pro-Stalin propaganda that had been spread, not without a large element of cynicism, by Western governments and the Western press), plus the relative free-

what the implementation of the principle of 'equal opportunity' would mean in practice. Imagine, under these circumstances, that in this same Rumania or Yugoslavia, or in some other war-weakened state, you have this so-called 'equal opportunity' for, let us say, American capital—that is, the opportunity for it to penetrate unhindered into Rumanian industry, or Yugoslav industry and so forth: what, then will remain of Rumania's national industry, or of Yugoslavia's national industry?"—*Problems of Foreign Policy* (Moscow, 1949), pp. 207–14 (cited in Lloyd C. Gardner, "New Deal, New Frontiers and the Cold War," in Horowitz (ed.), *The Corporations and the Cold War*).

[15] This showdown policy is analyzed at length in Alperovitz, *op. cit.* P. M. S. Blackett, in *Military and Political Consequences of Atomic Weapons* (1948), was the first to point out that the atomic bombs dropped on Japan fulfilled diplomatic objectives vis-à-vis the U.S.S.R. rather than military objectives which could be accomplished by other means. On the attempt to mobilize conventional forces, cf. Alperovitz, pp. 117, 129, 224.

dom which Stalin in fact permitted in Eastern Europe in 1945 and the restraint he imposed on the Communist parties of Western Europe, it was not possible to secure public support for an immediate showdown with Russia. Congress rejected Truman's plan for universal military training, while popular sentiment reflected in demonstrations among the armed forces overseas compelled the return home of large numbers of troops,[16] and, as Harriman admitted later: "Only by keeping our military forces in being after Germany and Japan surrendered could we have attempted to compel the Soviet Union to withdraw from the territory it controlled." [17]

In the ensuing period, the United States carried forward the basic "showdown" strategy, under the program officially labeled "containment"; this rejected the idea of a negotiated settlement and disengagement and envisaged, instead, a buildup of Western strength to put pressure on the weakened Soviet state in order to induce its withdrawal from the armistice line. This pressure was spearheaded by the diplomatic campaign against the Kremlin-backed governments of Eastern Europe, and supported by a global military encirclement of the Soviet land mass. The aims of this buildup (short of the preventive war which some cabinet members and top-ranking generals openly proposed) were to "overload" the Soviet political and economic system by adding the burdens of rearmament to the already considerable strains of postwar reconstruction and to "delay" Russia's recovery and development until a breakdown occurred.[18] The combination of these pressures, it was hoped, would "liberate" Eastern Europe (and the Soviet Union) without a fighting war.

---

[16] On August 31, 1945, total U.S. forces numbered 11.9 million, compared with 10.6 million Russian. However, the bulk of the U.S. forces were stationed in the Far East.

[17] Cited in Alperovitz, *op. cit.*, p. 224.

[18] The cold war strategy of "Overload and Delay" was formally worked out in 1951 or 1952, although it was clearly implicit in the containment program and Kennan's "X" analysis—*The New York Times*, June 9, 1959.

In its defensive aspect the containment program was directed toward the restoration of the conservative structure of European society, which had been dangerously weakened by depression, fascism and war and was now under challenge from the Communist left. The military buildup of NATO fitted in well with this political purpose,[19] as did the effort to create out of the Western zones of the defeated Reich a bastion of anti-Communism at the center of socially and politically unstable Europe. In the words of the House Special Committee on Postwar Economic Policy and Planning (December 1946): "Germany is the special responsibility of the Western powers, and on its fate mainly depends the future of Europe in relation to Communism." In the context of the overall anti-Communist containment program the policy of reviving German strength soon began to have distinctly ominous overtones of the anti-Comintern Pact of the inter-war years, with consequent implications for the cold war's development.

For with U.S. assistance, West Germany quickly became a major European power, harboring grave political and territorial "grievances" vis-à-vis Eastern Europe, with no possibility of satisfying them short of a new war. Nor was this recapitulation of the German past merely a superficial phenomenon; it also had structural roots. Restoration of German capitalism was accompanied by the restoration of those same economic rulers who had supported Hitler as an ally against domestic and international Communism;[20] it was followed, further, by the return to power and then elevation within the NATO military command of those same German generals

---

[19] From a strictly military point of view, there was no need for the NATO buildup at all. The failure of Stalin to invade the "renegade" state of Yugoslavia showed that Russia's power was already effectively contained, or self-contained. The Warsaw Pact was formed six years after NATO, only after Western Germany had been rearmed and integrated into the NATO alliance.

[20] James Stewart Martin, *All Honorable Men* (Boston: Little, Brown, 1950).

who had led Hitler's drive to destroy the "Jewish-Bolshevist system" in the East.[21] The political hardening of the cold war divisions—the failure to achieve a mutual withdrawal from the armistice line and the integration of Eastern Europe into the Soviet system—were integrally connected to the conflict over these German developments; the insolubility of the problems of the European division remained long afterward largely a result of the insolubility of the German problem.[22]

Three months after the Special Committee report, President Truman formally launched the cold war in his "Doctrine" speech of March 1947, announcing an ideological crusade against Soviet Communism, while at the same time

---

[21] Adolf Heusinger, Hitler's Chief of Operations and a war criminal, to pick only one obvious example, became the chairman of the Standing Military Committee of NATO in Washington. The phrase cited was used by von Manstein to explain to his troops in 1941 the necessity of extramilitary slaughter on the Eastern front ('The soldier must show severe revenge on Judaism, the spiritual carrier of the Bolshevist terror'), but the idea was basic to Nazism. Von Manstein was sentenced to eighteen years for his crimes, but according to the *New York Times* correspondent Arthur J. Olsen (in 1959), von Manstein was regarded as 'the most prestigious German soldier who survived the war . . . with honor.'—cited in T. H. Tetens, *The New Germany and the Old Nazis* (London: Secker & Warburg), 1961.

[22] This was the clear implication of Lippmann's critique of containment (1947) when he concluded that the role assigned to Germany in the program entailed "the most dangerous and destructive consequences of [the] policy of firm containment." It was confirmed by George Kennan, the "author" of the containment idea, in his Reith lectures of 1957 and his lecture at the Graduate Institute of International Studies (Geneva) in May 1965, in which he stated: "From the moment [NATO was formed], the peaceful solution of Europe's greatest problems on any basis other than that of the permanent division of Germany and the continent, with the implied consignment of the Eastern European peoples to inclusion for an indefinite period in the Soviet sphere of power, became theoretically almost inconceivable. . . ."

declaring an open-ended commitment to contain armed revolution wherever it developed. In his speech, Truman referred to an irreconcilable conflict between democratic and undemocratic "ways of life." But inasmuch as the specific action which the Doctrine underwrote was the defense of a foreign-imposed undemocratic government in Greece against an indigenous and popularly based revolutionary movement, it was clear (and confirmed by the whole tenor of the subsequent U.S. cold war program) that the real enemy pursued by Washington was not Soviet totalitarianism at all,[23] but the older enemy, the Soviet *revolution*, with its appeal to classes which did not have property "to obtain a share by process of government rather than by individual ['free'] enterprise." Here was the "threat at existing social order in all countries" that the U.S. cold war program was organized to contain.

The global terms of the Truman Doctrine (which had been conceived as early as autumn 1945) and the stark ideological choice presented in it reflected the recognition by American leaders that the postwar problems confronting them extended far beyond Eastern Europe and that the fundamental issue was not restricted to the terms of the postwar peace settlement but encompassed the very survival of the "free world" capitalist system. At the time, this threat to the system lay not in the military or economic strength of the war-ruined,[24] non-nuclear, semi-underdeveloped Soviet

---

[23] The extremely liberal attitude (to put no worse interpretation on it), which U.S. policy took toward the surviving agents of Nazism in occupied Germany, also betrayed a somewhat less zealous antitotalitarian commitment than the rhetoric of the Truman Doctrine suggested. See below, pp. 185–86.

[24] ". . . no nation in the history of battle ever suffered more than the Soviet Union in the Second World War. At least 20 million lost their lives. Countless millions of homes and families were burned or sacked. A third of the nation's territory, including two-thirds of its industrial base, were turned into a wasteland—a loss equivalent to the destruction of this country east of Chicago."— J. F. Kennedy, June 10, 1963.

power, which had suffered a serious famine in the year preceding the Doctrine and still faced (in conditions of severe manpower and capital shortage) one of the most daunting tasks of postwar reconstruction; the real threat lay in the accumulated failures of the system itself.

For the orderly structure of international capitalist society had been violently and profoundly disrupted in 1914 and its equilibrium had not been restored since. So shallow had been even its partial stabilization in the inter-war period, so ubiquitous the signs of disintegration, that the interconnection of particular and "local" social catastrophes during these years became not merely a Marxist but a generally held perspective. "We live," as one extremely conservative economist wrote in 1934, "not in the fourth, but in the nineteenth year of the world crisis." [25] In the unemployment and poverty of the Great Depression, this crisis of world monopoly capitalism found its deepest economic expression; in the barbarities of Nazism and the war, its moral and political nadir.

The cumulative consequences of the long-term crisis confronted the leaders of the supreme capitalist power, in 1945, with a series of grave problems. Internally, the United States faced the massive task of converting from war to peacetime production in an economy which had not solved the structural problems that had led it into the impasse of the thirties (as late as 1941, for example, when war production entered full swing, eight million workers were still idle). Externally, in Europe, as a consequence of the economic crisis and the rise of fascism, mass communist movements, particularly in France and Italy, emerged to challenge the capitalist status quo. Finally, in the underdeveloped world, the old colonial empires were in an advanced stage of disintegration, partly as a consequence of the inter-imperialist conflict of the war which had resulted in the devastation and exhaustion of the imperial powers themselves, partly as a consequence of

---

[25] Lionel Robbins, *The Great Depression* (1934).

the clash between Japanese imperialism and the white colonial powers in Asia and partly because of the rise during the preceding period of armed nationalist and communist movements.

U.S. leaders regarded not only the domestic problem, which they saw primarily as a question of markets, in economic terms, but the apparently political, foreign problems as well. To be sure, they understood the political dimensions of the crises they faced, and the ideological crusade against Soviet Communism was certainly a recognition of the importance of this factor. But the basis of the challenges, the ground in which they took root, was understood by U.S. leaders to lie in the economic domain. Thus, the man who drafted the "Truman Doctrine," with its emphasis on the political menace emanating from Russia, confided in private only two weeks before the speech his view of the crisis as primarily an economic problem.

"There are many signs," he wrote, "that the world is approaching this year the greatest crisis since the turn in the tide of the war in November 1942. It is primarily an economic crisis centered in Britain and Empire, France, Greece and China. . . . If these areas are allowed to spiral downwards into economic anarchy, then at best they will drop out of the United States orbit and try an independent nationalistic policy; at most they will swing into the Russian orbit." If *either* of these eventualities were to occur [i.e., "nationalist" independence of the U.S. open door empire or absorption into the Soviet sphere], the United States would face "economic isolation," in which case, he said, "I do not see how we could possibly avoid a depression far greater than that of 1929 –1932, and crushing taxes to pay for the direct commitments we would be forced to make around the world." [26]

---

[26] Letter of Joseph M. Jones to Assistant Secretary of State for Public Affairs William Benton, February 26, 1947. Cited in Henry W. Berger, "A Conservative Critique of Containment," in Horowitz (ed.), *Containment and Revolution*.

In the event, the U.S. cold war programs articulated in the Truman Doctrine, the Marshall Plan of economic aid to Europe and the NATO alliance resulted in an impressive restoration of political and economic equilibrium in the developed capitalist world. During the two postwar decades following the proclamation of the Truman Doctrine, a measure of stability was achieved such as had not been experienced in Europe since 1914, or in the United States since 1929. To some extent, the dramatic character of this reversal was the result of an overestimation of the postwar conversion problem in the United States; here hindsight showed that the forced savings of the wartime period, the backlog of unmet consumer demand and the requirements of postwar construction provided sufficient markets to sustain the economy in the initial switch from war to peacetime production. If there was a significant new factor in the postwar economic recovery, it was the unprecedented willingness of the U.S. government to provide massive public loan and aid capital to European industry and government to restore European production and international trade, and to open up new foreign markets for U.S. corporations (both in terms of direct foreign investment and export trade in military and economic goods).[27]

Yet, if the postwar recovery and its resultant equilibrium were impressive by contrast with what had preceded, they did not give any ground for supposing that the basic tendencies toward instability and *dis*equilibrium in the capitalist system had been removed by the kind of structural reforms that many of the most perceptive defenders of the system had

---

[27] Cf. Oliver C. Cox, *Capitalism and American Leadership* (New York: Philosophical Library, 1962), especially Chap. 4. Cox discusses the evolution of U.S. loan policy in terms of the U.S. assumption of the leadership role in the international capitalist system. On the postwar aid program itself, cf. Alavi and Khurso, "Pakistan: the Burden of U.S. Aid," *New University Thought* (Chicago) Autumn 1962. In the context of the Open Door program, see Williams, Gardner, and David Eakins, "Business Planners and the Development of American Postwar Economic Policy," in Horowitz (ed.), *The Corporations and the Cold War*.

considered inevitable toward the end of the inter-war period. Thus, despite the widespread introduction of Keynesian monetary and fiscal techniques for damping the postwar trade cycle,[28] neither of the two fundamental *structural* reforms advocated by Keynes as essential for long-term stability, namely the "socialization of investment" and the redistribution of wealth,[29] was implemented anywhere in the capitalist world.[30]

What made these vital reforms wholly impracticable was the distribution of social and political power in these societies which, like the distribution of wealth, flowed from the ownership and control of productive capital. The same class structure profoundly affected the spending pattern of the Keynesian state, so that those forms of investment which tended to expand social welfare and therefore to redistribute social wealth were either severely limited, or even curtailed,[31] while the most destructive and *politically* destabilizing form of state

---

[28] For an analysis and critique of these techniques from the point of view of their very limited effect, cf. J. M. Gillman, *Prosperity in Crisis* (New York: Marzani and Munsell, 1965).

[29] His proposal for a drastic reduction of interest rates amounted to the same kind of reform from a social point of view.

[30] For example, "Since about 1949, wealth inequality has been growing in [the United States], the rate of increase being more than twice as fast as the rate of decline between 1922 and 1949. . . . There is little evidence to suggest that Britain has not been following the same path since the end of the 1940s."—R. M. Titmuss, in his Introduction to R. H. Tawney, *Equality* (London: Allen & Unwin, 1964). Cf. Titmuss, *Income Distribution and Social Change* (Allen & Unwin, 1962); Gabriel Kolko, *Wealth and Power in America* (New York: Praeger, 1962). On the old contours of the "new" postwar capitalism, cf. Robin Blackburn, "The New Capitalism," and John Westergaard, "The Withering Away of Class: A Contemporary Myth," in *Towards Socialism* (Ithaca: Cornell University Press, 1966). Cf. also Blackburn, "The Unequal Society," in *The Incompatibles* (Baltimore, Md.: Penguin Books, 1967).

[31] For example, see Huberman and Sweezy, "The Kennedy-Johnson Boom," in Gettleman and Mermelstein (eds.), *The Great Society Reader* (New York: Random House, 1967).

spending—on arms production and deployment—was vastly extended.[32] The long-term destabilizing effect of this arms spending, moreover, was not limited to its impact in the inter-state sphere. For the failure to deal with developing domestic social crises in the United States in the areas of urban planning, housing, crime, education and race relations exacerbated social tensions and promoted political polarization in an atmosphere of increasing social violence.

In the United States—the critical case because of its dominant position in the capitalist world economy—the increase of federal government spending since 1929 was overwhelmingly dominated by the expansion of the military sector.[33] Moreover, in terms of effective demand, and the sustaining of postwar capitalist prosperity, the arms economy was unquestionably of decisive significance. For while there were such important factors as a major technological revolution, a postwar population boom and the vast expansion of available credit[34] to support the upswing, in the period taken as a whole, "defense expenditure played twice as powerful an expansionist role as private investment," [35] accounting at times for as much as 60 percent of gross domestic fixed capital for-

---

[32] For the structural causes of the inability of capitalist governments to pursue welfare programs on a scale commensurate with welfare needs or comparable with military spending, cf. J. Robinson, "Marx, Marshall and Keynes," in *Collected Economic Papers* (Oxford: Blackwell, 1960), Vol. II. Paul Baran and Paul Sweezy, *Monopoly Capital* (New York: Monthly Review Press, 1966); K. Kurihara (on Hansen) in *Applied Economic Dynamics* and Michael Kidron, *Western Capitalism Since the War* (London: Weidenfeld & Nicolson, 1968).

[33] F. M. Bator, *The Question of Government Spending* (New York: Harper, 1962).

[34] In 1967 consumer debts amounted to an unprecedented 55 percent of consumer incomes.—"End of the Boom," *Monthly Review*, April 1967.

[35] Alvin Hansen, *The Postwar American Economy* (New York: Norton, 1964), p. 28.

mation.[36] In the words of one of Keynes's most distinguished
Cambridge collaborators, "whatever might have been, in fact
Keynesian prosperity has been a by-product of the Cold
War." [37] Not only was this "prosperity" deceptive from a social point of view, but the combination of Keynesian-military
deficits and the monopolistic price structure of the key corporate sectors generated inflationary pressures which threatened to undermine its *economic* foundations.[38]

In Europe many of the factors contributing to the postwar economic equilibrium were different from those in the
United States, although the arms-stimulated vitality of the
U.S. economy undoubtedly lay at the basis of the European
recovery and expansion, which would not have been possible
without it. Among the major elements of the European "mir-
acle" were the demand generated by the destruction and exhaustion of the European capital structure, the almost unlimited capital aid and investment from the United States and
the flow of cheap immigrant labor. In Europe, too, a greater
and earlier use of Keynesian monetary and fiscal techniques, a
larger public sector and the introduction of indicative "planning" bodies helped to stabilize and sustain the economic expansion.

However, these factors were also either of a temporary
nature or remained largely superficial in terms of the deeper
forces at work in the system. For in Europe, as in the United
States, revolutionary structural changes were not undertaken;
corporate power was not surrendered or subordinated to social
power; corporate planning (for corporate profit) was not re-

---

[36] United Nations, *Economic and Social Consequences of Disarmament*, 1962, cited in Kidron, *op. cit.*

[37] Joan Robinson, "Latter-day Capitalism," in *Collected Economic
Papers*, Vol. III; Harry Magdoff, "Problems of U.S. Capitalism,"
in *The Socialist Register*, 1965 (New York: Monthly Review
Press, 1965).

[38] Paul Baran, *The Political Economy of Growth* (New York:
Monthly Review Press, 1962), pp. 123–27.

placed by social planning (for social need); and the fundamental contradiction between the tendency toward "unlimited" expansion of the productive forces and the systematically limited growth of effective demand [39] was not solved but continued to threaten the system with the dissolution of its newly found economic equilibrium.

A final factor sustaining the postwar equilibrium, particularly in the sphere of inter-national capitalist relations (but domestically as well), was the really new element in the postwar social equation: a large, and—as its wartime victories had shown—potentially very powerful anticapitalist bloc. In the presence of this bloc (and the large Communist movements supporting it in the West), inter-capitalist antagonisms were moderated and inter-capitalist conflicts contained. On a political level, cooperation was achieved through the agency of the NATO alliance, and on an economic level through the various new international trade and monetary agreements,

---

[39] With the Keynesian revolution in economic theory and the return of orthodox economics to the classical problems of macrodynamic development and growth, this fundamental contradiction ceased to be a preoccupation solely of Marxists and other economic heretics. As a Keynesian pioneer of modern growth theory formulated it: "In a private capitalist society where [the distribution of income] cannot be readily changed, a higher level of income and employment at any given time can be achieved only through increased investment. But investment, as an employment-creating instrument, is a mixed blessing because of its [capacity-increasing] effect. The economy finds itself in a serious dilemma: if sufficient investment is not forthcoming today, unemployment will be here today. But if enough is invested today, still more will be needed tomorrow. . . . [Therefore] as far as unemployment is concerned, investment is at the same time a cure for the disease and the cause of even greater ills in the future."—Evsey D. Domar, *Essays in the Theory of Economic Growth* (New York: Oxford University Press, 1957), p. 101. The "advantage" of military investment by the state, from the perspective of this model, is that it creates employment without causing a comparable increase in productive capacity.

which, however, represented no real surrender of national sovereignties.[40]

To some extent these restraints on economic nationalism were influenced by the disastrous inter-war experience, while in the early postwar years the appearance of "internationalism" was greatly enhanced by the fact that no capitalist power had the strength to challenge the international order established by the United States. Even with the recovery of European industry and the development of political and economic schisms in the Western camp, dissident and dominant capitalist governments showed a marked reluctance to go to the "brink," and inter-capitalist antagonisms did not begin to approach the magnitude of the inter-war years. There can be no doubt that the Soviet "menace" was a decisive factor inducing this spirit of mutual adjustment.[41]

Ultimately, however, because of the structural characteristics of monopoly capitalism, which had been modified but in no sense overcome, the end of the general equilibrium was inevitable. The day of reckoning might be delayed, but sooner or later it would come.

---

[40] As the American author of the U.S. proposals on world currency reform put it in 1945: "Our solution is international cooperation, but our point of view is as purely American as that of the most rigid economic isolationist."—Gardner, *op. cit.*, p. 290.

[41] For discussion of this phenomenon in relation to the international monetary crisis of the sixties, cf. "$ and Gold: Four Articles on Monetary Problems and Crises of the World Capitalist System," *Monthly Review*, December 1966. The Soviet bloc had a stabilizing effect on the capitalist system in other ways as well. For example, the extent of economic fluctuations was limited by the fact that part of the trading world was excluded from them. Furthermore, the challenge of "competitive coexistence" was an important stimulus to internal reforms in the capitalist countries and to intensified efforts to maintain internal economic stability and full employment. Cf. Joan Robinson, "Has Capitalism Changed?," in *Collected Economic Papers*, Vol. III.

Even while the postwar stabilization and containment program in Western and Southern Europe initially appeared to be an unqualified success from Washington's point of view, elsewhere—and especially in Asia—the picture was more complicated.

The disintegration of the colonial empires, under the combined impact of Japanese expansion and defeat, nationalist revolution, and the military and economic exhaustion of the European colonial powers, presented the United States both with opportunities and problems. Although exhibiting a somewhat ambivalent attitude toward overt *colonial* empire, Washington was in no doubt about its own stake in the political and economic organization of a *post*-colonial capitalist status quo and, as in Europe, assumed early a guardian role with respect to the vested interests of the international capitalist system in the underdeveloped regions.

It was the United States, and the United States alone in this period, that was able to supply billions of dollars in economic and military support for the last-ditch struggle to preserve the Open Door in China,[42] as it was the United States

---

[42] "Although unable to commit its own armies openly at the time, Washington devoted immense resources to the struggle, eventually providing the Kuomintang with twice the military and economic support in the three postwar years of civil war, as it had in eight years of war against the Japanese."—John Gittings, "The Sources of China's Foreign Policy," in *Containment and Revolution*. U.S. support for Chiang's regime provides further insight into the class nature of Washington's anti-Communist policy. For it was known to the State Department at the time that Mao was independent of Moscow and even at odds with its policies. Moreover, Chiang's Kuomintang provided no alternative whatsoever, in terms of the ideology of Western "freedom," to Stalin's Communist party on which it was explicitly modeled. As for the regime itself, it was one of the most brutal military dictatorships of modern times. Hundreds of thousands of people were *officially* executed for varying political crimes by the Chiang regime, which rested on police terror, censorship and all the familiar trappings of the dictatorial state. Its social policy was one of systematic plunder of the

alone that was able to provide the means for the other imperial powers to shoulder what burdens they could in the global
struggle to defend the "free world" against communist and
left-wing nationalist revolutions. Thus, more than half the
military and economic assistance to the French under the
Marshall Plan and NATO was used not to protect metropolitan France against the mythical Soviet threat, but to restore
her colonial control in Algeria and Vietnam. Similarly, Bel-
gium and Portugal's sole need for NATO arms was to preserve their colonial enclaves in Africa, while Britain was able
to make use of her "defensive" weapons only against nationalist revolt in the colonies and former colonies of her empire.

U.S. readiness to sustain its side of the cooperative effort,
however, proved to be very much dependent on the development of her own military resources and economic interests,
and whenever the occasion presented itself she quickly revealed her own particularist stake in these counterrevolutionary alliances. Already in victory the United States had eased
German and Italian economic interests out of Latin America
and drastically reduced the economic claims of Britain and
France throughout the Western hemisphere (including Can-
ada), while at the same time securing liens on the major British military bases in the Caribbean. In the initial postwar period the United States further "inherited" from Britain her
spheres in Greece and the Mediterranean, Iran, Jordan and
the Middle East. (Before the Second World War, for example, U.S. corporations owned only 13 percent of the oil of the
Middle East, whereas by 1960 they owned 65 percent while
the corresponding British share *declined* from 60 to 30 percent). From defeated Japan the United States openly seized
Okinawa and her Pacific bases, while moving into a dominant
position in South Korea and Taiwan; from France, she

---

weakest and poorest sections of society for the aggrandizement of
its own corrupt officials and the enrichment of the traditional parasitic classes of Chinese society. But, of course, it was a willing
agent of America's Open Door policy in the Chinese market.

secured Indochina, after first pouring in massive aid and materiel to support the vain attempt by the French forces to retain their colonial foothold on the peninsula.

Notwithstanding Washington's early and committed display of global "responsibility" and interest, however, its containment program in the underdeveloped world failed to achieve the conservative stabilization which it sought. While the revolution in Greece was defeated, the more momentous revolution in China was not, and even where containment was temporarily successful, the stability achieved proved precarious, the path to self-sustained development elusive and the "threat" of revolution more or less permanent.

Underlying this failure was a deeper cause than the inadequacy of the particular policies and programs of the new guardian capitalist world power. As the succeeding decades would make more and more plain, at the heart of the failure of counterrevolutionary containment lay the failure of the system itself: the historic bankruptcy of the bourgeois revolution and the approaching close of its epoch.

III

THE RUSSIAN REVOLUTION

AND ITS FATE

5. The Modern Revolutionary Framework

> . . . they themselves must do the ut-
> most for their final victory by clarifying
> their minds as to what their class inter-
> ests are, by taking up their position as
> an independent party as soon as pos-
> sible and by not allowing themselves
> to be seduced for a single moment by
> the hypocritical phrases of the demo-
> cratic petty bourgeois into refraining
> from the independent organization of
> the party of the proletariat. Their battle
> cry must be: Permanent Revolution.
> —Marx and Engels, 1850

> A permanent revolution versus a per-
> manent slaughter: that is the struggle
> in which the future is man.
> —Trotsky in *Pravda*, Sept. 7, 1917

The fate of the bourgeois revolution in the cold war period (and during the entire era following the nineteenth-century colonial expansion) adhered very much to the course indicated in the original Bolshevik perspective. Despite the massive official attention paid to the problems of underdevelopment and the so-called "aid" programs of the developed capitalist powers, and moreover despite the proclaimed commitment of the most important of these powers to promote and defend the "democratic revolution," not a single underdeveloped country remaining within the framework of international capitalism was able to achieve a stabilized bourgeois-democratic revolution and development in the manner of Western Europe and the United States.[1]

As a result, these countries were all beset by a complex of "insoluble" problems, including those of social backwardness, economic stagnation, industrial and agricultural underdevelopment, hence "overpopulation," and, as a surface expression of these deeper currents, chronic political instability. Virtually everywhere in the backward and exploited regions the democratic gains that were made proved superficial and impermanent; in their very impermanence they seemed to confirm Marx's warning after the revolutionary defeats of 1848: "Every revolutionary upheaval, however remote from the class struggle its goal may appear to be, must fail until the revolutionary working class is victorious, . . . every social reform remains a utopia until the proletarian revolution and the feudalistic counter-revolution measure swords in a *world war*." (Emphasis in original.)[2]

The proper starting point for an analysis of the contemporary framework of revolution in the underdeveloped world is, inevitably, the first proletarian conquest of power to take

---

[1] Cf. Barrington Moore, Jr., *Social Origins of Dictatorship and Democracy* (Boston: Beacon Press, 1967). He regards the U.S. Civil War as the last capitalist revolution and the Radical Republicans as the last true capitalist revolutionaries: "From the perspective of a hundred years later, they appear as the last revolutionary flicker that is strictly bourgeois and strictly capitalist, the last successors to medieval townsmen beginning the revolt against their feudal overlords. Revolutionary movements since the Civil War have been either anticapitalist, or fascist and counterrevolutionary if in support of capitalistm."—p. 142.

[2] Introduction, *Wage Labour and Capital* (1849). Marx, of course, was thinking of Europe and in a sense this war was and yet was not fought in 1914–1918 and again in 1939–1945. See below, pp. 174 ff. The "feudalistic" counterrevolution has since been subordinated to the counterrevolution organized by the metropolitan bourgeois capitalist powers who attained undisputed supremacy in 1945. But the incompletion of the bourgeois revolution and the impermanence of its reforms remain valid notions.

place in a backward environment—the Russian Revolution of 1917. The question that such an analysis must answer is why this revolution, which began in February 1917 as a bourgeois-democratic revolution against Czarist autocracy and feudal backwardness, was unable to stabilize itself, and instead was compelled to develop into a proletarian revolution against the capitalist status quo. In other words, what were the sources of the Bolshevik October?

We have already outlined a perspective on belated bourgeois revolutions generally, and the Russian Revolution in particular, which provides an answer to this question.[3] In order to arrive at an intelligible theory of contemporary revolutionary developments, however, it is necessary to take the analysis somewhat further and to examine, in closer detail, the social forces and conditions forming the framework of those events.

The earliest and still most adequate explanation of the peculiarities of the Russian 1917, was given by Trotsky, who, with Lenin, was the most important theoretician of the Bolshevik revolution,[4] as well as being the actual organizer and leader of the October insurrection.[5]

The framework of Trotsky's analysis was provided by the so-called laws of "uneven" and "combined" development. World historical evolution, he observed, was characterized by great inequalities in its levels of development. For while in

---

[3] See above, pp. 23–28.

[4] Prior to Trotsky's split with the party's leadership, this view would not have seemed heterodox. Thus, during the first five years of the Communist International, before Stalin imposed his own orthodoxy on party theory, Trotsky's book *Results and Prospects* (1905) was published widely (and in foreign languages) as an official theoretical interpretation of the forces of the Russian Revolution.

[5] "All the work of practical organization of the [October] insurrection was conducted under the immediate leadership of the president of the Petrograd Soviet, Comrade Trotsky."—J. V. Stalin, *Pravda*, November 6, 1918.

some regions very advanced stages of social and technical achievement were attained, in others the most primitive forms of backwardness continued to exist. Under the "whip" of the capitalist world market, however, which "prepares and in a certain sense realizes the universality and permanence of man's development," backward countries are compelled to assimilate the material and intellectual conquests of the advanced areas. This does not mean that the backward countries follow the advanced ones "slavishly," reproducing all the stages of their past. On the contrary, late-emerging societies do not take their steps in the same order as their forerunners but are forced to make leaps in their progress: "The privilege of historic backwardness—and such a privilege exists—permits, or rather compels, the adoption of whatever is ready in advance . . . skipping a whole series of intermediate stages. Savages throw away their bows and arrows for rifles all at once, without traveling the road which lay between those two weapons in the past." Thus, in the real world, development takes a course very different from that suggested in the *schema* of discrete and progressive historical stages. Instead, everywhere more advanced social elements combine with those that are retrograde to produce mixed rather than "pure" social forms, and "the development of historically backward nations leads necessarily to a peculiar *combination* of different stages in the historic process." [6]

In Czarist Russia, as Trotsky pointed out, elements of the bourgeois "future" were already grafted directly onto the feudal present, and it was the resultant hybrid development (or, in his terminology, *combined* development) that gave birth to the hybrid revolutions of 1917. Russian industry, for example, while small in relation to the economy as a whole, was technically very advanced and highly concentrated, as well as being greatly subordinated to foreign capital. The

---

[6] Trotsky, *The History of the Russian Revolution*, Chap. 1. See also especially Volume III, Appendix II.

confluence of such factors peculiar to Russian development (which meant, for example, the absence of large middle sectors of small businessmen) rendered the Russian bourgoisie weak and isolated. By contrast, the Russian proletariat had developed "abnormal" strength for this "stage" of the historical process. In fact, the strength of the proletariat rested on the same advanced factors of technical and social organization (the concentration of workers in huge modern enterprises, for example) that produced the relative isolation and weakness of the bourgeoisie. In addition, the proletariat was armed with an advanced revolutionary ideology developed by the much older and politically more mature working classes of Western Europe. Thus, as in Germany before, the revolutionary stage was set very differently in Russia in 1917 from the way it had been for the great bourgeois-democratic revolution in France.

The French bourgeoisie had been in a strong and independent position to lead both the democratic and agrarian revolutions against the feudal nobility and to withstand the unfocused left challenge of the *sans-culotte* and laboring masses; but the Russian bourgeoisie, because of the peculiarities of its *combined* development—its lack of independence, its entanglement with the landed aristocracy, its very fear of the socialism of the relatively advanced proletariat—proved inadequate to its historic tasks, and fell to an organized and mature working-class revolt. "Russia was so late in accomplishing her bourgeois revolution," as Trotsky summarized the difference, "that she found herself compelled to turn it into a proletarian revolution." [7]

Lenin was already convinced in 1905, that only the proletariat and the peasantry would stand consistently behind the democratic revolution and form its real vanguard. Hence, he had put forward the program of distrust of the bourgeoisie in

---

[7] *The History of the Russian Revolution*, Introduction to Volumes II and III.

its "own" revolution and struggle for the *revolutionary-democratic dictatorship of the proletariat and peasantry*. Trotsky, in the same period, and from the same perspective, had gone even further. He did not believe that such a revolutionary power could or would stop at the stage of bourgeois reforms. To defend its gains, "to safeguard its political supremacy," the proletariat, once in power would be compelled to push the revolution forward, to put *socialist* problems on the revolutionary agenda.[8]

Twelve years later, when the February Revolution of 1917 deposed Czar Nicholas and established the "dual power" of the provisional (bourgeois) government, on the one hand, and the soviets of workers and peasants, on the other, Lenin responded with a new program, the famous "April Theses," which reflected a perspective similar to that of Trotsky's 1905 analysis. In the existence of the soviets, which exercised effective power in the revolution, Lenin saw the revolutionary-democratic dictatorship of the proletariat and the peasantry "already accomplished in reality." The formula was, therefore, "already antiquated." [9] The new task facing the Bolsheviks was "to effect a split *within* this dictatorship between the proletarian elements . . . and the small-proprietor or petty-bourgeois elements," while calling for a transfer of all state power to the Soviets—in other words, to organize for a proletarian, i.e., a *socialist* conquest of power.

---

[8] Cf. Rosa Luxemburg, *The Russian Revolution, 1917* (Ann Arbor: University of Michigan Press, 1962): ". . . the Russian Revolution has but confirmed the basic lesson of every great revolution, the law of its being, which decrees: either the revolution must advance at a rapid, stormy and resolute tempo, break down all barriers with an iron hand and place its goals ever farther ahead, or it is quite soon thrown backward behind its feeble point of departure and suppressed by counterrevolution."—p. 36. To a large extent, Trotsky, in his forecast, was merely extrapolating from the revolutionary experience of 1905.

[9] "Letters on Tactics," in *Collected Works*, XXIV, 45. Cf. also "The Tasks of the Proletariat in the Present Revolution," in the "April Theses," *ibid.*, p. 21.

While recognizing the extreme difficulties besetting any attempt to put into effect "socialist changes" in "one of the most backward countries of Europe amidst a vast population of small peasants," Lenin stressed that "it would be a grave error, and *in effect even a complete desertion to the bourgeoisie* to infer from this that the working class must support the bourgeoisie, or that it must keep its activities within limits acceptable to the petty bourgeoisie, or that the proletariat must renounce its leading role [in promoting] practical steps towards socialism," including nationalization of the land and of the banks, "for which the time is now ripe." [10] (Emphasis added.)

In fact, Lenin's 1917 program of going beyond the bourgeois-democratic revolution had been inherent in his 1905 perspective. "From the democratic revolution," he had written, "we shall begin immediately and within the measure of our strength—the strength of the conscious and organized proletariat—to make the transition to the socialist revolution. We stand for uninterrupted revolution. We shall not stop half way." [11]

What divided Trotsky, who had been alone in actually *predicting* an uninterrupted transition or permanent revolution in Russia, and Lenin, who advocated it,[12] was their differing analyses before April 1917 (when the adoption of Lenin's famous theses eliminated any programmatic differences between them)[13] of the strength and dynamism of the bourgeois

---

[10] "Resolution on the Current Situation," adopted by the Seventh (April 1917) All-Russia Conference of the Bolsheviks, *Collected Works*, XXIV, 311–12.

[11] "Social Democracy's Attitude toward the Peasant Movement," *Collected Works* IX, 236–37. The above translation is from Carr, *The Bolshevik Revolution*, I, 68.

[12] Lenin regarded the victory of the democratic revolution consistently from the point of view of establishing an advanced position for the proletariat in its struggle for a *socialist* revolution. Cf. "Two Tactics of Social Democracy in the Democratic Revolution," *Collected Works*, Vol. IX.

[13] The chief differences between Lenin and Trotsky had been

revolution in Russia. In Lenin's perspective prior to 1917, the bourgeois revolution itself could be successfully challenged only with the support of a European socialist revolution because the Russian proletariat could not hold power without the backing of the basically nonsocialist peasantry. In Trotsky's view, owing to the peculiarities of Russian backwardness, the "democratic dictatorship" would not be able to stabilize itself; the Russian bourgeois revolution would prove powerless to fulfill its historic tasks, and therefore the Russian proletariat would *necessarily* come to power and set in motion a *socialist* revolution, with or *without* the aid of the proletariat of Europe.[14] "The essence of the dispute about the question of permanent revolution from 1905 till 1917," Trotsky later wrote, "reduces itself . . . to the question whether a bourgeois revolution really capable of solving the agrarian problem[15] was still possible in Russia, or whether for the accomplishment of this work a dictatorship of the proletariat would be needed." [16]

As events actually turned out, the February Revolution in Russia was unable to distribute land to the peasants, and therefore proved unstable. To "solve" the agrarian problem—which had been one of the historic tasks of the bourgeois revolution in France, but which the Russian bourgeoisie had not the will to solve, and the peasantry had not the independence or organization to solve for itself—the peasant classes of rural Russia were obliged to support the October Revolution, the *proletarian* conquest of power.

---

over party organization. These were resolved when Trotsky joined the Bolsheviks in July 1917, taking the position that Lenin had been right.

[14] For the *construction* of socialism in Russia, however, as opposed merely to the establishment of collective ownership—its "legal premise"—Trotsky agreed with Lenin on the necessity of international revolution.

[15] That is, as a problem of distribution.

[16] Trotsky, *History of the Russian Revolution*, Vol. III, Appendix II.

What was true in regard to the question of land was also true in regard to the other great and intimately related social question of the revolution—the question of peace. For the major classes and their parties divided on the distribution of the land in the same way as they divided on the issue of ending the imperialist war. The coalition of bourgeois "revolutionary" parties, for example, opposed the immediate distribution of the land and the consequent up-ending of the social structure while supporting the war. They supported the war not only because they wished to preserve their alliance with the other bourgeois powers and to obtain control over the Dardanelles and the territory in the Balkans promised under the secret London Treaty of 1915, but because they saw in the war—with its military controls and patriotic fervor—a profoundly conservative force. As the Russian historian and liberal foreign minister of the first Provisional Government commented in early April 1917: "Perhaps something will be preserved as a result of the War; without the War everything would break up more quickly." [17]

Predictably, the moderate parties, socialist and nonsocialist alike, vacillated hopelessly over the main questions of the day. While opposing the annexationist war aims of the Czarist government, they were prepared to continue the war, without the Czar but under the social, economic and political regime of the old ruling classes, as a "war for democracy." Similarly, while sympathizing with the peasants' desire for land, which was leading to insurgency in the countryside and sapping the morale of the army, they were not ready to break with the bourgeoisie (or the aristocracy) or to jeopardize the war effort by promoting domestic upheaval. So momentous a decision as land reform, they held, should be decided by a constituent assembly. But when the bourgeois ministers insisted on delaying the assembly, fearing that such a body convened at the height of the revolution would be too radical,

---

[17] Milyukov, cited in Chamberlin, *op. cit.*, I, 107.

the socialist ministers "sacrificed the assembly to save the coalition." [18]

Of all the organized *parties*, therefore, only the Bolsheviks were ready to break decisively with the bourgeoisie and the landowners on the questions of land and peace, while among the consistently revolutionary *classes* only the urban proletariat was willing and able to seize *state* power.

To what extent this pattern of dynamic revolutionary forces is repeated in subsequent upheavals in the underdeveloped world can be suggested by comparing the Russian experience with the other great and, in many ways, even more characteristic revolution of the age, the revolution in China. One immediate difference between the two events was that the Bolsheviks had to struggle against nationalist sentiment on the war question, whereas the Chinese Communists were able to take the lead in a national struggle against Japanese imperialism. It is extremely significant, therefore, that despite this difference in the situations, the line-up of class forces on the basic issues of the belated bourgeois-democratic revolution remained the same. In China, as in Russia, it was not the party of the bourgeoisie that led, or consistently supported, the popular revolutionary struggle on the agrarian, democratic and national questions, but the armed and independently organized Communist Party, which mobilized the revolutionary-nationalist ferment among the lower classes. In Russia the Bolsheviks supported the demands of the non-Russian nationalities for self-determination. In China the bourgeois party was itself a nationalist party, but when confronted by an independent force mobilizing and leading the agrarian revolution, it subordinated national interests to class interests—a policy which eventually led to its defeat. [19] "Except for the Commu-

---

[18] Isaac Deutscher, "The Russian Revolution," in *The New Cambridge Modern History*, XII, 401.

[19] Cf. Chalmers A. Johnson, *Peasant Nationalism and Communist Power* (Stanford, Calif.: Stanford University Press, 1962). John-

nist Party," wrote Mao at the end of the thirties, "no political party (bourgeois or petty bourgeois) is equal to the task of leading China's two great revolutions, the democratic and the socialist revolutions, to complete fulfillment." [20]

In one respect, however, the Chinese Revolution did represent a major departure from the Russian. In contrast to the Russian Marxists, the Maoists based their revolutionary party on the peasantry and carried their revolutionary struggle from the countryside to the towns. The Russian experience had seemed to confirm both Lenin's and Trotsky's stress on the proletariat as providing the only viable class basis for a revolutionary conquest of power.[21] However, many different circumstances in China (not least the prolonged national war of liberation) altered the social assumptions on which Lenin's and Trotsky's analysis had been based, and therefore vitiated its conclusions.[22]

Unlike the Bolsheviks, the Chinese Communists arrived at the conception of their own role, as leaders in the *bour-*

---

son's thesis is that the national struggle takes primacy over the class struggle in determining the Communists' success. In fact, what his material shows is that in China and Yugoslavia (the countries studied) the class character of the contending parties determined their national orientation (in the way outlined above) and their ability to take the lead in the nationalist struggle.

[20] *Selected Works,* II, 331. In Cuba, the revolutionary experience provided a similar conclusion: "In the present historical conditions of Latin America the national bourgeoisie cannot lead the anti-feudal and anti-imperialist struggle. Experience demonstrates that in our nations this class—even when its interests clash with those of Yankee imperialism—has been incapable of confronting imperialism, paralyzed by fear of social revolution and frightened by the clamor of the exploited masses."—*Second Declaration of Havana,* February 4, 1962.

[21] Cf. Chamberlin, *op. cit.,* II, 458.

[22] For an appraisal of the Chinese Revolution in terms of the classical framework and these altered assumptions, see Isaac Deutscher, "Maoism—Its Origins and Outlook," in *Ironies of History* (New York: Oxford University Press, 1966).

geois "stage" of the revolution, only after bitter experience and tragic defeats.[23] The pragmatic nature of the Chinese gravitation toward a "Leninist" strategy of permanent revolution seems to confirm the rootedness of that strategy in the social realities of belated bourgeois development. "The bourgeois-democratic revolution in present-day China," wrote Mao in 1939, "is no longer of the general, old type, which is now obsolete, but of the special, new type. This kind of revolution is developing in China as well as in all other colonial and semi-colonial countries, and we call it the new-democratic revolution." [24] This "new-democratic" revolution, according to Mao, embraces the stages of both the bourgeois and socialist revolution; the first providing the conditions for the second,[25] and the two taking place consecutively, i.e., *"without allowing any intervening stage of bourgeois* dictatorship." [26] (Emphasis added.) A 1958 resolution of the Central Committee of the Chinese Communist Party expressed this theoretical position: "We are partisans of the Marxist-Leninist theory of permanent revolution. We hold that there is not and cannot be a great wall between the democratic revolution and the socialist revolution . . ." [27]

This formulation by the Chinese, in classical Marxist terms, owed its parentage not to Trotsky, whom the Chinese

---

[23] Cf. Harold R. Isaacs, *The Tragedy of the Chinese Revolution* (London: 1938) for the authoritative account of these defeats.

[24] "The Chinese Revolution and the Chinese Communist Party" (n.d., 1939?), in Stuart Schram, ed., *The Political Thought of Mao Tse-tung* (New York: Praeger, 1964), p. 161; also in *Selected Works* (Peking, 1965), Vol. II.

[25] Cf. Lenin, "Two Tactics of the Social-Democrats in the Democratic Revolution," in *Collected Works*, IX, 84–86, 95, 112.

[26] "On New Democracy" (1940), in *Selected Works* (Peking: 1965), II, 360.

[27] *Jen-min Jih-pao*, December 19, 1958, cited in Schram, *op. cit.*, p. 53. This perspective was also pragmatic in origin. The "radicalization" of the Chinese Revolution toward a socialist program having taken place only under the impact of an imperialist offensive in Asia.

in their neo-Stalinist vein, still reviled,[28] but to Lenin. "Beginning in *April* 1917," Lenin had explained in his postrevolution polemic against Kautsky, "long before the October Revolution, that is, long before we assumed power, we publicly declared and explained to the people: the revolution cannot now stop at this stage, for the country has marched forward, capitalism has advanced, ruin has reached unprecedented dimensions, which (whether one likes it or not) will *demand* steps forward, to *Socialism*. For there is *no* other way of advancing [than by this path] . . . To attempt to raise an artificial Chinese Wall between the first and second [stages], to separate them by anything else than the degree of preparedness of the proletariat and the degree of its unity with the poor peasants, means monstrously to distort Marxism, to vulgarize it, to substitute liberalism in its place. It means smuggling in a reactionary defense of the bourgeoisie against the socialist proletariat by means of quasi-scientific reference to the progressive character of the bourgeoisie as compared with medievalism." [29] (Emphasis added.)

. . . . . .

> . . . the rule of monopoly capitalism and imperialism in the advanced countries and social and economic backwardness in the underdeveloped countries are intimately related, [and] represent merely different aspects of what is in reality a global problem.
> —Paul Baran, 1957

In his own theoretical analysis of the October insurrection, Trotsky had laid down as the fundamental and general *prem-*

---

[28] The term "permanent revolution," which in the Stalinist and neo-Stalinist canon is the technical term for Trotskyite heresy, was first "rehabilitated" by Liu Shao-ch'i in a speech on May 5, 1958 (Schram, *op. cit.*).

[29] Lenin, *The Proletarian Revolution and the Renegade Kautsky* (Peking, 1965), pp. 97–98.

ise of revolution the inability of the existing social structure to solve the urgent problems of national development. A revolution only becomes possible, he added, when there is a class "capable of taking the lead in solving the problems," while to prepare and actually achieve a revolution, it is necessary to make "the objective problems . . . find their way into the consciousness of living human masses," to change this consciousness, and thereby to "create new correlations of human forces." [30]

To establish that the notion of "permanent," or "uninterrupted," or "new-democratic" revolution indicates a general model for belated bourgeois development and social transformation and therefore provides a basis for understanding the general instability of underdeveloped states in the capitalist world orbit, it would have to be shown (1) that the urgent problems of national development in these countries cannot be solved within their existing social structures; (2) that the nascent bourgeoisies, because of the peculiarities of their development, are either unwilling or unable to undertake the revolutionary tasks necessary to solve them. In fact, a major attempt to formulate a theory along these lines was made in the mid-fifties by the American economist Paul Baran.[31]

In his analysis, Baran showed how penetration by the monopolistic combines of the economically advanced capitalisms skewed the internal formations of the weaker, industrially backward countries; it distorted their investment patterns and altered their class structures in directions which destroyed the very conditions of self-sustaining capitalist de-

---

[30] *The History of the Russian Revolution*, Vol. III, Chap. 6 ("The Art of Insurrection").

[31] Cf. Paul A. Baran, "On the Political Economy of Backwardness" (1952), reprinted in Feinstein, ed., *Two Worlds of Change* (New York: Anchor Books, 1964); "Economic Progress and Economic Surplus," *Science and Society*, Fall 1953; *The Political Economy of Growth* (New York: Monthly Review Press, 1956). Baran's theory owes much to his teacher, the Bolshevik theorist E. Preobrazhensky, author of *The New Economics* (New York: Oxford University Press, 1965; originally published 1924–26).

velopment and growth. If the penetration of these quasi-feudal and tribal societies by the advanced capitalisms had been total, Baran argued, if there had been "a *complete* substitution of capitalist market rationality for the rigidities of feudal or semi-feudal servitude," this "would have represented in spite of all the pains of transition, an important step in the direction of progress." But under the circumstances of "partial penetration" (i.e., *combined* development), what happened was that "age-old exploitation of the population by their domestic overlords was freed of the mitigating constraints inherited from the feudal tradition." This "superimposition" of capitalist exploitation over traditional oppression resulted in a compounded form of exploitation, "more outrageous corruption, and more glaring injustice." [32]

In India, for example, the British land and taxation policy ruined the native village economy, substituting the economy of "the parasitic landowner and moneylender." [33] British commercial policy "destroyed the Indian artisan and created the infamous slums of the Indian cities filled with millions of starving and diseased paupers"; British economic policy "broke down whatever beginnings there were of an indigenous industrial development," promoting instead "proliferations of speculators, petty business men, agents, and sharks of all descriptions eking out a sterile and precarious livelihood in the meshes of a decaying society." [34] As for politics, the British consolidated their rule "by creating new classes and vested interests" tied up with that rule and by a conscious policy of "creating divisions among Indians, of encouraging one group at the cost of the other." [35]

---

[32] Baran, "On the Political Economy of Backwardness."
[33] Baran, *The Political Economy of Growth*, p. 149. Cf. also Rene Dumont, *Lands Alive* (New York and London: 1965), pp. 139 ff.
[34] Baran, *The Political Economy of Growth*. Cf. M. Barratt-Brown, *After Imperialism* (London: Heineman, 1963), pp. 174 ff.
[35] Jawaharlal Nehru, *The Discovery of India* (New York: John Day, 1946), pp. 304 ff.: ". . . nearly all our major problems today have grown up during British rule and as a direct result of British

Not only in India but throughout the underdeveloped world, the seemingly intractable problems of economic and social stagnation (and their appalling consequences) can be traced to penetration by the advanced powers of the capitalist world system.[36] This domination of backward economies and their subordination to the metropolitan markets characteristically leads to the siphoning off of the economic surplus whose investment is the source of economic expansion and to an internal utilization of the surplus inimical to self-sustaining growth.[37]

Thus, the *net* flow of capital *from* the underdeveloped world *to* the United States between 1950 and 1965, as a result of its direct foreign investments, was $16 billion.[38] In the case of a capital-starved country like India, during roughly the same period in which the foreign investment stake doubled, "foreign investors as a whole [took] out of the general currency reserve nearly three times as much as they contributed directly." [39] In other words, the investment of foreign private capital, far from resulting in a capital flow *to* the underdevel-

---

policy: the princes; the minority problem; various vested interests, foreign and Indian; the lack of industry and the neglect of agriculture; the extreme backwardness in the social services; and above all, the tragic poverty of the people."

[36] As Professor Josue de Castro, author of *The Geography of Hunger* and former president of the United Nations Food and Agriculture Organization commented in the early 1960's: "[Neo-] colonialism is the only cause of hunger in Latin America."—cited in John Gerassi, *The Great Fear in Latin America* (New York: Collier, 1965), p. 265. Cf. Edward Boorstein, *The Economic Transformation of Cuba* (New York: Monthly Review Press, 1968), Chap. 1, "Imperialism."

[37] Baran, *The Political Economy of Growth*, Chaps. 5–7.

[38] H. Magdoff, *Economic Aspects of U.S. Imperialism,* pamphlet, (New York: Monthly Review Press, 1966). Cf. A. G. Frank, "Services Rendered," *Monthly Review,* June 1965; Huberman and Sweezy, "Foreign Investment," *Monthly Review,* January 1965.

[39] Michael Kidron, *Foreign Investments in India* (New York: Oxford University Press, 1965), p. 310.

oped country, acts as a suction pump drawing much needed capital *away* from it to the rich metropolitan power.

The so-called economic aid programs of the developed capitalist countries do not alter this flow significantly because in the main they represent little more than export credit schemes, labeled "aid" for propaganda purposes.[40] Tied to agreements not only to buy goods from the donor country but also to guarantee and promote foreign private investment, the "aid" programs constitute a primary mode of modern imperialist penetration.[41] As a former director of the foreign trade branch of the U.S. Bureau of Foreign and Domestic Commerce told the Chicago World Trade Conference in 1950, the real "substance and essence" of the Point Four aid program (the forerunner of the Alliance for Progress) was "the stimulation of private enterprise and private investments in underdeveloped areas." [42] The structure of U.S. aid programs has been thoroughly consistent on this point. As one Cambridge economist summed up the position: "The aim of aid is to perpetuate the system that makes aid necessary." [43]

---

[40] I. M. D. Little and J. M. Clifford, *International Aid* (London: Allen & Unwin, 1965). Cf. also I. M. D. Little, *Aid to Africa* (New York: Pergamon Press, 1964). The amount of U.S. aid which is "tied" in this way ranges from 80 percent to more than 90 percent.

[41] The American business magazine *Forbes*, for example, describes the Agency for International Development (the chief distributor of U.S. aid funds) as "the principal agency through which the U.S. government finances business abroad. . . . AID distributes about $2 billion a year. Of this, 85 percent is spent in the United States for American products and raw materials." (Most of the money is distributed in the form of loans, often at high interest rates.) Cited in Carl Oglesby and Richard Shaull, *Containment and Change* (New York: Macmillan, 1967), p. 81. Cf. David Eakins, "Business Planners and the Development of American Postwar Economic Policy," in Horowitz (ed.) *The Corporations and the Cold War.*

[42] Statement by August Maffry cited in Rollins, *op. cit.*

[43] Joan Robinson, *The New Mercantilism*, pamphlet (New York: Cambridge University Press, 1965).

Backed by their own state powers,[44] the monopolistic combines of the metropolitan countries block the formation of domestic industries in the satellite countries which are vital for economic advance but competitive with their own operations;[45] they secure the exploitation of natural resources for raw material export rather than for internal development; they pump out scarce capital not only via retained profits but also through discriminating financial arrangements and the manipulation of commodity markets;[46] furthermore, as institutions and agencies of a class society, they actively promote parasitic and nonproductive employments of the national economic wealth.[47] Nor is this the whole story. The growth-stunting domination of merchant over industrial capital and the catastrophic subordination of the economic life of the satellite countries to the severe fluctuations of primary commodity markets are direct consequences of their overall dependent economic relations to foreign capitalist powers and their financial-corporate interests.

It is clear, therefore, that such countries cannot be regarded as underdeveloped in the orthodox sense, i.e., in the sense of being at a prior stage along the path of development taken by the advanced capitalisms. On the contrary, their typical characteristics are not characteristics of the immature stages of the now-developed capitalist societies but of the *combination* of advanced and backward stages produced by "partial penetration." These economies are not "dual" (part

---

[44] Not merely in a military-political sense, moreover. Such putative "international" institutions as the World Bank, controlled by the United States government (and usually headed by a U.S. banker), are used to pressure underdeveloped nations to yield to the wishes of U.S. corporate and financial interests.

[45] This applies to the development of technologies as well. Cf. Kidron, *op. cit.*, pp. 282 ff.

[46] For example, cf. Fitch and Oppenheimer, *Ghana: End of An Illusion* (New York: Monthly Review Press, 1966), Chap. 3.

[47] Baran, *op. cit.* For example, the production of luxuries and the marketing of inessential commodities associated with high-consumption economies.

capitalist, part feudal), as is sometimes suggested, but "hybrid" or "mutant." [48] Their problems stem not from a *failure* to develop but from a *distorted* development, one that leads not along a path to eventual self-sustaining growth but into an economic cul-de-sac. In other words, real growth in these mutant economies cannot be achieved by organic, evolutionary processes within the basic existing structures (least of all by an influx of foreign private capital), but only through a revolutionary transformation of the structures themselves and a cutting of the dependent and dependency-generating ties.[49]

This conclusion is, of course, directly contrary to the doctrine promulgated by W. W. Rostow, the director of the policy-planning staff of the U.S. State Department.[50] According to Rostow, whose thesis serves as an official rationale for U.S. antirevolutionary intervention in the underdeveloped world, "communism" (i.e., anti-imperialist, anti-capitalist social revolution) is a "disease of the transition" from underdevelopment to self-sustaining growth. The above analysis, supported by the historical evidence to date, points rather to the opposite conclusion—that *such a revolution is an indispensable precondition of the transition's ever taking place.*

This thesis is confirmed by the one historical case of a capitalist "take-off" into self-sustaining growth in the period following the imperial expansion and penetration of the backward regions in the nineteenth century.[51] The underdeveloped country in which this take-off occurred, namely Japan,

---

[48] For a critique of "dualistic" theories, see Andre Gunder Frank, "The Myth of Feudalism in Brazilian Agriculture," in *Capitalism and Underdevelopment in Latin America* (New York: Monthly Review Press, 1967).

[49] For a case study of the failure of an attempt to achieve development without such a revolution, cf. Fitch and Oppenheimer, *op. cit.*

[50] W. W. Rostow, *The Stages of Economic Growth* (New York: Cambridge University Press, 1960).

[51] This generalization is meant to apply only to those countries where a traditional or feudal society already existed and was then penetrated by a developed capitalist power. This excludes settled countries like Australia and New Zealand, or South Africa.

was distinguished as "the only country in Asia that escaped being turned into a colony or dependency of West European or American capitalism that had a chance of independent national development." [52]

Japan's escape from imperialist domination and distorted underdevelopment depended on a constellation of circumstances (including a temporary stalemate between the imperialist rivals) which has proven to be unrepeatable. Once penetrated, underdeveloped countries find the Japanese road of conscious imitation of Western capitalism closed to themselves,[53] as they do the path of classical bourgeois revolution. For while their middle classes are able to lead a struggle for formal *political* independence from the imperial powers, they are unable to break the chains of *economic* dependence and are incapable of carrying through the internal social and economic changes that are required for self-sustaining growth.

On the one hand, because of the profound effects of partial penetration, including the lack of an indigenous independent and integrated industrial sector, the growth in independent power of the nascent bourgeoisies is critically stunted. On the other hand, there is a critical sapping of the revolutionary will of the middle classes and their allies as a direct consequence of the ideological maturity, the revolutionary change in consciousness of the doubly oppressed masses.

Indeed, on any count, a prime factor in estimating the potential and direction of a revolutionary transformation of the underdeveloped regions in the post-1917 epoch must be this revolutionized consciousness of their peasant and working classes. The rise of socialist radicalism in the underdeveloped regions, inspired by the Bolshevik revolution and spread by its organs, has had the effect of instilling "a mortal fear of

---

[52] Baran, *The Political Economy of Growth*, p. 158.
[53] Cf. Mao Tse-tung's comments in "On People's Democratic Dictatorship" (1949) on the attempt in China to follow the Japanese example and its failure as the result of imperialist intervention.

expropriation and extinction" in the minds not only of economically retrograde but "of *all* property-owning groups"
and has tended "to drive *all* more or less privileged, more or
less well-to-do elements in . . . society into one 'counterrevolutionary' coalition." In other words, "whatever differences
and antagonisms [exist] between domestic and foreign interests [are] largely submerged on all important occasions by
the over-riding common interest in staving off socialism," or,
to use the battle language of the cold war, in *containing communism*. With this hybrid conservatism of the rising bourgeoisie, in the underdeveloped areas this anticommunist degeneration of liberalism, "the possibility of solving the economic
and political deadlock prevailing in the underdeveloped countries on the lines of a progressive capitalism [has] all but
disappeared." [54]

While fear of expropriation has certainly been the basis,
ideologically speaking, for the stillbirth of the bourgeois revolution in the post-1917 period, it by no means represents the
whole explanation. By the same token, it is not merely the
idea of socialism or communism which has stimulated the revolutionary impulse among the oppressed masses. For since 1917
the socialist revolution has existed as a history as well. The
actual course which the Russian Revolution took and the
deeds with which socialism in its name became identified have
constituted powerful factors in making the revolution a pull
for the poverty-stricken masses, on the one hand, while making it a repellent force for middle-class (and not only middle-
class) liberals on the other.

For this reason, and because the policies of the Communist states themselves have had a profound impact on the
prospects of later upheavals, the actual course taken by the
Bolsheviks in Russia stands as a key to the whole subsequent
historical development, and in particular, to the shifting paths
of the *world* socialist revolution.

---

[54] Baran, *loc. cit.*

6. Uninterrupted Revolution: From Lenin to Stalin

> The . . . power in the hands of the proletarian state of Russia is quite adequate to ensure the transition to Communism. What then is lacking? Obviously, what is lacking is culture among the stratum of Communists who perform administrative functions.
>
> —Lenin, March 1922

> . . . the misfortune which has fallen upon us is an international misfortune. . . . there is no way out of it but international revolution.
>
> —Lenin, April 1921

To understand the evolution and transformation of Russia under Soviet power, it is as necessary to take into account the phenomenon of uneven and combined development as it was to understand the conditions which made possible the initial triumph of the Bolsheviks. This fact is not generally appreciated, however, and the distortion of perspective which results from the attempt to impose an abstract theory of "pure" historical stages onto the complex Russian reality afflicts not only Marxist but also anti-Marxist accounts and appraisals of the revolution. As a consequence, the fate of liberal democracy in post-Czarist Russia is as generally misunderstood as the more complicated, but equally uncomprehended, fate of post-Czarist socialism.

To many historians, for example, the stillbirth of liberal

democracy in Russia was not a result of the relatively late, Prussian-style introduction of capitalism[1] into an extremely backward economic and political environment, but was caused by the activities of Lenin and the Bolsheviks. The assumption underlying this interpretation of events is that Czarist Russia was embarking on the path of social development previously taken by the democratic capitalisms of Western Europe when deflected by war and Bolshevism from its "proper" historical course. Such an assumption, however, ignores the fact that the victory of the Bolsheviks (very much a minority party at the beginning of 1917, even in the cities) was made possible not only by their own tactical skill, but by the very weakness, indecisiveness and even incoherence of the bourgeois and anti-Bolshevik socialist parties, who were unable, in the course of the struggle, to maintain their initial popular support.

Far from being an arbitrary stroke, the Bolshevik victory was—given the framework of existing political and social forces—a "logical" outcome of the open contest of 1917. Thus the authoritative liberal history of the Russian Revolution sums up that struggle in the following illuminating terms: "The steady swing to the Left which set in immediately after the breakdown of the Imperial regime and reached its culmination in the seizure of power by the Bolsheviki seems, in retrospect, logical and inevitable, incredible and outrageous as it must have seemed to the wealthy and middle classes while it was going on. The Provisional Government, in which was embodied the irresolute softness and mildness which were characteristic of many pre-War Russian liberals and radicals, was quite helpless in the face of the elemental

---

[1] That is, not through the growth of small, competitive business, but as a process of "combined" development through the direct transfer from abroad of advanced monopolistic enterprise. The term appears to originate with Lenin. Cf. Baran, "Economic Progress and Economic Surplus," *Science and Society* (Fall 1953); and Veblen, *Imperial Germany and the Industrial Revolution*.

popular demand for land, peace and socialism, which, to the average uneducated worker, meant plundering the rich for the benefit of the poor. It could neither make war nor make peace. It could neither place itself boldly at the head of the huge peasant movement and decree a radical expropriation of the big estates, nor enforce respect for the property rights of the landlords. Under these circumstances it is scarcely surprising that, when Lenin decided that the moment had come to strike for power in November, 1917, the Provisional Government collapsed for sheer lack of defenders." [2]

Those views that project the possibility of a classical "Western" path of development onto the Russian situation in 1917 ignore not only the balance of social forces in Russia, but also the general experience of *belated* bourgeois revolutions, which would contradict such optimism and any notion that there is a singular path of Western social development.[3] As if to emphasize the point, imperial Germany, in the ashes of military defeat, embarked yet again on a belated revolution against feudal autocracy, and in contrast to Russia, the "moderate," "democratic" parties were able this time to retain state power.[4] But—and the proviso here is crucial—they were able to hold power only in league with Prussian militarism and the forces of German social reaction. During the revolution, to preserve bourgeois "law and order" the "socialist" Minister of War, Noske, resorted to the notorious *Freikorps*, the prototype of Hitler's storm troopers, financed by big German capital (Krupp, Kirdorf, Stinnes, etc.) to crush the radical left.[5]

This triumph of the German Kerenskys and defeat of

---

[2] William H. Chamberlin, *The Russian Revolution* (New York, 1965), II, 453. Cf. Lionel Kochan, *Russia in Revolution, 1900–1918*, p. 267.

[3] See above, pp. 48 f.

[4] For a comparison of the extremely feeble character of these liberal forces with those of 1848, see A. J. P. Taylor, *The Course of German History* (London: Methuen, 1966), pp. 211–12.

[5] It was this group that murdered Rosa Luxemburg and Karl Liebknecht.

German Leninism did not result in a stable democratic development, as the notion of a "Western" path in Russia would seem to imply. Instead, precisely because the price of the triumph was the preservation of German capitalism and the principal forces of Germany's autocratic, nationalistic and militarist past—the "dung of medievalism," in Lenin's phrase[6] —it produced chronic economic and political instability, the rapid rise of Nazism, the fascist counterrevolution and ultimately the barbarism of the Second World War.[7]

The revolution of Russia under a Weimar-type regime, if such had been possible, would undoubtedly have been very different from the German experience (reflecting principally the much lower level of Russia's capitalist and industrial development); but the savage and semibarbarous forces rooted in the social and cultural soil of the Russian Empire and manifested in the Czarist pogrom, in the ferocity of the White and Red Terrors and later in the Stalinist blood purges would hardly have been exorcised by a mere retention of parliamentary forms throughout the year 1917 and the convocation of a Constituent Assembly.

In fact, the long-promised Constituent Assembly was convened on January 18, 1918, only to be dispersed after the first session by the Bolsheviks—an act which is taken by many to symbolize their destruction of parliamentary democracy in Russia. If anything, it shows, rather, how insubstantial the basis of parliamentary democracy was in the already existing Russian framework. For, according to Chamberlin's previously cited account (and amply confirmed by other authori-

---

[6] *Collected Works,* XXXIII, 300.
[7] For an analysis of Nazism within the framework of the class forces of the German revolution and counterrevolution, and the expansionist tendencies of German capitalism, compare Neumann, *Behemoth,* and the discussion below (pp. 176 ff.). The situation in Russia in 1917 was in many ways even more analogous to the situation in Italy in 1922, just before the triumph of fascism: cf. Robert A. Brady, *Business as a System of Power* (New York: Columbia University Press, 1943), pp. 56–58.

tative sources), "the dissolution of Russia's first and sole freely elected parliament evoked scarcely a ripple of interest and protest, so far as the masses were concerned."

Chamberlin adduces two reasons for this reaction. First, the Bolsheviks had already enacted "the decisions which the majority of the people wanted on the engrossing questions of land and peace" and had thereby "robbed the deliberations of the Assembly of most of their interest." Second, the assembly collapsed "because Russia was conspicuously lacking in all the conditions which historical experience indicates as essential to the effective functioning of parliamentary democracy." The larger implications of this structural environment are also evident to this liberal historian: "For . . . the same reason the alternative to Bolshevism, had it failed to survive the ordeal of civil war, the first shots of which were already being fired, would *not* have been . . . a Constituent Assembly, elected according to the most modern rules of equal suffrage and proportional representation, but a military dictator, a Kolchak or a Denikin, riding into Moscow on a white horse to the accompaniment of the clanging bells of the old capital's hundreds of churches." [8]

To appreciate fully how hostile the Russian environment was to the institutions of democracy in 1918, as well as to understand the tragedy that followed, it must be remembered that the Bolsheviks did not intend to establish a political dictatorship[9] as the agency of socialist transformation. In 1905, for

[8] Chamberlin, *op. cit.*, I, 371.
[9] The concept of the "dictatorship of the proletariat" is that of a *class* dictatorship, paralleling the "dictatorship of the bourgeoisie," which operates in normal circumstances through the constitutional medium of bourgeois democracy. The essence of the concept of the dictatorship of the proletariat lies in the recognition that when the existential base of the bourgeoisie (private property) is threatened, it will not confine itself to legal and constitutional methods of defense. Hence, acceptance of the dictatorship concept by a revolutionary party means the readiness to use force against the counterrevolution even if that entails going outside the framework

example, in terms consistent with his whole approach to the
two revolutions, bourgeois and socialist, Lenin had written:
"We Marxists should know that there is not, nor can there be,
any other path to real freedom for the proletariat and the
peasantry, than the path of bourgeois freedom and bourgeois
progress. We must not forget that there is not, nor can there
be at the present time, any other means of bringing socialism
nearer, than complete political liberty, than a democratic republic, than the revolutionary-democratic [class] dictatorship
of the proletariat and the peasantry." [10] Shortly before the
revolution of 1917 Lenin reiterated this theme, emphasizing
that the struggle for democracy was no diversion, but that
"just as socialism cannot be victorious unless it introduces
complete democracy, so the proletariat will be unable to prepare for victory over the bourgeoisie unless it wages a many-
sided, consistent and revolutionary struggle for democracy." [11]

---

of legal institutions set up in the old society under the class rule
of the same bourgeoisie. "When a revolutionary class is fighting
the propertied classes that offer resistance, the resistance must be
crushed. And we shall crush the resistance of the propertied
classes, using *the same means as they used* to crush the proletariat—
no other means have been invented."—Lenin, *Collected Works*,
XXVI, 354.

[10] *Ibid.*, IX, 112.

[11] Cited in the editor's Introduction to Trotsky, *Terrorism
and Communism* (Ann Arbor, 1963). The citation is from an
article by Lenin entitled "The Revolutionary Proletariat and the
Right of Nations to Self-Determination" written in 1915. Cf. *Collected Works*, XXI, 408. The point is so fundamental and so
generally misunderstood that the passage is worth quoting at
length: "From what [Radek] says, it appears that, *in the name of*
the socialist revolution, he scornfully rejects a consistently revolutionary program in the sphere of democracy. He is wrong to do
so. The proletariat cannot be victorious except through democracy,
i.e., by giving full effect to democracy and by linking with each
step of its struggle democratic demands formulated in the most
resolute terms. . . . We must *combine* the revolutionary struggle
against capitalism with a revolutionary program and tactics on *all*

The political form of democracy which the Bolsheviks advocated was embodied in the workers' and peasants' councils, or soviets, which they regarded as providing an incomparably more direct and advanced mode of democratic participation in government than that provided by parliamentary institutions.[12] Addressing a meeting of soldiers shortly after his return to Russia in April 1917, Lenin declared: "All power in the state, from top to bottom, from the remotest village to the last street in the city of Petrograd, must belong to the Soviets of Workers', Soldiers' and Peasants' Deputies. . . . There must be no police, no bureaucrats who have no responsibility to the people, who stand above the people; no standing army, only the people universally armed, united in the Soviets—it is they who must run the state." [13] Introduced

---

democratic demands: a republic, a militia, the popular election of officials, equal rights for women, the self-determination of nations, etc. While capitalism exists, these demands—all of them—can only be accomplished as an exception, and even then in an incomplete and distorted form. Basing ourselves on the democracy already achieved, and exposing its incompleteness under capitalism, we demand the overthrow of capitalism, the expropriation of the bourgeoisie, as a necessary basis both for the abolition of the poverty of the masses and for the *complete* and *all-around* institution of *all* democratic reforms." (Emphasis in original.)

[12] Thus, in *State and Revolution* (Moscow, n. d.; pp. 77, 149–50), Lenin cites with approval Marx's remarks on the Commune: "The Commune [wrote Marx] was to be a working, not a parliamentary, body, executive and legislative at the same time. . . . Instead of deciding once in three or six years which member of the ruling class was to represent and repress the people in Parliament, universal suffrage was to serve the people, constituted in Communes, as individual suffrage serves every other employer in the search for the workers, foremen and bookkeepers for his business." "If we look more closely into the machinery of capitalist democracy," wrote Lenin, ". . . we shall see restriction after restriction upon [genuine] democracy . . . in their sum total these restrictions exclude and squeeze out the poor from politics, *from active participation in democracy*."

[13] Cited in *The New Cambridge Modern History*, p. 403.

as a cardinal point in Lenin's April Theses, "All power to the Soviets!" became in due course the slogan of the October Revolution.

The conflict between the Constituent Assembly and the soviets reflected the basic conflict between the two revolutions (bourgeois-democratic and proletarian-socialist) which were so inextricably intertwined in 1917. Precisely because the bourgeois-democratic forces had previously failed to carry through their revolution in a consistent manner and to convene the assembly when they had the power, the issue arose in a fundamentally changed context. For by then the bourgeois-democratic revolution had been superseded by its Bolshevik successor. It was, therefore, by the new *soviet* power that the assembly was convened. Furthermore, the struggle against the feudal-military counterrevolution, in which the democratic forces had hopelessly vacillated in the preceding year, was far from over. When the assembly was finally called by the Bolsheviks, General Kaledin and the Cadet party, backed by foreign capitalist powers, had already begun the military counterrevolution against the soviet regime. The Constituent Assembly was not outside this struggle but at the very center of it. The Kaledin-Cadet forces rallied behind the slogan "All power to the Constituent Assembly" (which they had previously sought to prevent or delay), precisely because the assembly promised to be a more conservative power than the triumphant soviet regime. In the circumstances, the only condition under which the soviet regime was prepared to tolerate the assembly was that the assembly itself be prepared to support the regime in the emerging civil war, i.e., "to proclaim it unreservedly recognises Soviet power, the Soviet revolution, and its policy on the questions of peace, the land and workers' control, and to resolutely join the camp of the enemies of the Cadet-Kaledin counter-revolution." [14] When this condition, which was announced

---

[14] "Theses on the Constituent Assembly," *Pravda*, December 26 (13), 1917, in Lenin, *Collected Works*, XXVI, 383.

three weeks in advance of its opening, was rejected by the assembly, its dissolution was inevitable.

But the soviets themselves were not destined to survive the civil war as democratic institutions, nor to initiate a "higher form of democracy" in Russia, as Lenin intended. For the basic conditions of a soviet democracy—a multi-party system,[15] no standing army, no state police—all vanished in the bloodshed and violence of the civil war. On the one hand, the Bolsheviks did not stint to meet terror with counter-terror and escalation was inevitable. On the other hand, the stringent measures which they took—including the retention of the death penalty and the creation of the secret police which contributed to the emergence of a ruthless dictatorial state—were taken amidst a storm of treason, counterrevolution and open insurrection against the regime by all forces of the opposition. In the end, the demise of democracy in Russia could hardly be laid at the door of one party or faction. For, in the words of E. H. Carr: "If it was true that the Bolshevik regime was not prepared after the first few months to tolerate an organized opposition, it was equally true that no opposition party was prepared to remain within legal limits. The premise of dictatorship was common to both sides of the argument." [16] By the end of the civil war a brutalized and iso-

---

[15] A multi-party system was not one of the conditions mentioned by Lenin, mainly because the issue never arose. There had been a multi-party system even under the more limited bourgeois democracy and it had never been part of any Marxist program to change that. See p. 147 below.

[16] The Bolshevik Revolution 1917–1923 (Penguin edition), I, 190; Isaac Deutscher, The Prophet Armed (New York: Oxford University Press, 1965), Chaps. 10–13, The Prophet Unarmed (New York: Oxford University Press, 1965), Chap. 1. Cf. also J. P. Nettl, The Soviet Achievement (London: Thames & Hudson, 1967), p. 55: "The concept of exclusive power to one party thus sprang not primarily from doctrinal predisposition, but from a revolutionary situation in which neutrality or indifference was meaningless. Those who were not with the Bolsheviks were against them."

lated Bolshevik party emerged "victorious" to exercise monopoly state power over a predominantly illiterate and basically medieval society and its underdeveloped,[17] primarily agricultural, economy.

The nation the Bolsheviks now presided over, having defended and consolidated their power against armed foreign intervention and domestic counterrevolution, was in a state of virtual dissolution. By the end of the conflict and just before the devastating drought and famine, which was severe enough for cannibalism to appear in the countryside, the national income was only one-third of its level in 1913. Industry produced less than one-fifth of the goods, the coal mines yielded only one-tenth, and the iron foundries only one-fortieth of their normal output. In addition, the railways were destroyed, and all stocks and reserves utterly exhausted. Exchange of goods between town and country had ceased altogether. Russia's cities and towns, previously the centers of revolutionary strength and Bolshevik support, had become so "depopulated" [18] that in 1921 Moscow had only one-half and Petrograd one-third of its former inhabitants; typhus was rampant and "the people of the two capitals had for many months lived on a food ration of two ounces of bread and

---

[17] "On the eve of the [1914] war, Russian industry produced 30 kg. of iron per head of population, compared with 203 in Germany, 228 in Great Britain and 326 in the U.S. The output of coal per head of population was 0.2 tons in Russia, 2.8 in Germany, 6.3 in Great Britain and 5.3 in the U.S. . . . Russia possessed only the beginnings of electrical and machine-building industries, no machine-tool industry, no chemical plants, no motor-car factories."—*New Cambridge Modern History*, p. 388. Cf. Dobb, *Soviet Economic Development Since 1917* (New York: International Publishers, 1948), pp. 36 ff.

[18] On the importance of this dispersal of the working class for the evolution of the totalitarian party and state, see Deutscher, *The Prophet Unarmed*, especially Chapter 1; cf. also E. H. Carr, *The Interregnum* (New York: Macmillan, 1954), pp. 327–28, and *Socialism in One Country* (New York: Macmillan, 1960), I, 99 ff.

a few frozen potatoes and had heated their dwellings with the wood of their furniture." [19]

Such was the ruined condition of the nation in the *fourth* year of the revolution. Moreover, not only was there to be no outside help to alleviate this situation, but the external pressure on the regime, both direct and indirect, was not to be significantly lessened (except, of course, in an overt military sense).

If the problems which the Bolsheviks faced at the outset were formidable, their long-term prospect as a proletarian socialist party possessing state power in a hostile environment of profound social and economic backwardness was no less ominous. The problems which pressed on them and threatened their stability and very survival found immediate expression in a set of grave difficulties, rooted in what Bolshevik theoreticians referred to as the "contradictions" between town and country, industry and agriculture, the proletariat and the peasantry.

Underlying these contradictions was the basic fact that five years after the end of the civil war nearly 85 percent of the population of the country in which the proletarian revolution had first triumphed lived in rural areas and worked in rural occupations. If the Bolsheviks were to construct out of the ruins of the Czarist empire a socialist union of soviet republics, that is, an educated, technologically advanced,[20] fully democratic industrial society, they knew they would first have to win the peasantry, representing the mass of the population, to the socialist cause. But at the same time, to build

---

[19] Deutscher, *op. cit.*, p. 4. Cf. Victor Serge, *Memoirs of a Revolutionary* (New York: Oxford University Press), Chaps. 2, 3.

[20] "The primitive technological state of the main sector of the economy was recorded in the 1910 census, which showed that 10 million wooden plows and *soklias* and 25 million wooden harrows were in use as opposed to only 4.2 million iron ploughs and less than a half million iron harrows. More than one-third of the farmsteads possessed no implements at all."—*New Cambridge Modern History*, p. 387.

such a society—one able, moreover, to withstand the expected military intervention from the hostile capitalist powers—they would also have to carry out a full-scale industrial revolution, which had the daunting prerequisite of a "primitive socialist accumulation of capital." [21] In these conflicting necessities lay the horns of a tragic dilemma for the Bolshevik revolution in Russia.

For while the peasantry would "the more voluntarily and successfully take the road of collectivisation, the more generously the town [was] able to fertilize their economy and their culture," [22] it was precisely such a task that the Russian town, with its abysmally low level of industry and culture,[23] was unable to fulfill. At the most basic level the quality of the town product, insofar as the goods even existed, was poor, its price too high. As a result, the peasant responded by hoarding his produce. The cities, representing Russia's rudimentary industrial and cultural centers, verged on starvation.

The prevailing tendency of the social economy was to strengthen rural agriculture at the expense of urban industry, and in general to slide back into economic, cultural and social primitiveness. What small accumulation was achieved within this framework was mainly an accumulation by the richer kulak peasantry, based on its exploitation of the poorer peasants and landless laborers, under conditions that were in many

---

[21] Cf. Preobrazhensky, *The New Economics* (New York: Oxford University Press, 1965).

[22] Trotsky, *History of the Russian Revolution* (New York: Macmillan, 1967), p. 1241.

[23] This is not to say that there was no culture in prerevolutionary Russia, merely that it was mainly confined to the numerically inconsiderable upper and middle classes and the few large urban centers; those who were cultured, moreover, were generally hostile to the revolution and in a great number of cases either left voluntarily or were driven into exile. In European Russia only a third of the males and a quarter of the females were literate in 1920, while the corresponding figures for Siberia were one fifth and one tenth.

cases even worse than those that had existed under the *ancien régime*. Another class of accumulators was formed by the middlemen and speculators who flourished under the New Economic Policy which had been adopted by the Bolsheviks in 1921 as a concession to the strength of the capitalist tendencies in the economy.

In the steadily increasing power of these antisocialist forces, the Bolshevik regime was faced with a growing political threat. The Bolsheviks, therefore, had to do more than merely preside over a natural evolution of the economy in an industrial-socialist direction. They were confronted, rather, with the increasingly urgent necessity of taking steps to force the social economy, against its grain, toward such a progressive development. It was the magnitude of this task and the dangers it presaged that made the early Bolshevik leaders shrink from the prospect, and look to the aid of industrialized socialist allies (particularly a socialist Germany) as indispensable for the transition to advanced socialist development.

Military considerations aside, such allies were required to supply capital and technology for the perilously weak industrial sector and also a civilizing ideological and cultural influence for the backward Russian society. This was important not only because the mass of illiterate muzhiks vastly outnumbered the party workers, but because the moral, cultural and educational level of the party itself was staggeringly low (and this included the level of its Marxism).[24] In this period, Lenin described the Bolshevik state apparatus as "deplorable" and even "disgusting," and stressed the importance of finding a way to combat its defects, "bearing in mind that these defects are rooted in the past, which although it has been over-

---

[24] ". . . we hear people dilating at too great length and too flippantly on 'proletarian culture.' For a start, we should be satisfied with real bourgeois culture; for a start, we should be glad to dispense with the cruder types of pre-bourgeois culture, i.e., bureaucratic culture or serf culture, etc."—Lenin, "Better Fewer, But Better," March 2, 1923. Cf. also Note 25.

thrown, has not yet been overcome. . . ." [25] (As late as 1932, a soviet report revealed that in some of its sections, as much as 50 percent of the bureaucracy was composed of former Czarist officials.)[26]

In sum, the less external capital there was available to the regime to expand the industrial sectors and induce the peasants to yield up their surplus, the more the peasants would have to be squeezed, administratively, to provide it. The less available the advanced technical and ideological influence, the more primitive and brutal would the primary accumulation become, the more desperate and fierce the popular resistance to it.

The prospect of such a violent minority social revolution (for a complete transition would mean nothing less) was so unacceptable to the Bolshevik leaders—even if they had supposed they might win this second civil war—and the idea of a forced industrialization so repugnant that they refused to

---

[25] Lenin, "Better Fewer, But Better." Reporting to the Eleventh Party Congress, Lenin remarked on the relation between the 4,700 Communists in the Moscow administrative apparatus and the vast number of civil servants carried over from the old state machine and asked, "Who is directing whom?" The culture of the non-Communist bureaucrats, he said, "is miserable, insignificant, but it is still at a higher level than ours. Miserable and low as it is, it is higher than that of our responsible Communist administrators, for the latter lack administrative ability. Communists who are put at the head of departments—and sometimes artful saboteurs deliberately put them in these positions in order to use them as a shield—are often fooled. This is a very unpleasant admission to make, . . . but I think we must admit it, for at present this is the salient problem."—*Collected Works*, XXXIII, 288–89. Cf. Carr, *Socialism in One Country*, I, 112 ff. Cf. also Maxim Gorky, *Untimely Thoughts* (New York, 1968), pp. 95–96. Gorky opposed the Bolshevik Revolution precisely on the grounds that the Russian masses were too uncultured and savage to be capable of building a socialist society.

[26] Cited in Barrington Moore, Jr., *Soviet Politics—The Dilemma of Power* (New York: Harper Torchbooks, 1965), p. 163.

contemplate them. On this point, Lenin was categorical: "The work of [socialist] construction depends entirely upon how soon the revolution is victorious in the most important countries of Europe," he said in 1919. "Only after this victory can we seriously undertake the business of construction." And on the third anniversary of the October insurrection he stated flatly, "We have always emphasized that we look from an international viewpoint and that in one country it is impossible to accomplish such a work as a socialist revolution." [27]

This had been the perspective not only of Lenin but of Trotsky, Bukharin, Stalin and the whole Bolshevik leadership up to 1924.[28] They too saw that the fate of socialism in one backward country, where the proletariat had come prematurely to power, depended not so much on the domestic productive forces as on the revolution's ability to take advantage of an inter-national division of labor within a community of industrialized socialist nations. Their program was to hold power, to educate the population and to lay the foundations of a socialist construction (gradual introduction of planning, gradual and voluntary collectivization of agriculture).[29] They did not think of carrying through such a construction alone.

In 1923, however, with the final crushing of the left in Germany which seemed to close off the immediate possibilities of revolution in Europe, and consequently to seal Russia in her isolation, the perspective of the party began to undergo a profound change and to turn inward. This process which had been developing for some time was hastened by the death of Lenin and the massive influx of new elements into the party apparatus. (Party membership increased thirty-fold between 1917 and 1922 alone, and five-hundred fold in the first

[27] Cited in Deutscher, *The Prophet Unarmed*, p. 290n. The second clause of the sentence last appeared in the 1928 edition of Lenin's *Collected Works*. It has been removed from all subsequent editions.

[28] Cf. Stalin's remark of April 1924, cited above, p. 13n.

[29] Lenin, *Collected Works*, XXIX, 210; XXXI, 525.

decade of the revolution.) It was Stalin who gave expression to the new mood, elaborating tentatively at first, and then more affirmatively, a line based on the hitherto rejected idea of national self-sufficiency and the possibility of building "socialism in one country."

This line, which was to have the most far-reaching consequences, did not express a carefully thought-out analysis and program. Even when he elevated the slogan into a party dogma, for example, Stalin did not put forward the program of rapid transition and forced industrialization which he was to promote later. On the contrary, during the next few years he waged a fierce struggle against the left oppositionists led by Trotsky, subsequently joined by Zinoviev and Kamanev, who called for the introduction of gradual collectivization and the acceleration of industrial development. Stalin dismissed these proposals—which were far more moderate than the measures he himself was to put into practice—as "utopian" schemes to "exploit" the peasantry and fan class struggle in the countryside, and as the fantasies of "super-industrializers."

Stalin's own "doctrine" of "socialism in one country," seemed to sum up, from a national point of view, the situation in which the regime found itself and to make a virtue of its necessity. For the untheoretical General Secretary the slogan was valuable because it was welcomed by party workers who longed for a respite and stability, who were weary of the insistent denigration of "backward" Russia associated with the old perspective, and who resented being dependent on constantly deferred non-Russian revolutions—who were open, in a word, to its implicit nationalist appeal.[30] At the same time, the slogan proved an ideal foil to that of "permanent revolution," which was identified with Trotsky, and under which he attempted to defend the old internationalist analysis and outlook.

Where Trotsky's slogan and analysis implied risk, con-

---

[30] Cf. Carr, *Socialism in One Country*, II, 47–48.

tinuing turbulence and struggle, and a "pessimism" with regard to the national potential, "socialism in one country," particularly as it was translated into practice in its first years, appeared to offer the opposite: a national mission, yet an *evolutionary* development (the perspective of the "kulak's growing into socialism"), and hence a disinclination to embark on programs which would alienate or antagonize (as any serious industrialization or collectivization program must) those classes which had been increasing their strength under the New Economic Policy. The cautiousness of the faction which consolidated its rule in the party under the banner of "socialism in one country," was perhaps best reflected in the official draft of the first five-year plan (1927). For this plan projected a state budget at the *end* of the five years of only 16 percent of the national income, or *less* than the prewar budget of Czarist Russia, which had been 18 percent! [31] Within two years, however, Stalin was prompted, partly by circumstances, partly by his own will, to take action on a scale and in a direction which neither he nor anyone else had hitherto foreseen as possible.[32]

---

[31] *The Platform of the* (Joint) *Left Opposition*, 1927 (published also in Trotsky, *The Real Situation in Russia*). It was written by Trotsky, Zinoviev, Kamenev, Smilga, Piatakov and others. An interesting early analysis of the inner party struggle of this period by a former member of the Central Committee of the German Communist party and the Executive of the Comintern can be found in Arthur Rosenberg, *A History of Bolshevism* (New York: Anchor Books, 1967).

[32] "The unpremeditated, pragmatic manner in which he embarked upon the [collectivization] would have been unbelievable if, during the preceding years, from 1924 until late in 1929, Stalin had not placed his views on record. Up to the last moment he shrank from the upheaval, and he had no idea of the scope and violence which it was to assume. In this he was not alone. Not a single Bolshevik group, faction, or coterie thought of an industrialization so intensive and rapid or of a collectivization of farming so comprehensive and drastic as that which Stalin now initiated."—Deutscher, *Stalin*, pp. 319–20. An admirable, technical account of the

From his exile, in the very year (1929–1930) in which "the great change" took place, Trotsky surveyed the experience of the preceding period through the classic internationalist perspective that had been common to all the Bolsheviks prior to 1924. "The maintenance of the proletarian revolution within a national framework," he wrote, "can only be a provisional state of affairs, even though, as the experience of the Soviet Union shows, one of long duration." In the proletarian dictatorship which is isolated, "the internal and external contradictions grow inevitably along with the successes achieved. If it remains isolated, the proletarian state must finally fall victim to these contradictions. The way out for it lies only in the victory of the proletariat of the advanced countries." [33]

Much that had occurred in the preceding period served to corroborate this analysis. The tensions besetting the Bolshevik state since the close of the civil war had become stronger, the obstacles which confronted it greater, and yet its own ability to cope with them significantly less. Isolated externally at the outset, the regime became ever more isolated internally, as it was forced by the catastrophic condition of the economy to strengthen those classes most hostile to socialism and to expand their base in the still-predominant capitalist sectors. Simultaneously, the party suffered a serious deterioration in its own morale and internal posture as its methods became more and more permeated by the bureaucratic, arbitrary and brutal techniques characteristic of the Stalin era and its leaders ever more contemptuous of those whom they led.[34] As its inner democracy was more and more stifled, the party's ability to reflect currents and forces outside itself and to respond rationally to challenges atrophied; its dependence on terror (both internally and externally) increased.

---

debates of the preceding period is to be found in Alexander Erlich, *The Soviet Industrialization Debate, 1924–1928* (Cambridge: Harvard University Press, 1960).

[33] *Permanent Revolution*, Introduction to the Russian edition.

[34] Cf. the section on the party, in the *Platform of the Opposition*.

By 1928 the national product was only just at the level of 1913, the market held full sway over the economy, and there had been no serious attempt to collectivize the poorer peasants or to increase the pace of industrialization. As a direct consequence, the chronic food crisis, which reflected the most basic contradiction of the social economy, was approaching proportions that threatened the party and its urban base with ultimate catastrophe. As the kulaks "blockaded" the cities, refusing to sell their grain at the fixed prices and thus "took the regime by the throat," Trotsky's analysis seemed about to be fully confirmed.

It was at this moment that Stalin broke through the threatening impasse by reversing course and carrying out a new revolution. Troops were sent to rural areas, first to confiscate the stocks of grain, and then to drive the peasants by armed force into collectives. The class struggle was "fanned" in the countryside in a manner in which the Bolshevik Party would not have dreamed of fanning it previously. "We must smash the kulaks," Stalin proclaimed, "eliminate them as a class." [35]

The ensuing bloodshed, in what rapidly became a civil war against *all* strata of the peasantry, was incalculable. Stalin even told Churchill later that the collectivization had created an internal situation more perilous than any Russia faced in the Second World War. The peasants responded to the confiscation by burning their crops and destroying their livestock, so that—according to official figures—almost eighteen million horses, thirty million large cattle and nearly a hundred million sheep and goats were killed between 1929 and 1934. [36] Vast tracts of land were left untilled, with the result that famine once again appeared in the Russian steppes.

In contrast to the October Revolution, this upheaval "came at the lowest ebb of the nation's social awareness and

[35] J. V. Stalin, *Leninism* (London: Allen & Unwin, 1940), pp. 325–26.
[36] *Ibid.*, p. 498.

political energy." It was "a revolution from above, based on the suppression of all spontaneous popular activity. Its driving force was not any social class, but the party machine." To Bolsheviks like Trotsky, therefore, whose thought was steeped in the European tradition of classical revolution, "this upheaval was . . . no revolution at all—it was merely the rape of history committed by the Stalinist bureaucracy." Yet, as Deutscher rightly pointed out, "however 'illegitimate' from the classical Marxist viewpoint, Stalin's revolution from above effected a lasting and, as to scale, an unprecedented change in property relations, and ultimately in the nation's way of life." [37]

By transforming property relations, and with them the Russian social structure, by decisively defeating the domestic forces of restoration, and by establishing a firm industrial base, Stalin's reversal falsified Trotsky's perspective (which posed the alternatives of revolution in the advanced countries *or* Soviet collapse). But it had no such implications for the general analysis from which the perspective had grown. On the contrary, the very fact that Stalin's upheaval represented a *reversal* of the previous "gradualist" policy, that it *was* a revolution—infinitely more costly and perilous in its outcome for not having been expected or properly prepared—was the debt which "socialism in one country" was compelled to pay to the forces of permanent revolution and to the analytic foresight of the theories of Trotsky and Lenin. Seen in perspective, "forcible industrialization and collectivization" were alternatives to "the spread of revolution," while "the liquidation of the Russian kulaks" was but the substitute "for the overthrow of bourgeois rule abroad." [38]

[37] Deutscher, *The Prophet Outcast*, pp. 110–12.
[38] *Ibid.*

7. Uneven and Combined Development: The Stalin Era

In a sense, Bolshevism has "Westernized" the essential framework of Russian society. But it could do so only by itself becoming "Orientalized." This mutual interpenetration of modern technology and Marxist socialism with Russian barbarism formed the content of the Stalin era.

—Isaac Deutscher

Stalin's revolution from above, which ruthlessly drove a primitive and barbarous culture into the atomic era, was an epoch-making event. Yet, its immediate impact was profoundly contradictory and ambiguous. This ambiguity was rooted in the very nature of the upheaval, which was as hybrid and dual, as much a product of the combined development of Russian society, as the October Revolution had been before.

Just as Russia's late and backward development had previously given her anti-feudal revolution its proletarian character, so now it was her relative earliness of development that made her advanced socialist revolution so backward. In the former upheaval, the immaturity of the Russian social structure had weighed heavily against the old regime, making it possible and even necessary for the working class to assert itself "prematurely" and take the lead in the revolutionary process; now that vast and ponderous primitiveness weighed down on the revolutionary forces themselves, dominating and eventually distorting the transformation which still had to be carried through.

The "dual" nature of Russia's historical development has generally been seen as a product of the Euro-Asian framework of Russian society, influenced by the fact that the Russian empire was situated, as Lenin put it, "on the border-line between the civilized countries and the countries which this war[1] has for the first time definitely brought into the orbit of civilization." It was Russia's Oriental backwardness that made her such a weak link in the capitalist chain in 1917. It was her proximity to the advanced European West that involved her so directly and so destructively in the conflict, and imbued her revolutionaries so early with a powerful and mature Marxist vision.

Perhaps the best expression of the dual or combined character of the second Russian Revolution, and its historical place in the Russian framework, was its very "illegitimacy," from a Western Marxist point of view. For such a view regarded the self-conscious action of class, and not the bureaucratic terror of a party apparatus, as the proper agency of socialist transformation. However, it was by no means "illegitimate" when viewed in terms of the national environment in which the revolution had now been sealed and by which in a partial yet profound sense it had been overwhelmed. Thus, to an extraordinary extent in prerevolutionary Russia, a centralized autocratic state had also dominated every level of society. Even the highest nobles were but "the first slaves of the Tsar," possessing "no security against sudden and arbitrary execution accompanied with the confiscation of their property." [2] More importantly, this state itself, historically, had been the main agency of Russian social development and reform.[3]

Stalin's revolutionary despotism placed him in the tradi-

---

[1] The First World War.

[2] Chamberlin, *The Russian Revolution* (New York: Universal Library, 1965), I, 6.

[3] The liberal historian Milyukov, for example, held that, in contrast to the West, in Russia the state had actually created the estates.

tion of the Czars in more ways than one. Indeed, in the descriptions of Peter the Great, who also attempted to carry out a "Westernizing" revolution from above, there are uncanny reverberations of the awesome upheaval over which the General Secretary later presided: "His beneficent actions were accomplished with repelling violence. [His] reform was a struggle of despotism with the people, with its sluggishness. He hoped through the threat of his authority to evoke initiative in an enslaved society, and . . . to introduce into Russia, European science, popular education, as the necessary condition of social initiative. . . . The interaction of despotism and freedom, of education and slavery—this is the political squaring of the circle, the riddle of which we have been solving for two centuries from the time of Peter, and which is still unsolved." [4] This was written well before Stalin's own autocratic and brutal transformation from above shattered the medieval framework of Russian society and culture, ushering her irrevocably into the modern age.

Stalin was able to square the circle and solve the riddle where the Czars had failed before him, because while they had based their own autocratic revolutions on the existing structure of society and the preservation of its traditional class institutions, Stalin based his firmly on the gains of October. The October Revolution had destroyed the legal premise of class rule in Russia and had laid the basis for planned economy. Moreover, it had raised to power a party dedicated to a revolutionary program.[5]

Precisely because Stalin's revolution *was* a revolution from above, however, based not on a class but on a bureaucracy, not on a popular upsurge but on the suppression of the popular will, it inevitably remained restricted and contradic-

---

[4] V. Kluchevsky, *The Course of Russian History*, cited in Chamberlin.

[5] The key role of the party in preserving and carrying forward revolutionary gains in the post-1923 period, though denied by Trotsky and his followers, is well brought out in Carr, *Socialism in One Country*, I, 124–36.

tory in its progress, and ultimately incomplete. Moreover, it promoted, in its course, developments which even looked reactionary from the vantage point of 1917.

Thus, while the Stalin regime liquidated class rule in the countryside, it regimented the lives of the peasants in their new collectives, as it did a whole generation of laboring Russians. In laying the foundations of rapid industrialization, it conscripted workers in military style for the urban industries, destroying what modicum of autonomy had been preserved by the trade unions until then, and in general drastically *curtailing* the freedoms that had been thought won in the Bolshevik October. While breaking the back of rural individualism, the Stalin regime fostered a furiously competitive Stakhanvoism among the traditionally collectivist Russian working class. While encouraging learning and the acquisition of scientific knowledge on an unprecedented scale, it propagated unscientific and anti-intellectual doctrines,[6] and launched witch-hunting attacks on those sections of the intelligentsia that sought to assert any independence. While introducing large-scale social welfare services and glorifying human labor, it reintroduced in the penal camps the most hateful form of labor. While proclaiming its object to be a "classless" society, it created extensive inequality and privilege. While exorcising religion in the name of Marxism and scientific rationality, it made Marxism itself a religion and deified both the ruler and the state.[7] And finally, while proclaiming its own

---

[6] For example, those associated with Zhdanovism and Lysenkoism or the notion that Einstein's theory of relativity was somehow bourgeois and therefore wrong.

[7] Underlying this development was a primitive reaction to Russia's isolation and weakness. The necessity and yet the impossibility of deliverance made it necessary to believe in a superhuman deliverer. Marxism bestowed the divine miracle-working power, and Stalin ("the Lenin of his time") was both its prophet and its pope. Cf. Deutscher, *Russia After Stalin*. The glorification of the "thoughts of Chairman Mao" and the attribution to them of semimystical, semidivine powers during the Chinese Cultural Revolution represent a similar phenomenon.

continuity with "Leninism," it encouraged the resurgence of Russian nationalism, the rejection of which had been the very basis of the Leninist break with social democracy and the creation of the Communist International.

This forward-backward progess, this amalgam of the Gothic with the modern, the irrational with the scientific, the inhumane and barbarous with the enlightened and progressive, was the distinctive form of the Stalinist development of Russia; and this development was itself the consequence of the combination of advanced and backward elements in the national framework within which the revolution had become so firmly enclosed.

The nationalist course which the revolution took was a direct consequence of Russia's international isolation; but just as the course of international revolutionary developments had a profound impact internally, so, too, this nationalist course had important international reverberations. For the failure of advanced revolutions to materialize in the 1917–1923 period not only left Russia's national backwardness to dominate the progress of its revolution, but also paved the way for Russian Communism to dominate the Communist International and thus to impose its own primitive elements on the Communist movements of other countries. In this international environment, moreover, the contradictory elements within the national progress had ambivalent and "uneven" consequences, corresponding to the fundamental unevenness of world development.

In the underdeveloped regions the more progressive features of the Stalinist transformation naturally exerted the more important influence. Agricultural Russia's forced ascent within two decades to an urban, industrialized development inevitably had a revolutionary impact on the aspirations of the backward, poverty-stricken areas of the world. The practicality of such epochal development within even a single generation emphasized all the more painfully the incalculable degradation and misery, the irredeemable sacrifice of *both* present and future generations, to which an exploited position in the capitalist world system doomed an underdeveloped nation.[8]

Equally important, the industrial and military power of Stalinist Russia ensured to other revolutionary states at least a partial protection against the kind of isolation and armed intervention which had helped to promote the conditions in which Stalinism had been born. There can be little question, for example, that Russia's possession of atomic weapons in the early 1950's was a powerful deterrent to the ambition of certain top U.S. political and military leaders who wanted to subject revolutionary China to a catastrophic nuclear attack at the time.[9] The survival of revolutionary Cuba and North Vietnam may similarly be said to have hinged on Russia's military might.

Moscow's early alliance with Peking not only protected China from attack, but also pushed the Chinese Revolution forward, easing the path to industrial development. Thus, Maoism, for all its Stalinist features, rooted as in Russia in

---

[8] "It could hardly escape the notice of Asian and African leaders . . . that the Russians did more in a quarter of a century for the education of the peoples living in the Arctic circle and in the Caucasus, who in 1917 had not even a written language, than the British did in India in an occupation of nearly two hundred years." Geoffrey Barraclough, *An Introduction to Contemporary History* (Baltimore, Md.: Penguin Books, 1967), p. 224.

[9] Among those who are known to have held such objectives or publicly proclaimed them are General Douglas MacArthur, Supreme Commander in the Far East until 1951, Secretary of Defense Louis Johnson and Secretary of the Navy Francis P. Matthews. Admiral Radford "told a congressional committee that Red China had to be destroyed even if it required a fifty-year war [and] argued, as Chairman of the Joint Chiefs of Staff for the use of 500 planes to drop tactical A-bombs on Vietminh troops before the Fall of Dienbienphu. If China openly came into the picture, we are unofficially told, Peking was to be given atomic treatment." —C. Wright Mills, *The Power Elite* (New York: Oxford University Press, 1956), pp. 210–11.

"the conflict between the strivings of the revolution and the pre-industrial conditions of society" [10] cannot without serious distortion be equated with Stalinism. Indeed, China's ability (in a struggle by no means over) to wrest herself free from the horrors of backwardness and foreign exploitation without incurring the supreme costs of the Russian ascent (though there have been very heavy costs) naturally enhances the socialist prospect in the eyes of the underdeveloped world and drives the engine of revolutionary change with redoubled force.

If the Russian Revolution, particularly in its second phase, imparted a direct and powerful impetus to indigenous revolutionary movements in the backward regions its influence in the advanced capitalist countries was decidedly more contradictory and complex. On the one hand, there was the growth of mass Communist parties in several European countries as a direct consequence of the Revolution and the activities of its Comintern. On the other, there was the arrest of these movements, where they existed, and their failure to develop at all in some of the most important capitalist countries.

While many factors certainly contributed to the political stabilization of advanced capitalism, particularly in the first two decades of the postwar "cold war" period, there can be little doubt that the success of the anti-Communist crusade was a major one. Nor can it be doubted that the excesses of Stalinism were major factors in making possible the success of this crusade. For in countries which already possessed the material base that the Stalinist ascent attempted to achieve, it was only natural that the backward features of the Russian development should have made the most significant impression.

An equally important factor in determining the impact of the Revolution in the West was the character and perspec-

---

[10] Isaac Deutscher, "Three Currents in Communism," in *Ironies of History* (New York: Oxford University Press, 1966).

tive of the Western Communist parties themselves. Regarding the defense of the Revolution as a primary task, taking a subordinate position within the International to the stronger Russian party, and naturally deferring to its successful revolutionary record, these parties patterned themselves to an extraordinary degree on the Russian model. This course was fostered by Lenin himself,[11] who failed to grasp in this a profound implication of the law of uneven development. It was not missed by Rosa Luxemburg, however, who had previously warned against the danger of taking backward Russia as a socialist model.

"It would be demanding something superhuman from Lenin and his comrades," she had written, "if we should expect of them that under such circumstances [i.e., of Russia's ruin and isolation, and the allied intervention] they should conjure forth the finest democracy, the most exemplary dictatorship of the proletariat and a flourishing socialist economy." Lenin and the Bolsheviks, by their revolutionary determination and unbreakable loyalty to international socialism, had "contributed whatever could possibly be contributed under such devilishly hard conditions." But, she warned, "the danger begins . . . when they make a virtue of necessity and want to freeze into a complete theoretical system all the tactics forced upon them by these fatal circumstances, and want to recommend them to the international proletariat as a model of socialist tactics. When they get in their own light in this way, and hide their genuine, unquestionable historical service under the bushel of false steps forced upon them by necessity, they render a poor service to international socialism for the sake of which they have fought and suffered; for they want to place in its storehouse as new discoveries all the distortions prescribed in Russia by necessity and compul-

---

[11] For example, in the twenty-one conditions he laid down for membership in the Third International. Cf. also the documents in H. Gruber, *International Communism in the Era of Lenin* (New York: Fawcett, 1967).

sion—in the last analysis only by-products of the bankruptcy of international socialism in the present world war." [12]

What had been a tendency under Lenin's leadership became the rule under Stalin's, and as a result the international parties reflected in their advanced environments the backward features of the Russian development even more sharply. In this way, the previous unbalancing, in Russia, of the equilibrium of world revolutionary forces found its partial redress. For the acceleration of the international revolution, as a consequence of the weakness of one of the most backward eastern links in the capitalist chain, was now reversed as the revolutionary process in the stronger West was retarded by the Stalinization (in effect, the primitivization) of the most advanced ranks of the international revolutionary vanguard.

This retarding influence of the Russian Revolution is not only a complex phenomenon but, more important, an unstable one. In its very instability lies the basis for a potential realignment of forces which could profoundly affect the cold war and the course of world revolutionary development. To gain insight into the dynamics of this process, it is necessary to look again at the relationship between the actual revolution in its autarchic Eastern development and socialism as a revolutionary program in the advanced West.

An immediate and far-reaching consequence of the Bolshevik party's adoption in the mid-twenties of the doctrine of national self-sufficiency was the opening of a serious gap, which had not existed before, between party proclamation and the realities of Soviet life. The adoption of a program to build, alone, an advanced socialist society in a situation of extreme backwardness, and in the face of tremendous internal and external hostility, naturally invited the creation of consoling and self-supporting myths. Where frankness among the Bolsheviks about the gravity of their plight (failing help from

---

[12] Rosa Luxemburg, *The Russian Revolution* (Ann Arbor: University of Michigan Press, 1962), pp. 78–79.

abroad) had been previously the rule, the party leaders now began systematically to understate the difficulties involved in the construction of socialism in one country, stifling those sections of the party which dissented, and to exaggerate the progress already made toward its completion. Such myth making not only provided self-justification to a bureaucracy suspended above the masses, as the party had found itself at the end of the civil war, but the deception was also felt by many to be necessary to stave off the destructive and self-defeating despair that was endemic to such desperate times.[13] In any event, the deception which began in a mild and half-defensive manner, grew rapidly into an immense and uncontainable lie.

At the Fifth Party Conference in November 1926, Stalin recalled the program for a new socialist order that had been laid down by Engels in his *Principles of Communism* seventy years earlier: "Engels said that the proletarian revolution with the above program could not succeed in one single country alone. The facts, however, show that . . . such a revolution in its most essential parts has already been carried through in one single country alone, for we have carried out nine-tenths of this program in our country." [14]

---

[13] Trotsky strongly dissented from such reasoning: "The worker who understands that it is impossible to build a socialist paradise, like an oasis in the hell of world capitalism; that the fate of the Soviet Republic and therefore his own fate depend entirely on the international revolution, will fulfill his duties toward the USSR much more energetically than the worker who is told that what we already possess is presumably 90% socialism."—*The Third International After Lenin*, p. 68.

[14] Compare Lenin's remarks three years earlier: "The most harmful thing would be to rely on the assumption . . . that we have any considerable number of elements necessary for the building of a really new state apparatus, one really worthy to be called socialist, Soviet, etc. No, we are ridiculously deficient of such an apparatus, and even of the elements of it, and we must remember that we should not stint time on building it, and that it will take

Stalin's remarks indicate how great was the gap already opening up between party doctrine and truth to cover the disparity between reality and goal which the civil war and isolation had bequeathed to the victorious Bolshevik remnants. For it could hardly be said that a country in which the presence of poverty, misery, unemployment and illiteracy had hardly abated in the decade since the revolution,[15] and in which there was still no political democracy for *any* class, had advanced far along the path to a socialist society. Certainly it had not gone most of the way, as Stalin was then contending.

Yet this claim rapidly became a central tenet of party dogma, and the gap between party statement and the harsh facts of Soviet existence, far from closing in the ensuing period, continued to grow at an awesome rate. Thus in 1931, after the draconian collectivization had plunged the countryside into bloody civil war, resulting not only in a prodigal toll in human life but in the destruction of well over half the nation's livestock as well—in these near-famine and still pre-industrial conditions (only seven thousand tractors being available in the whole of the U.S.S.R. at the inception of the collectivization)—Stalin announced that Russia had at last "entered the era of socialism."

As if this distortion were not enough, in the mid-thirties, that is to say, in the throes of Russia's industrial revolution, at a time when inequality and privilege were expanding at a frenzied pace, when grinding poverty was still the lot of the vast mass of the people, when the life of the nation was regimented and terrorized as never before, when the labor camps were packed with political prisoners, when the state—far from withering away—had become a more oppressive and

---

many, many years."—"Better Fewer, But Better." It has been said of Stalin that, like Lenin, he knew how to retreat when necessary; the difference was that Stalin presented the retreats as advances.
[15] Industrial unemployment, for example, which had been 2,600,000 in 1913, and 1,250,000 in 1921–22, was 1,900,000 in 1925. Statistics are from Carr, *Socialism in One Country*, I, 218.

more glorified institution than at any time since 1917, when
the infamous purge trials were just beginning and would end
in the liquidation of virtually the entire old Bolshevik leadership, including the whole Politburo as it had been constituted
under Lenin, Stalin declared: ". . . the complete victory of
the Socialist system in all spheres of the national economy is
now a fact." And what does this mean? "It means that
the exploitation of man by man has been abolished, eliminated. . . ."

To crown this "transformation," Stalin ordered the
drafting of a new Soviet constitution, which his propaganda
proclaimed "the most democratic in the world" and which,
among other things, abolished the Soviet system of election
(via local organizations organized around centers of work)
and replaced it with the bourgeois concept of the universal
vote of an atomized population. With this document, the reduction of socialist goal to self-justifying ideology reached
the pinnacle of its development. In it, the single-party system,
previously introduced by the Bolsheviks as a temporary expedient in perilous civil war conditions, became enshrined as a
socialist *principle*, the organizational expression of the alleged
classlessness and conflictless harmony of the new order. Here
was not only a mockery of the existing Russian reality of
1936—the camps, the firing squads, the labor conscripts—but
a mockery of the socialist ideal in Marxian doctrine as well,
which had had nothing in common with one-party dictatorships.[16] It was also based, needless to say, on a caricature of
the Marxian class concept. For economic classes are often het-
erogeneous in social composition, and a single class generally
provides the basis of several parties.[17] Unhappily, this did not

---

[16] On Marx's anti-authoritarian attitude to the pre- and post-
revolutionary state, see R. Miliband, "Marx and the State," *The
Socialist Register, 1965* (New York: Monthly Review Press, 1965).
[17] For example, the Mensheviks and the Bolsheviks! Cf. Trotsky's
discussion of party and class in his critique of the Constitution in
The Revolution Betrayed (New York: Pioneer, 1965).

prevent the now-Stalinized world Communist movement, and particularly the movement in the West, from assimilating the new principle of "socialist" reconstruction into its own programs.

From the beginning Trotsky, as the leader of the Left Opposition, had decried the growing distortion of the real situation in Russia, and had continued to warn of its inevitable consequences. "One could not find a more anti-socialist and anti-revolutionary assertion," he wrote in a brief to the Comintern Executive in 1928, "than Stalin's statement to the effect that 'socialism has already been 90 percent realized in the U.S.S.R.'" For as long as the Soviet Union was a poverty-stricken and backward country such statements could serve only to "hopelessly discredit the idea of a socialist society in the eyes of the toiling masses." [18]

After Stalin proclaimed Russia's *entry* into the era of socialism in 1931, Trotsky wrote again from exile, again attacked the misrepresentations of the official propaganda, the euphoric picture of Soviet society and the equally unrealistic nineteenth-century image of the conditions of the masses under advanced capitalism that the party was promoting. To tell the Soviet people that their oppression, hunger and privation were the fruits of socialism, wrote Trotsky, was to kill their desire for socialism altogether and to make them its enemies. He even went so far as to denounce this as Stalin's "greatest crime," for it was a crime perpetrated against the deepest aspirations of the working classes which threatened to compromise the future of the revolution and its movement.[19]

As events turned out, these apprehensions proved to have far less revelance to Russia, the chief object of Trotsky's concern, than to Europe and the advanced capitalist West. Three main factors were responsible for this. In the first place, the socialist ideal as a postindustrial, democratizing and rationalizing transformation had little relevance for an illiterate, "pre-

[18] Trotsky, *The Third International After Lenin*, p. 66.
[19] Isaac Deutscher, *The Prophet Outcast* (New York: Oxford University Press, 1965), p. 103.

capitalist," peasant society, possessing underdeveloped means of production and enjoying no tradition of democratic rule. Hence, the "failure" of the ideal in terms of such a transformation, that is, in the terms in which it would inevitably be seen from an advanced capitalist vantage, was also felt far less in backward Russia.

In the second place, the positive changes which the Stalinist revolution brought about in the structure and quality of Russian life, were formidable. Thus, the industrialization, education and modernization of the old Czarist empire, the liberation of a continent from ignorance and backwardness—in a word, the transformation with which socialism became identified in Russia—made it possible to maintain at least the quiescence of the masses (which sheer terror alone would not have accomplished) and to achieve later their acquiescence and even support, though in Stalin's lifetime the balance was often a precarious one.

Finally, Stalin gave to the "socialist" transformation in Russia a frankly nationalist expression.[20] In 1931, for example, he justified the rapid and ruthless ascent as necessary to avoid the hapless plight of "old Russia," which the Bolsheviks had previously denounced as an imperialist exploiter of small nations, but which Stalin now portrayed as having been "ceaselessly beaten for backwardness" by the Mongols, the Turks, the Swedes, the Japanese and others. "We are fifty or a hundred years behind the advanced countries," declared Stalin. "We must make good this lag in ten years. Either we do it or they crush us."

Within a decade of this warning, Russia was in fact invaded by the Nazi armies, though ironically the Father of the People was unprepared for the actual assault when it came,[21]

---

[20] Of course, in one sense, Stalin was merely giving overt expression to a nationalist pattern latent in Bolshevism from the outset. See Carr, *Socialism in One Country*, I, 8 ff.

[21] A week before the Nazi invasion, Stalin attacked the British ambassador for spreading "rumors" of an impending war between Russia and Germany. Though informed by the British of the

and through his purges, particularly in the army, had drastically weakened the nation's defenses. It was in the "Great Patriotic War" that followed, when Russia's newly won technological prowess allowed her to repulse an army twice the size of that by which she had been defeated in the First World War, that the Stalin regime and its version of industrializing "socialism" implanted itself firmly in Russian soil.

For similar reasons the identification of "socialism" with the Stalinist ascent in conditions of extreme scarcity, far from compromising the ideal in the underdeveloped regions, did much, on balance, to enhance it. As Toynbee has observed: "Considering how overwhelming the West's ascendancy over most of the rest of the World had been during the preceding quarter of a millennium, Communist Russia's feat of turning the tables on the West was impressive. Indeed, in the eyes of anti-Western-minded Asians, Africans, and Indian Americans . . . Russia was an example and an inspiration . . . because Russia had been the first non-Western country that had had the courage to stand up to the modern West and the ability to beat it at its own game by mastering Western weapons and doing better than their Western originators in the use of them." [22] In this way the nationalist development of the "socialist" revolution in Russia was linked directly and positively to the nationalist revolution in the colonial world.

In the advanced capitalist West, by contrast, the identification of socialism with the Russian ascent had profoundly negative consequences for the revolutionary movement. Here Stalin's exaggerations of Soviet achievements (and lies about

---

exact date of the German attack, Stalin failed to mobilize his troops on the scale necessary and move them up to the frontier. He did not want to provoke Hitler into breaking the neutrality pact. As a result, and also because of the purges which had demoralized the defending forces, the whole buffer zone he had gained by his pact with Hitler was lost immediately to the invading armies.

[22] Arnold Toynbee, *A Study of History* (New York: Oxford University Press, 1961), XII, 536–37.

the frame-ups of the Communist oppositionists) compromised those Socialists and Communists in the West who repeated them, while the grim horror of much of Soviet reality served to discredit their program and ideal, even as the horrors of industrializing England had discredited capitalism in the eyes of the early socialists. In the end, the Stalinist identification of socialism with the hell of Soviet primitive accumulation discouraged and demoralized many more Socialists in the West than in Russia itself, where the oppression and poverty were really felt, but where the transformation made its deepest impression as well.

It is just in the further progress of the transformation in the East, however, that the seeds of a possible reversal in the West may be seen to lie. For by this very transformation, Stalinism has already rendered itself an anachronism in its own Russian context. Where the Europe-oriented Bolshevik vanguard had been overwhelmed by the barbarism of primitive Russia, the nation-centered Stalinist bureaucracy was able by its despotism to overcome and dissolve that framework, and to create out of its backwardness and "on the bones of its builders" a modern twentieth-century culture. By electrifying and industrializing an archaic economy by drawing a generation of muzhiks out of the darkness of medieval superstitution and icon-worship, and educating them in scientific technologies and the industrial arts, and by schooling them in the elements of Western culture, Stalinism destroyed the only soil in which its peculiar brand of Byzantine Marxism and ritual terror could flourish. As Isaac Deutscher has succinctly observed, "A nation which has successfully coped with the problems of nuclear technology well ahead of the old industrial nations of Europe—such a nation can no longer be ruled by a 'rising Sun' and a 'Father of the People' and held in awe by the whole set of Stalinist totems and taboos which belonged essentially to a much earlier and lower phase of civilization." [23]

---

[23] Deutscher, *Ironies of History*, p. 21.

With the modernization and urbanization of Soviet Russia, the practice and theory of primitive Stalinism became incompatible with its social integument and was accordingly burst asunder. But the post-Stalin reform of Stalinism, though far-reaching in its consequences, still stopped well short of revolution. Like the Czarist reforms, which it resembled in this, de-Stalinization came from above as an incomplete measure, a concession—in this case to preserve the power and privilege of the ruling Stalinist bureaucracy and its base in the party-state. It brought, therefore, no restoration of the democracy of the Soviets, no revival of trade union autonomy, no full freedom of expression and association, no crack in the monolithic structure of the party, in which control of economy and state remained vested.

Yet this new socio-political equilibrium was itself unstable. For just as the Russian environment had become incompatible with Stalinism, so it showed signs of becoming inhospitable to the bureaucratic rule of a privileged minority and the glaring inequalities which that rule defended. On the one hand, increasing economic abundance was divesting such rule of its material basis. (For where there is scarcity, there will be inequality and minority privilege, and where there is inequality and privilege, there will tend to be an inequality of power to enforce it.)[24] On the other hand, the ending of Russia's isolation was depriving the party autocracy of its ideological buttresses, as the influx of democratic ideas from other revolutionary movements and the West strengthened the democratic currents within the U.S.S.R. itself. In other words, the close of the Stalin era was witnessing the evening up of levels of development between East and West.

In one important sense, however, social relations in Russia had already outstripped those in the capitalist world. For

---

[24] Cf. Leon Trotsky, *The Revolution Betrayed*, especially Chapter 3.

the introduction of planned economy in the Soviet Union had
not only permitted a rapid ascent from backwardness, but
also a far more rational, more socially beneficial allocation of
basic resources than was possible in the advanced capitalist
countries. Thus, by mastering the blind forces of the economy, the Russians were able to avoid the suffering and waste
resulting from the chronic unemployment and underutiliza-
tion of existing capacity which was endemic to capitalist
economies. In the prosperous period between 1953 and 1964,
for example, it was conservatively estimated that the output
lost through these causes in the United States alone was $550
billion,[25] or more than twice the annual income of the entire
underdeveloped world.

Even when fully utilized, moreover, resources in the advanced capitalist countries were grossly *mis*used, indeed
wasted, from a social point of view. Thus in the United States
the income spent on advertising amounted to nearly three
times the budgets of all U.S. institutions of higher learning
taken together.[26] On the other hand, the U.S.S.R., with half
the *per capita* income of the United States, allocated to education a percentage of its national product between two and
three times greater.[27]

By the mid-sixties, despite the irrationalities inherited
from the past, and others transmitted from the West (e.g.,
the necessity for a debilitating arms program[28]), the U.S.S.R.
was beginning to attain something approaching the material

---

[25] Leon Keyserling, *Progress or Poverty*, Conference on Economic
Progress (Washington, D.C., 1964), p. 91. Keyserling was chairman of the Council of Economic Advisors to President Truman.
[26] *Monopoly Capital*, pp. 307–8. The figures are taken from various
U.S. Congressional reports. If aggregate advertising expenditure is
combined with sales efforts of all kinds, such as annual style
changes in automobiles, the sum is equivalent to all the expenditure on education at all levels.
[27] *Ibid.*
[28] See above, p. 78 and Note.

base originally prescribed in the Marxian program for the socialist transition. How the process of Soviet development would go forward, however, and how far it would progress in the classical socialist direction remained open questions even a decade after the intial de-Stalinization. For as long as the monopoly of power (not merely of the party, but of a single faction in the party[29]) still remained unchallenged, the question of whether the rule of a privileged stratum could survive this monopoly remained unanswered and unprobed.[30] Half a century after the Bolshevik October, the road to socialism in Russia still remained the road through the democratic revolution to which Lenin had pointed in 1905.[31]

One important relationship seemed clear, however: the liberalization in Russia had already produced the revival of an advanced socialist Left in the Western capitalist states, particularly among the intelligentsia and the students; every advance in the de-Stalinization process, every move toward a resurrection of the Soviet (and Soviet bloc) Left, every step toward an authentic socialist development in the U.S.S.R. (and in other bloc states like China and Cuba) would prompt

---

[29] The rule outlawing factions was introduced as an expedient measure in a perilous situation at the end of the civil war. (Cf. Carr, *The Bolshevik Revolution*, I, 205 ff.) Like many other "temporary" measures, however, it has been maintained to serve other purposes and remains in force in most Communist parties.

[30] "In [Soviet] society, no automatic economic mechanism keeps the masses in subjection; it is sheer political force that does it. True, the bureaucracy derives part of its strength from the uncontrolled commanding position it holds in the economy; but it holds that, too, by means of political force. Without that force it cannot maintain its social supremacy; and any form of democratic control deprives it of its force."—Isaac Deutscher, *The Unfinished Revolution* (New York: Oxford University Press, 1967), p. 106. Cf. also Deutscher, "Ideological Trends in the USSR," *The Socialist Register 1968* (New York: Monthly Review Press).

[31] See above, p. 121.

the revolutionary impulse once again to flow in earnest from "East" to "West." [32]

---

[32] Within months of the completion of this manuscript, events in France served to confirm this thesis. Militant students of the "New Left," ideologically inspired by the Cuban and Chinese revolutions, and encouraged by the recent de-Stalinization reforms and student demonstrations in Czechoslovakia and by similar New Left student rebellions in Germany and the United States, rose in protest and triggered a general strike and the most insurrectionary situation in the West since the Second World War.

IV

COEXISTENCE AND

REVOLUTION

8. Russia, the Comintern and the West

> Only after we have overthrown, finally vanquished and expropriated the bourgeoisie of the whole world, and not merely of one country, will wars become impossible.
>
> —Lenin, 1917

From the outset, the impact and influence of the Russian Revolution extended far beyond its borders in a single country. That impact was not confined to the Revolution's role as a model for other revolutionary movements. For the possession of *state* power added a dimension to the scope and activity of the Russian leaders which went far beyond their ability to influence by example. Moreover, this "state significance of the revolution" [1] imposed on the Kremlin its own necessities and responsibilities, and exerted a corresponding conservative influence on the policies and outlook of the revolutionary regime.

Despite, or perhaps because of, its complexity, Soviet foreign policy has often been portrayed in a one-sided and therefore unsatisfactory manner. Thus, the Stalin regime has been seen by many as inspiring and instigating all foreign upheavals, while at the same time it has been castigated as the

---

[1] The phrase was used by Steklov, the editor of *Izvestia*, in a leading article which suggested the possibility of receiving aid from America because of its rivalry with German and Japanese imperialism. The article appeared on March 15, 1918. Cited in Carr, *The Bolshevik Revolution*, III, 79.

conservative representative of bureaucratic national interests and the gravedigger of the international revolution. The reality is far from being so one-sided, and to grasp its dynamics is essential to understanding the shape of the world struggle in the post-October era.

Just as classical Marxism had conceived of a socialist revolution taking place only on the basis of highly developed productive forces, so the early Bolsheviks regarded the revolution in Russia as the spark, not the center, of the world revolution. "To the Russian proletariat has fallen the great honour of *beginning* the series of revolutions which the imperialist war has made an objective inevitability," wrote Lenin in March 1917, "but the idea that the Russian proletariat is the chosen revolutionary proletariat among the workers of the world is absolutely alien to us." Because of Russia's backwardness, "the Russian proletariat, single-handed, cannot bring the socialist revolution to a *victorious conclusion*." However, the revolutionary drive of Russia's peasantry "*may*, to judge from the experience of 1905, give tremendous sweep to the bourgeois-democratic revolution in Russia and *may* make our revolution the *prologue* to the world socialist revolution, a *step* toward it." [2] (Emphasis in original.)

Defending these ideas a decade later against the doctrine of "socialism in one country," Trotsky wrote: "The colossal importance of the Soviet Union lies in that it is the disputed base of the world revolution and not at all in the presumption that it is able to build socialism independently of the world revolution." [3] "We have always and repeatedly pointed out to the workers," Lenin had declared in February 1921, "that the underlying chief task and basic condition of our victory is the propagation of the revolution at least to several of the more advanced countries." In accordance with this perspec-

---

[2] "Farewell Letter to the Swiss Workers," *Collected Works*, Vol. XXIII.

[3] *The Third International After Lenin*, p. 63.

tive, two years earlier the Bolsheviks had formed the Comintern, an International of revolutionary Communist parties.

For a few short years after its formation, and especially in the period coinciding with overt capitalist intervention in Russia, the Comintern largely held to its revolutionary program. But with the failure both of the intervention and of the hoped-for European revolution, and following a wave of recognition for the new regime from the capitalist states,[4] the Kremlin's perspective on the International underwent a profound change. From the periphery of the world revolution the enterprise in Russia was now moved to its very center. Instead of seeing their own socialist development as dependent on the progress of foreign revolutions, Russia's leaders adopted an outlook in which other socialist revolutions were to wait on their development. The primary task of the Comintern, in their view, was no longer to inspire and aid new revolutions internationally (for which there was held to be no prospect and which disturbed Russia's advantageous relations with capitalist states[5]) but to defend the revolution already made at home. Thus, in the eyes of the Russian leaders the aim of Comintern policy became not to promote the Communist conquest of power in the capitalist countries, but to exert pressure on the ruling classes of these countries to coexist with Communism in the Soviet Union.

In this way the doctrine of "socialism in one country"

---

[4] In 1923, 1924 and 1925, recognition was granted by Britain, Italy and several other states; commercial treaties were signed and there was a general détente between Russia and the West.

[5] An indicative and highly significant incident at this time concerned the famous "Curzon Ultimatum," which complained of the activities of the Comintern and threatened, if nothing was done, to denounce the trade agreement that had been concluded in 1921. The enfeebled Soviet government yielded to this pressure and bound itself "not to support with funds or in any other form persons or bodies or agencies or institutions whose aim is to spread discontent or to foment rebellion in any part of the British Empire." This promise was given in June 1923. Cf. Carr, *The Interregnum* (New York: Macmillan).

came to represent a radical reversal of the Leninist perspective on the Comintern and revolutionary internationalism. Of course, neither the Russian party nor the Russian-dominated Comintern were ready to abandon the revolutionary ideas and programs of their still-recent origins and past. But if the forms of Communist doctrine were more or less preserved for a while, by the mid-twenties their practical content had already undergone a critical transformation.

The first important expression of this change was to be seen in the strategy which the Comintern promoted in the Chinese Revolution of 1925–27. China's development as a backward, semifeudal/semicapitalist society, whose belated bourgeois-democratic revolution had already demonstrated its feebleness and inability to solve the urgent questions of national and democratic development, suggested the compelling relevance of the classical Bolshevik perspective. Yet the Comintern imposed on the Chinese Communist party a diametrically opposed strategy which led to disastrous results. Declaring that the Chinese Revolution, because of its context of backwardness, was "unripe" for a socialist conquest of power and would be confined wholly within the bourgeois-democratic stage, the Comintern—in contrast to the essence of Lenin's approach in Russia—assigned to the Chinese bourgeoisie the leading role in the "anti-feudal," "anti-imperialist" struggle, and ordered the Communists who had previously joined the Kuomintang to submit to Kuomintang party discipline.[6] Although a bourgeois-nationalist party,[7] the Kuomin-

---

[6] "Our revolution is a bourgeois revolution, the workers must support the bourgeoisie—say the worthless politicians from the camp of the liquidators. Our revolution is a bourgeois revolution, say we who are Marxists. The workers must open the eyes of the people to the fraud of the bourgeois politicians, teach them not to place trust in promises and to rely on their *own* forces, on their *own* organization, on their *own* unity, and on their *own* weapons alone" (emphasis in original).—Lenin, cited in Trotsky, *The Third International After Lenin*, p. 179.

[7] That is, in terms of its program. Its composition reflected the

tang was even allowed representation in the Communist International, with the rights of an associate member, while Chiang Kai-shek was given an honorary seat on the Comintern Executive.

The tragic denouement to which this strategy led, was readily foreseeable within the framework of the Marxist theory of belated bourgeois revolution. Finding themselves caught between two revolutions, and under pressure from the imperialist powers, the bourgeois and landowning leaders of the Kuomintang soon moved to halt those forces which were driving events beyond the bourgeois-democratic stage (and their own dominion). Heading these forces was China's urban working class, supported, as in Russia before, by the gathering storm of peasant revolution.

The conflict between the two revolutions, bourgeois and socialist, was drawn to a climax in 1927 when the workers of Shanghai rose en masse to take control of the city. When Chiang Kai-shek's Kremlin-trained army appeared on the scene, the Communist leaders, instead of defending their position, used their influence (on Kremlin orders) to *disarm* the workers and thereby maintain the "anti-imperialist" alliance with the Kuomintang. With the workers thus disarmed, Chiang's forces proceeded to massacre tens of thousands, including their hapless Communist leaders. The purge of Communists by the Kuomintang was carried well beyond the Shanghai events (the toll of political executions mounting to hundreds of thousands by 1931), as were the futile Kremlin-directed attempts by the Communists to continue to collaborate with Chiang by helping to contain the leftward surge of the Chinese masses.[8] In the end, Chinese Communism took

---

combined and belated development of the revolution, consisting of war lords and landowners, as well as bourgeois elements.

[8] The pattern in respect to the agrarian revolution was tragically similar to that of the revolt of the urban working class. Cf. H. R. Isaacs, *The Tragedy of the Chinese Revolution*, Chap. 13; also C. Brandt, *Stalin's Failure in China* (New York: Norton, 1966), Chap. 5.

years to recover from these crushing blows (and never recovered in the cities), but when the party did finally reemerge as a power under the leadership of Mao Tse-tung, it did so only because it was able to disregard the Comintern's refurbished [9] but fundamentally unaltered advice, and to rediscover, in its own terms, the Bolshevik theory of permanent revolution.[10]

The immediate bases of the Kremlin's short-sighted and self-defeating policies in China lay, of course, in the internal and external isolation of the Russian regime and the emerging state-centered perspective of the party bureaucracy. Discounting the possibility of a successful Communist revolution in China (a skepticism maintained until the end of 1948) and dominated in their outlook by the short-term security interests of the Russian state, the Kremlin leaders were rapidly led to subordinate revolutionary principle to *raison d'état*. In their bureaucratic perspective the primary necessities for Russia were to coexist with established power represented in China by the Kuomintang, and to avoid the dangers to Russia of the inevitable foreign capitalist intervention, should the Chinese Communists actually conquer power.

It can easily be seen that these considerations would apply generally to other Communist revolutions, and that so long as the Kremlin's new priorities remained unchanged, their perspective on such revolutions and their strategies would also remain the same.

In order to comprehend fully the post-Lenin shift in the

---

[9] Part of this refurbishing, in the interim, took the form of an equally suicidal "ultra-left" policy (see discussion below), the fruits of which were abortive risings and more massacres.

[10] The struggle over the China policy was the last great contest between Stalin and Trotsky before the latter was expelled from the party and exiled. Cf. Deutscher, *The Prophet Unarmed*, pp. 316 ff. As already noted, Mao's version of permanent revolution sought its basis in the rural peasantry rather than in the urban proletariat. But in its attitude toward bourgeois power and toward the importance of relying on its own forces, it remained one with the orientation of Lenin and Trotsky, and therefore diametrically opposed to that of Stalin.

perspective of the Comintern, however, it is necessary to bear in mind the organization's relation to the Second International, out of which it originally emerged. The Leninist revolt against the Second International was essentially a revolt against its reformist and nationalist ("social-patriotic") orientations, specifically its failure to oppose the imperialist World War or to attempt to transform that conflict into a struggle for proletarian power. In Russia, the Menshevik representatives of the Second International fully subscribed to its reformist and nationalist strategies, supporting what they regarded as a "defensive" war against Germany and a "revolutionary" bourgeois Provisional Government. It was Lenin's April Theses, opposing the war, breaking with the government, and proposing a *socialist* program beyond the bourgeois revolution, that drew the decisive line between the reformist-nationalist orientation of the Social Democratic movement and the revolutionary-internationalist orientation of its yet-to-be-born Communist successor.

Nationalism, as already noted, has an indeterminate social content, and can serve as a vehicle both for imperialist chauvinism and revolutionary self-determination. It can easily be seen to have a similar indeterminacy in respect to the revolutionary struggle within nations, its bias (counterrevolutionary, revolutionary or reformist) being determined by the configuration of other social factors, particularly the balance of class forces. In the orientation of the Second International, however, the phenomenon of nationalism was integrally and indissolubly linked with that of reformism.

In a famous phrase, the *Communist Manifesto* had proclaimed that "the worker has no country." The idea behind this phrase was that even as those who lacked property also lacked bourgeois rights and representation, and were therefore "outside" bourgeois society, so they lacked a real stake in the bourgeois nation. The *Manifesto*'s declaration that the workers had "nothing to lose but their chains" merely expressed the revolutionary implications of the same social pattern.

But, to the extent that capitalism in the course of its

evolution was able to integrate the workers, and the lower classes generally, into the bourgeois polity and society, that is, to give them something to lose besides their "chains"—to that extent, these classes gained a corresponding sense of their own identity and stake in the bourgeois nation. It was understandable, therefore, that the Leninist appeals for revolution during the First World War (i.e., for treason to the national state) fell on deaf ears in the West, where the largest and most powerful working-class organizations had won for the workers electoral representation, higher wages, legal protection and social benefits. Nor was it strange that in backward Russia, where the workers and peasants were still classes with "*radical* chains," classes *in* civil society but not *of* civil society, and hence classes for whom the plea to defend Czar and Fatherland had little comparable pull, the Bolshevik call should be answered with such epoch-making effect.

A basically reformist orientation in the Second International thus led directly to the nationalist distortion and moral collapse of 1914, the unwillingness to break with bourgeois society being camouflaged and expressed as patriotism, as defense of the Fatherland against Russian Czarism and reaction. The Third International did not spring directly out of the ideological and moral collapse of the Second, however, but from the subsequent Bolshevik upheaval in Russia. The theoretical issues were not different, but in practice they became polarized over a concrete historical event.

The reformist International had attacked the revolutionary politics of the successful Bolsheviks, and in effect had joined forces with the international counterrevolution. Lenin's call for a Third International was, therefore, equally a call for solidarity with the existing Soviet regime and an affirmation of its specific revolutionary path to power. Hence, in practice, the new parties of the Third International identified themselves as revolutionary parties by their concrete defense of the *Bolshevik* Revolution and its historical course, and (with much less justification) by their readiness to adopt specifically Bolshevik forms in their own party organizations.[11] Already at its inception, therefore, Communist international-ism was internationalism of a very special kind, expressing, as it did, solidarity with a *particular national expression* of the world social revolution.

Historical developments led, moreover, not to the lessen-ing of this nationalist emphasis in Communist internationalism but to its intensification. For years the Russian Revolution remained unique—an island of "socialist" promise in a sea of capitalist and feudal reaction. Inside Russia, isolation led to the ascendance of the Stalinist leadership with its sharply na-tionalist and bureaucratic orientation. The combination of these factors led directly to a reformist orientation among the various parties of the Comintern. Working within the bour-geois stage of the revolution instead of pushing it toward its socialist stage, supporting the national bourgeoisie and adopt-ing thereby a reformist posture toward bourgeois power and the capitalist status quo, all these were various facets of the one basic intent to avoid collision between the bourgeois state system and socialism in one country. Primary emphasis on external coexistence with bourgeois nation-states inevitably led, therefore, to a policy of coexistence between social classes *within* these national states. The nation-centered inter-nationalism of the Comintern therefore resulted in a reform-ism not unlike that of the Second International. But because of its inescapable identification with the Revolution in Russia and the uneven levels of world development, Communism on a world scale remained an ambiguous formation, retaining still a potential for revolution, as the Chinese, Vietnamese and Yu-goslav parties subsequently showed.

The principal apparent exception to the general reform-ist pattern of the Third International in the inter-war years was the ultra-left policy adopted by the Comintern Congress in 1928, when the prospect of imminent revolution and a final

---

[11] See above, 143 f.

offensive against the imperialist system produced a radical change in Communist party tactics and programs. In fact, however, this exception (to the extent that it actually was an exception[12]) only confirmed, in its fundamentals, the more general orientation of the Comintern parties: it was but another expression of their inverted internationalism, the domination of their revolutionary perspective by the national development of the Revolution in Russia.

For the temporary and extreme shift in Comintern strategy was not caused by any comparable change in the balance of class forces within the capitalist system[13] but rather by the sharp, bureaucratic left turn in the Soviet Union, and in particular the struggle with the Bukharin faction in the Russian party,[14] and the collectivization and liquidation campaign against the Russian kulaks. The abrupt end to peaceful coexistence between the internal sectors and classes of the Soviet economy was reflected in an equally abrupt end to the International's previous perspective of a fifteen- to twenty-year period of "peaceful coexistence" with the capitalist powers. It was further reflected in the Comintern's shift from an attempted rapprochement with the parties of the Second Inter-

---

[12] In the Spanish Revolution, during this period, for example, the Communists combined ultra-left tactics, including the rejection of demands for democratic liberties and the identification of all reformist and bourgeois parties as "fascist," with a strategic perspective of staying within the bourgeois-democratic limits of the revolution. Cf. Hugh Thomas, *The Spanish Civil War* (Baltimore, Md.: Penguin Books, 1965), pp. 106 f., and Deutscher, *The Prophet Outcast*, p. 160.

[13] Although the catastrophic economic crisis predicted by the Comintern in 1928 did come to pass the following year.

[14] The Bukharinists had been the chief exponents of the evolutionist line with respect to the development of the Russian economy. They had also dominated the International and formulated its line of peaceful coexistence and accommodation with the capitalist powers and the bourgeois ruling classes. When the Stalinist struggle against this faction was brought into the Comintern, it took the form, for tactical reasons, of a struggle against this line.

national to extreme attacks on them as constituting the "main danger."

While the sharpness of the shift in Russian policy (exacerbated by the bureaucratic and monolithic structure of the party and its civil war mentality) was the result of a sharply polarized internal social situation, the shift in the line of the international Communist parties reflected no such reality and took place in wholly different social contexts. Their ultra-militancy, therefore, only served to expose their own weakness and to intensify their already evident isolation, while in the most crucial area—Germany—it led directly to catastrophe and defeat.

In Germany during the years preceding the Nazi rise to power the main anti-fascist force, represented by the working class, had been fatally weakened by the antagonism between Social Democrats and Communists and by their refusal to form a united anti-fascist front. The split between the two factions predated the Comintern's ultra-left policies, but the new characterization of the reformists as "social fascists" ("the more to the left, the more dangerous") and as representing no real alternative to Hitler, contributed to a decisive widening of the gulf. The Social Democrats, for their part, reciprocated the hostility: in January 1933, for example, only a few days before Hitler's accession to power, their leading theorist, Hilferding, wrote in the party journal that the primary aim of the Socialists was the fight against communism.[15] The resulting disorientation of the working-class movement enabled the Nazis to conquer and crush it, virtually without a struggle. This collapse of the anti-Nazi opposition was, in turn, no small factor in shaping the totalitarian character of the Hitler era.

Two years later, in 1935, with the collectivization struggle in Russia concluded and the first five-year plan complete, and at a time when Moscow had already begun to seek pro-

---

[15] Cited in Neumann, *Behemoth*, p. 36.

tective alliances with Western governments against the Nazi menace, the Comintern met again and reversed the policy of the preceding period. Defense of democracy now became the watchword of the hour, popular fronts with liberals and social democrats the agency. For the next four years the Soviet Union and the Comintern formed the backbone of the struggle against fascism in Europe, as they did later during the Nazi occupation. This period witnessed the greatest expansion of the Communist parties of the West and was the time of Russian Communism's greatest prestige in these countries.

Like its predecessor policy, the Popular Front tactic was wholly subordinated to the narrowly conceived interests of the Soviet state, with the result that the front was constantly compromised and weakened by the opportunistic maneuvers of the Soviet leadership. This opportunism attained its acme, perhaps, with the Nazi-Soviet pact, when the International and its parties were compelled by Moscow, temporarily but with a terribly demoralizing effect, to abandon the anti-fascist struggle.

During the Popular Front period, the Soviet Union sought not only to coexist with the democratic capitalist powers, but to enter a defensive military entente with them against the fascist menace. But no matter how reformist and moderate the orientation adopted by the Comintern, the Kremlin found itself unable to allay the fears and hatred which the mere presence of its forces aroused in the hearts of the capitalist ruling classes, especially at a time when the system over which they presided was in the throes of a deep, pervasive and intractable crisis. In this period, the root contradictions of Soviet policy—between the national orientation of the Kremlin bureaucracy and the class character of the Comintern system, between coexistence and revolution—manifested themselves at every turn. They did so nowhere more tragically or more significantly than in the Spanish Civil War.

In 1931, in Spain, a belated bourgeois revolution had been marked by the fall of the monarchy. This was followed by an impasse in which several bourgeois governments failed either to contain the momentum behind the revolution or to carry it through. As in 1917 in Russia, the forces of the socialist future were already prominent in the bourgeois stage, their most significant expression being in the Spanish "October" of 1934, climaxed by the rising of the miners of Asturia. In 1936, a popular front ranging from the Communists to the liberals swept the elections, only to find itself at once confronted by a fascist military revolt, backed by Italian and later German intervention. The irresoluteness of the bourgeois government in the face of this threat from the Right —its unwillingness to arm the radical populace—immediately put the republic in grave danger, from which it was saved only by the spontaneous rising of the urban working class, whose councils and militias, formed on the spot, began rapidly to recall the "dual power" of 1917. In the Civil War which ensued, the Communists struggled not to transfer power to the working-class organizations, as the Bolsheviks had, but to vest it in the bourgeois central government. They sought not to push the revolution forward, but to hold it back, firmly within bourgeois limits.

As Russia came to the aid of Republican Spain and the Communists consequently gained a greater influence in the government, the brakes were applied hard to the already advanced social transformation. The elimination of the left-wing socialists from the administration had already been a primary condition of Soviet support. Now the revolutionary workers' councils and militias were dissolved,[16] workers' control of industries was halted and the agrarian upheaval was contained. In addition, partly as a reflex of the purges going on in Russia, agents of Stalin's G.P.U. were sent among the parties of the Left, where they assassinated many working-class leaders not amenable to the Communist line.

Stalin's motive in these maneuvers, which split and de-

---

[16] The dissolution of the militias had a plausible military justification. (Cf. Thomas, *op. cit.*, p. 340, 458.) But given the existing situation, its political consequences could not be separated from its military effects. Nor were they intended to be so.

moralized the Spanish Left and fatally weakened its resistance, was to avoid antagonizing the Western bourgeois governments, particularly Britain and France, with whom he
sought collective-security arrangements. Stalin hoped that by
forcing the Spanish Revolution into a thoroughly bourgeois
mold, protecting foreign and domestic investors and present-
ing the struggle purely as a conflict between fascism and democracy, that he could enlist the support of the capitalist
powers against the common menace. However, it proved impossible in practice to remove the class question from the
Spanish conflict, or indeed to separate the Spanish struggle
from the class struggle in the rest of crisis-ridden Europe,
where, despite Communist moderation, strikes and mass demonstrations already constituted mortal threats in the eyes of
the propertied social elements. Faced with the choice between the triumph in Spain of the iron heel of fascism or of
the poverty-stricken Spanish masses in arms, the British and
French ruling classes were in little doubt as to where their
interests lay (and in France were able to carry the governing
Social Democrats along). In the name of preserving European
"peace," and upholding the principle of "nonintervention"
(which had never been an obstacle to their own imperialist
aggressions in the past, and had already been thoroughly violated by the fascist powers) the European capitalist democracies sealed the fate of Spain's bourgeois republic and opened
the door to the Second World War.[17]

---

[17] "British and French policy . . . decided the outcome of the
Spanish civil war. The republic had greater resources, greater
popular backing. It could [have won] if it [had] received the correct treatment to which it was entitled by international law. . . ."
—Taylor, *The Origins of the Second World War*, p. 121. We may
note in passing that the United States government, which had refused recognition to the Soviet government for sixteen years, recognized the Franco fascist regime within four days of the fall of
Madrid (March 28, 1939).

9. World War and Cold War

> The socialist revolution begins on the national arena, it unfolds on the international arena, and is completed on the world arena. Thus the socialist revolution becomes a permanent revolution in a newer and broader sense of the word; it attains completion only in the final victory of the new society on our entire planet.
>
> —Trotsky

This second international struggle of the great powers had obvious diplomatic and political roots in the first,[1] but at the same time a more complex class character. Although generally neglected or misunderstood, this class dimension of the conflict provides the vital key to the events that followed. For while the First World War was climaxed by a concert of the victorious powers, who organized and presided over a postwar settlement, the close of the Second witnessed an abrupt dissolution of the wartime coalition, a dramatic and unprecedented reversal of alliances in the West—with the former enemies becoming intimate allies—and a new, even more bitterly engaged international conflict. (The fact that this conflict was contained within cold war limits by the deterrent factor of nuclear weapons does not alter the reality of the confrontation.) To omit or overlook the social character of

---

[1] Cf. A. J. P. Taylor, *The Origins of the Second World War* (New York: Atheneum, 1962), Chap. 2.

the wartime alliances and struggles and to dwell exclusively on their national or political content is simply to render this whole succeeding development opaque and unintelligible.

If the conflicts of the war and its aftermath are subjected to a class-oriented analysis, however, they can readily be seen to reflect the combined and uneven development of world social forces and the antagonistic property bases which formed the premise of that development in the East and in the West.

In the evolution of the conflict, the principal combatant states fell clearly into three distinct groups, corresponding to the three main historical routes to industrialization.[2] On the one hand, there were the globally preeminent Western allies, whose modern developments were more or less dominated by commercial capitalist classes and based on largely complete bourgeois-democratic revolutions.[3] Ranged against them were the three global latecomers Italy, Germany and Japan—the "renaissance powers," as Nazi writers described them—all either victims of the Versailles settlement or excluded from its benefits. Dominated by conservative bourgeois-aristocratic alliances, these countries' modern developments were at best

---

[2] Cf. Barrington Moore, Jr., *Social Origins of Dictatorship and Democracy* (Boston: Beacon, 1967); also pp. 48 f. above.

[3] Put baldly in this manner, the characterization may appear at first not to apply to England, where the relationship between bourgeoisie and aristocracy was extremely complex. To make possible an explanation of the difference between liberal and non-liberal or bourgeois and non-bourgeois capitalist developments, it is necessary further to distinguish between aristocracies, i.e., between those of the Junker type, based on labor-intensive agriculture ,and repressive forms of landlord-peasant relationship, and those of the gentry type, as in England, where the peasants were driven from the land and agricultural relations acquired a liberal commercial structure very early. Cf. Moore, *op. cit.* On Japan, cf. Norman, *op. cit.*, pp. 149 ff. On the peculiarities of English development, see the controversy between Perry Anderson and Edward Thompson in "Towards Socialism," in *The Socialist Register, 1965* and *New Left Review*, January–February, 1966.

based on belated and *incomplete* bourgeois revolutions (in the case of Japan there was no bourgeois revolution at all).

Allied with the Western powers up to the end of the war was Soviet Russia, a noncapitalist power, whose recent industrial ascent had been dominated by a bureaucratic-revolutionary elite, and whose course of development was based on a previous thoroughgoing proletarian-peasant revolution, which had swept away both the old landed and industrial ruling classes. The most important feature of this premature, autocratic socialist state, in terms of subsequent developments, was its connection through the International with the forces of revolution in both the industrial and colonial regions of the world, from Europe to China. For as we have seen, this served to sharpen the international class significance and impact of the Soviet state system, and therefore to intensify its inter-state tensions with the dominant capitalist powers in the West—tensions which the Soviet regime throughout the thirties, and afterward, sought futilely to repress and contain.[4]

It is in the two-front orientation of the fascist "anti-Comintern" axis, however, that the complex engagement of social forces in the conflicts of the Second World War finds its real focus and its underlying patterns become intelligible. For fascism as a form of capitalist development can be seen to represent an acute and qualitatively new stage of the permanent crisis of belated bourgeois revolution—a post-1914 and especially post-"October" deepening of this particular form of capitalist impasse. Thus, the factors associated with belated bourgeois revolution—the inveterate weakness of the liberal-democratic forces, the strength of the conservative feudal-military tradition, the internal social tensions generated by distorted development and capitalist crisis and the determining threat of the incipient socialist revolution (now signifi-

---

[4] In 1943, for example, as a gesture to his capitalist allies, Stalin even took the formal step of dissolving the Communist International.

cantly heightened by the Bolshevik triumph and the post-1917 rise of Communism)—all played critical roles in the fascist emergence both in advanced industrial areas like Germany and in more backward countries like Italy and Spain.

In the advanced and intensely monopolistic contexts of Germany and Japan the fascist development was more deeply based both in the structural evolution of the social economy itself [5] and in the pressure for military-imperialist expansion (the military emphasis being itself a consequence of late internal and external development). Thus, the necessity for total mobilization for imperialist war had a profound impact on the emergence of fascism in both countries[6] as well as on its totalitarian character, which was correspondingly less evident in less expansionist states.

Nazism in Germany, as a result of the peculiar features of Germany's development—its amalgamation of Eastern barbarism and Western industry, its late unification (by military conquest), its recent defeat and the economic, psychological and political consequences of that defeat—represented the most extreme form of the fascist phenomenon, and in this respect was atypical. Nonetheless, its principal features conformed to the general pattern.

Thus, antagonism to Western (especially English) liberalism and imperialism, which formed one characteristic pole of the Nazi program, was as rooted in the whole course of

---

[5] For example, ". . . business enterprise in Japan has, from the earliest days, unfolded its activities in an atmosphere largely, and at times, wholly dominated by principles, controls, and social philosophies which are internally coherent with what we in the Western world have come more recently to identify as Fascism." —Robert A. Brady, *Business As a System of Power* (New York: Columbia University Press, 1943), pp. 84–85.

[6] In Japan its influence was decisive, even the limited constitutional framework proving a serious obstacle to a program of military imperialism. On the role of the military in the emergence of Japanese fascism, see Tanin and Yohan, *Militarism and Fascism in Japan*.

Germany's belated emergence as was Germany's expansion toward the Slavic, Communist and non-Communist East. Neither the Versailles system, organized by Germany's capitalist rivals at the end of the First World War, nor the dissolution of the monarchy and establishment of the Weimar Republic (in which the armed presence of the Western powers also played a decisive role) represented any real steps toward destroying the structural bases of Germany's military-imperial expansionism. Because of the feebleness of German liberalism, including its social democratic form, and the reluctance of the capitalist victors to weaken the structure of Germany's social and economic status quo (in the face of what they regarded as an immediate Bolshevik threat), the revolution of 1918–19, even in its democratic aspect, was extremely partial; the forces of the old order—the imperial army, the absolutist bureaucracy and the Prussianized capitalist ruling class—were left intact and in possession of their bases of social and economic power. An immediate effect of this was to prevent the necessary widening of the internal market through income redistribution and control of the monopolies. The more general and related consequence was to ensure that the Weimar Republic would be little more than an interregnum before the triumph of the counterrevolution and the restoration of the interrupted course of Germany's prewar military-imperial expansion.[7]

The origins of this interregnum in defeat and its history in crisis had a profoundly negative effect on the political character of the restoration. Another factor, ironically, was the institution of parliamentary rule. This forced reaction to seek plebeian roots and compelled the holders of social and economic power in Germany to form alliances with popular, demagogic and "extremist" political forces, like Hitler's National Socialists. But this should not obscure the class charac-

---

[7] Cf. Taylor, *The Course of German History*, which makes eminently clear the character of fascism as a restoration rather than a revolution.

ter of the restoration itself.[8] Thus the Nazis' anti-Communism (which meant ruthless hostility to the working-class
organizations and socialist parties) as well as their authoritari-
anism, militarism and racial nationalism, were all basic compo-
nents of the traditional program of Germany's traditional
imperialist ruling class. This was evident in the dual ideological function of Nazi racism. For the doctrine of racial superiority provided, internally, an obvious surrogate for the class
struggle, directing anticapitalist resentments against a dispen-
sable ("non-Aryan") minority group; externally, it provided
a necessary justification for the program of military expansion against powerful European states.[9]

Moreover, the *anti*capitalist planks of the Nazi program,

---

[8] On the economic ruling class in Nazi Germany, cf. Neumann,
Behemoth, Brady, *op. cit.*, and Robert A. Brady, *The Spirit and
Structure of German Fascism* (London: Gollancz, 1937). On the
relation of ruling classes generally to mediating powers in the
social structure, cf. P. Anderson, "Socialism and Pseudo-Empiric-
ism," *New Left Review*, January–February, 1966.

[9] As Neumann points out, political nationalism (as opposed to
racial nationalism), which emphasizes the sovereignty of the
nation, tends to "equalize" all nations and thus to raise a barrier
against the assertion of national superiority. "Indeed, whenever
democratic states resort to [imperialist] expansion, they almost
invariably abandon the national concept and glorify racial and
biological traits that allegedly make them superior to the conquered." In England and America, as Neumann notes, such theories
served as an aid to expansion, but never attained the proportions
or significance they did in Germany. The reason he adduces is
that England and America conquered very weak states, so that
the services of such theories "were never required to organize the
total power of the nation for war." In the case of Germany, however, "expansion was and is directed against powerful states. When
Germany came forward as an active imperialist force, it found the
earth divided among the various military machines. Redistribution,
where it could not be achieved peaceably, required the force of
arms and an enormous outlay in blood and money. It required an
ideology that could justify the huge effort in the eyes of the people. The alleged superiority of the German Nordic race performed
this function."—*Behemoth*, p. 89.

which had been an important basis of the Nazi appeal to petty-bourgeois, peasant, and declassed social elements, were all dropped under the pressure of big capital, as the Nazis acceded to power.[10] (No similarly effective pressure was forthcoming to curb Nazi barbarism, however, for while Nazi methods were undoubtedly distasteful to some segments of the ruling elite in German society, opposition to them lacked the substance of a class interest, and carried no comparable weight.) The only "socialist" doctrine to be implemented by the Nazis was, significantly, that of "social imperialism," i.e., what the Nazis called "proletarian war" against the dominant capitalist states—which was merely the Nazi version of a "have-not" imperialism in a world of established imperial systems.[11] Such an "anticapitalism," of course, was not at all objectionable to Germany's expansion-minded, militaristic ruling class, even as such a war was for them the only course open within the given economic and international framework.

In the Far East the conflict with Japanese fascism showed striking similarities in origin and development to the conflict with Germany in Europe. For it was Japan's effort to establish a "Greater East Asia Co-Prosperity Sphere" to provide foreign markets and outlets for her intensely monopolistic economy[12] as well as the raw materials, which she lacked, for self-sufficient production that had brought her into collision with the dominant Western powers in Asia (the Netherlands, the United States and Britain)[13] just as surely as had Ger-

---

[10] This "betrayal" provoked a significant reaction and resulted in the famous "night of the long knives," in which the "radical" Nazis were purged.

[11] Cf. Neumann, *op. cit.*, pp. 165 ff.

[12] Japanese proponents of empire also spoke of the pressure of surplus population. However, "surplus population" was directly related to the narrowness of the internal market, which resulted in turn from the monopolistic structure of the economy.

[13] Vichy France collaborated with the Japanese in Asia, as with the Germans in Europe.

many's expansion in Europe. The way in which both Japanese and German statesmen pointed to the Monroe Doctrine area of the United States as providing a prototype for their own imperial concepts underlined the extent to which the Second World War was, like the First, an imperialist war of redivision in the strict Leninist sense.

Yet, important as this similarity of structure was, it should not be allowed to obscure the differences between the two world conflicts, which were rooted in the social developments of the intervening period. Among these, the most significant was the emergence of the Soviet Union and the world Communist parties and their role as major participants in the second conflict. This difference manifested itself most centrally in the revolutionary developments in Eastern Europe and China at the war's end, and played no small part in the subsequent reversal of alliances which initiated the postwar struggle. The principal problem for analysis raised by this development is to explain how the Western capitalist states came to find themselves in an unexpected and relatively firm alliance not only with the Soviet state but with revolutionary Communist parties (e.g., in Yugoslavia) in a struggle against other capitalist states.

Not the least part of the answer to this question lies in the very weakness of the Soviet Union at the beginning of the war (Western experts expected a rapid capitulation of Russia before the German onslaught), so that until the very end the Soviet forces never represented such a threat to the conservative camp as to cause its unification. The other part of the explanation, as the preceding analysis of fascism suggests, lies in the recognition that the inter-capitalist conflict of the Second World War represented not merely a struggle between national imperialist powers for hegemony within a single global system,[14] but to a significant extent a conflict be-

---

[14] This element of the struggle should not be underestimated, how-

tween imperialist social systems as such. For, despite their common capitalist frameworks, there was a profound historical gulf between the social and political orders of the fascist powers and the bourgeois democracies in the West. This gulf extended in varying degrees to the wider systems of the capitalist states, and found its clearest and most significant expression in the difference between the corporate imperialism under which the United States dominated and exploited the Monroe Doctrine area of Latin America (a system which was destined to become *the* postwar mode of imperialist relationship) and the "New Order" which Nazi Germany sought to impose on the states of central and eastern Europe. A similar though subtler difference was reflected in developments in Asia, where the Japanese "New Order" began its expansion with the incalculable advantage of an "anti-(white)imperialist" program, but was incapable of establishing a neo-colonial system in collaboration with nationalist, anti-Western forces, because of its own intensely chauvinistic, repressive and basically feudal concept of empire.

This conflict between imperialist systems had its basis in the divergent historical developments of capitalism in its

---

ever. For while many people at the time might have expected the British to make terms with Hitler, as a class ally, and while Britain's response to the Finnish war seemed to indicate the formation of a general capitalist alliance against Russia, the national outlook of leaders like Churchill, supported by the swell of popular feeling against the Germans after the occupation of the low countries, prevented such a course. A German conquest of Europe (against which British diplomacy and arms had been marshalled for a century) would have been fatal to British national interests, and therefore to the interests of the British ruling class as well; on the other hand, Russia was considered to be so weak that few expected her to survive the German attack, and no one expected the Red Army to emerge as the liberating force in Eastern Europe. When this did begin to seem a prospect, the military strategy of the British was oriented to prevent it, and to keep the main thrust of the German forces toward the Soviet Union.

bourgeois-democratic and belated feudal-military forms, and in this lay the source of the different character of the two world wars. For in the general crisis after 1917 this gulf was greatly deepened, and because of the prodigious military-industrial strength of the belated systems which made it possible for them to raise a serious challenge for global hegemony, the conflict of the war attained, in a real sense, the character of a struggle *for* the bourgeois-democratic revolution, and created the ground for a temporary alliance between bourgeois and socialist forces against the threat of antidemocratic, anti-Communist reaction.[15]

This alliance, however, did not (and in the nature of things could not) outlast the military defeat of the major fascist powers and the establishment of the absolute and unchallenged supremacy of the bourgeois system in the non-Soviet world. For, as was clear on analytic and historical grounds and confirmed in the prewar vacillation of these powers—their unwillingness to bloc with Soviet Russia and their readiness to accommodate, appease and make a substantial space for the fascist orders in Europe and Asia—the alliance between capitalist and anticapitalist "democratic" forces was necessarily conjunctural, and once the fascist threat to bourgeois hegemony was removed, and the U.S.S.R. had emerged as a potential world power, it was destined to be overridden by more basic class antagonisms.

Thus with the defeat of Germany and Japan the ground was laid for the inevitable realignment of national and social forces based on the realities of the international class struggle: the basic community of interest between propertied social classes, and their common fear of the resurgent threat of

---

[15] In Yugoslavia, for example, it was the Communist partisans who attained leadership of the *national* resistance to German oppression and of the struggle for self-determination, and it was precisely because the Communists were the leaders of the nationalist cause that the British were compelled to cooperate with them. Cf. note on pp. 104 f., above.

Communist revolution. For various reasons, not least of which were the strength of antifascist sentiment in the West and the solidarity forged by the preceding struggle, this realignment did not take place everywhere at once. In general, the illusion of a continuing Grand Alliance between Washington, London and Moscow survived many frictions and conflicts of the immediately ensuing period. There were areas, however, where the exigencies of the class struggle, as it emerged out of the wartime resistance, forced a sudden and dramatic reversal which threw a clear light on the nature of the cold war to come.

In Greece, for example, the suddenness of this reversal within the antifascist camp[16] was a major factor in deciding the outcome of the developing internal civil war. The Left, which had emerged through the resistance as the predominant power in Greece, with a program of democratic revolution,[17] did not foresee the antidemocratic, counterrevolutionary role which their previous ally Great Britain would play in the decisive next phase of the struggle. Consequently they were unprepared for the intervention when it came.[18] In effect, neither the Communists (whose outlook, for reasons already analyzed, was one of coexistence with "progressive" capitalisms) nor the non-Communist Left understood the dynamics of the international class struggle as it was emerging with the defeat of German and Japanese imperialism and the tremen-

---

[16] Of course, this reversal did not yet represent a split between the great state powers of the alliance, since the Soviet Union acquiesced in the British intervention.

[17] The points of the National Liberation Front (EAM) program are quoted in Gitlin, "Counter-insurgency: Myth and Reality in Greece," in Horowitz (ed.), *Containment and Revolution*, p. 144.

[18] Thus the Communist Z. Zografos wrote in retrospect: "The leadership of the Communist Party correctly directed all its efforts at ensuring allied victory over Hitler Germany. But it failed to expose and rebuff the intrigues of the British imperialists and to prepare the people to resist British intervention. . . ."—*World Marxist Review*, November 11, 1964 (cited in Gitlin, *op. cit.*).

dous wartime upsurge of the global revolutionary forces. Hence, they did not understand the threat which their own armed revolutionary presence posed, despite their limited demands, to "democratic" British and American imperialism. So sharp and unexpected was the transition in Greece from one phase of the international struggle to the next that demonstrating crowds of the left-wing, antifascist resistance were heard chanting "Long live Roosevelt! Long live Churchill! No King!" [19] even as they were shot down by British troops who had been sent (in American planes) to crush them, and to reimpose the hated rightist monarchy in collaboration with conservative, quisling and fascist elements.

The illusion that despite the tremendous power shifts of the war the capitalist states would remain allies of the Left, so long as the Left confined itself to the democratic struggle,[20] was dramatically shattered not only in Greece at this time, but on the other side of the globe as well. In French Indochina, where the forces of the Vietnamese resistance proclaimed a democratic republic in a document modeled on the American Declaration of Independence and closely according with the spirit of the Atlantic Charter, a similar realignment took place.

---

[19] A fourth slogan was "Down with Papandreou," the provisional Prime Minister. Two decades later, even Papandreou's conservative brand of liberalism and bourgeois nationalism was considered to be too dangerous by the United States and its monarchist and military allies in Greece. To close the liberal doorway to communism, a fascist coup was carried out in April 1967, just prior to general elections which Papandreou's party was expected to win. See below, pp. 227–28.

[20] In one area, namely Italy, this alliance not only worked (until 1947), but actually produced a bourgeois-democratic "revolution." This was mainly because of Italy's defeat in the war and the fact that the American occupation forces had played a major role in the actual liberation and were physically in control of many areas as the crucial negotiations were being conducted, and to some extent that the Americans did not have the kind of direct ties to the Italian monarchy as the British did to the Greek.

"We are convinced," said the Vietnamese in their declaration,[21] "that the Allied nations which at Teheran and San
Francisco [the U.N. Conference] have acknowledged the
principles of self-determination and equality of nations will
not refuse to acknowledge the independence of Vietnam. A
people who have courageously opposed French domination
for more than eighty years, a people who have fought side by
side with the Allies against the Fascists during these last years,
such a people must be free and independent." As in Greece,
incoming British troops were initially welcomed to Hanoi by
the resistance leaders, who regarded them as allies and libera-
tors. But instead of disarming the Japanese occupation forces
the British used them to maintain "order" while the French
troops prepared themselves to reestablish their colonial control of Vietnam. In the ensuing struggle the United States,
which had offered a modicum of aid to the Vietminh during
the struggle against the Japanese and their French collaborators, now threw their full support behind France's effort to
retain this resource-rich outpost of its dwindling colonial empire.[22]

In the East as in the West, at the end of the war, the
natural alliance of conservative class forces was reestablishing
itself in the face of the rising threat of socialist revolution. By

[21] A complete text of the declaration is reprinted in Marvin E.
Gettleman (ed.), *Vietnam* (Baltimore, Md.: Penguin Books, 1966).
[22] Indeed, the parallel between Vietnam and Greece, with respect
to the commitments of the Western powers and the tactics of revolutionary struggle goes much further. Just as the Vietminh in
1954 laid down their arms (under Sino-Soviet pressure) for a
worthless Western guarantee that political rights would be safeguarded and free elections held, so the Greeks nine years before
were induced to accept a similar arrangement under the Varkiza
agreements. Like the South Vietnamese, once they had laid down
their arms they were hunted by rightist forces and compelled to
resume their resistance under far less favorable circumstances. Cf.
Gitlin, *op. cit.*, pp. 158–60, 163n.

the early fifties, when the United States was openly providing massive economic and military support to sustain the fascist regime in Spain, the cold war "free world" alliance of propertied social forces, ranging from the parliamentary states of the developed capitalist world through the military dictatorships and feudal kingdoms of their dependent allies, was firmly sealed.[23]

The main stages of the transition to this realignment and its effect on the bourgeois-democratic revolution throughout the ensuing period were most clearly registered in the transformation of Allied occupation policies in the defeated fascist states. This was particularly true in the Far East, where the United States, the most bourgeois of the capitalist powers, exercised unilateral jurisdiction over the most "feudal," Japan, and where the complicating European factor of military confrontation between the great powers was not directly present.

Initially, the U.S. Occupation Command acted with apparent determination to bring Japan's archaic social and political structure fully into the bourgeois framework. A bourgeois-democratic constitution was introduced, the emperor being reduced to the status of a constitutional monarch; a trade union law was promulgated, guaranteeing the right to organize, bargain and strike, and a democratizing educational reform was undertaken. In addition, a move to deconcentrate Japan's intensely monopolized economy was initiated, as well as a bourgeois land reform aimed at the repressive, quasi-feudal

---

[23] By March 1955, of 71 countries in the "free world," according to one Congressional reporter, 49 were "outwardly or actually dictatorships or close oligarchies . . . of the remaining 22 nations, most of them truly have some claim to the adjective 'free' as far as their political governments are concerned, but certainly as far as the economic control of several of them is concerned, it is oligarchic and a small percentage of the nation is living off the backs of the other 99%."—Representative Thomas B. Curtis (cited from the Congressional Record in Mills, *The Marxists*, p. 24).

relations in agriculture. Finally, war crimes trials were held, and there was an administrative purge of the military and civil bureaucracies, as well as a general demilitarization and dismantling of the Japanese war machine.

Even from the beginning, however, these reforms were of a partial rather than a sweeping nature. For the U.S. authorities were restrained in their program by the desire not to weaken the conservative structure of Japanese society in the process of bringing it within the framework of the bourgeois system. Thus, the purges, while extensive, were nonetheless superficial, and the bureaucracy was left essentially intact.[24] Even the land reform, which fared far better, stopped short of fulfillment as a result of the reluctance of the authorities to stir up the class struggle in the countryside.[25] Another factor inducing restraint, and drastically reducing the practical impact of the reforms, was the post-liberal character of U.S. capitalism itself. Thus the crucial but half-hearted attempt to deconcentrate Japanese industry[26] and break up the *zaibatsu* proved almost wholly abortive, meeting even in its diluted form with stiff opposition from U.S. financial and corporate interests.

Additional forces behind the arrest of the Occupation Command's reformist impulse were the growing international and internal class tensions: the triumphant revolution in China, the Communist-initiated civil war and Western intervention in Korea and the rise of a Japanese Marxist Left. As

[24] The purge was carried out by category, so that the top officials were removed as a group, leaving their juniors in charge. This made the bureaucracy more tractable to the Occupation Command, but hardly represented a change in its outlook.

[25] An extensive account of the reform is given in R. P. Dore, *Land Reform in Japan* (New York: Oxford University Press, 1959).

[26] A list of 1,200 firms to be broken up was compiled and then progressively reduced until there were only 19 left. When nine of these had been dealt with, the board set up by the U.S. authorities, and composed of five prominent U.S. corporate leaders, decided that enough had been done. Cf. Jon Halliday, "Japan—Asian Capitalism," in *New Left Review*, July–August 1967.

early as February 1947 the Occupation banned a general strike on "economic grounds," while the following year civil servants and local government employees were prohibited from resorting to the strike weapon at all. In 1949 the Occupation's progressive labor laws were revised (at U.S. insistence) to restrict the power of the trade union movement, and in 1949 and 1950 there was a general purge of Communists in the unions, government, education and industry. At the same time, the Occupation authorized the Japanese government to review the applications of those removed in the original purge of fascists, and by 1951 almost all those originally affected had regained their political rights. Coincident with the anti-Communist repressions, which were accompanied by the reinvigoration of the Japanese police apparatus, a remilitarization campaign was begun (also under U.S. pressure, in alliance with the Japanese right-wing), so that, as in Germany, the last phase of the occupation witnessed a restoration of the forces of the old order, albeit within a partially reformed institutional context.

While the U.S. occupation of Japan is instructive because of the clear insight it provides into the characteristic relation between bourgeois and fascist forces[27] in the postwar epoch, and the fateful consequences of that relation for the bourgeois-democratic revolution, it does not give a full picture of the dynamics of the emergent cold war struggle. For this conflict was dominated in its initial stages by the confrontation between the great powers in Europe. It cannot be understood therefore without insight into the duality of Soviet state policy as well, and hence the temporary but far-reaching reorientation in the East, which reflected and interacted with the early postwar realignments in the West.

Initially, Stalin had attempted to approach the postwar period in the same nationalist manner in which he had approached the period leading up to the disasters of 1939. In-

---

[27] And hence "feudal" forces as well.

deed, this was the very basis of his agreements at Yalta with the Western allies. Just as he strove to keep the Spanish revolution within bourgeois limits in the interests of "coexistence" and defensive entente with the capitalist powers, so at the end of the war he sought to contain and even abort the Communist revolutions in Yugoslavia, China and Greece,[28] which were outside the sphere assigned to Russia under the Yalta agreements. In a similar spirit, he recognized the Badoglio regime in Italy,[29] and urged the French and Italian Communists to enter the conservative cabinets of De Gaulle and De Gasperi, and the latter even to vote for the reenactment of Mussolini's Lateran pacts with the Vatican.

His approach to the security zone in Eastern Europe, including the former Nazi satellites (over whom it was agreed Russia would have an influence comparable with that of the British in Greece), was initially in keeping with this conservative coexistence policy. While taking steps to ensure the pro-Soviet political orientation of the regimes, he left their social structures basically intact and proceeded to satisfy the demands of Russia's own devastated and perilously weakened economy by exacting reparations and tribute from the conquered regions (and even from the former devastated allies of Russia—Poland, Czechoslovakia and Yugoslavia). By these methods he began the slow replenishment of Russia's depleted economic base, while at the same time severely damaging any prospect of popular socialist revolution in the tributary areas for years to come.

However, even in this early period, when Stalin was pursuing a basically nationalist policy at the expense of revolutionary interests in Eastern Europe, deep cold war tensions

---

[28] The evidence for this comes mainly from Yugoslav sources, e.g., Dedijer, *Tito Speaks*, and Djilas, *Conversations with Stalin*, but has been confirmed by others as well. Cf. Gittings "The Origins of China's Foreign Policy" in Horowitz (ed.), *Containment and Revolution*.

[29] See p. 74, Note 4.

with the West were already making themselves felt. These tensions, though expressed in political and national power terms, were, in fact, rooted in the ineradicable antagonism between the economic systems of the contending states and their mutually exclusive institutional (class) bases. The class orientation of Western policy was amply evident in its whole effort to restrict Soviet influence in the guaranteed Eastern sphere and in Washington's parallel attempt to extend the Open Door system to the Soviet border. Nor was the Soviet Union any more capable in this particular context, of separating its national aspirations from the underlying class bias of its economic structure. For just as the West, to further *its* influence, reached out to anti-Communist conservatives, as well as to anti-Russian nationalists in the region of the former cordon sanitaire, so the Soviet Union inevitably found its "national" allies in the East European Communist parties and among those class forces which were pressing for a revolutionary transformation of the repressive and inequitable East European social order. Thus, even if Soviet policy in Eastern Europe had started from purely nationalist premises—in particular the Kremlin's intense regard for the area as a primary security zone—inevitably, in order to defend the zone the Kremlin would have found it necessary to block the open door penetration of U.S. private capital, and to attack the economic and social bases of anti-Soviet power, i.e., to restrict and curtail the influence of the old ruling groups and conservative class forces in the area.

To this general situation was added another element in the outlook of the officer corps of the occupying Red Army. For, as Deutscher has observed, while these men were instructed by the Kremlin to carry out a policy of "non-interference" in the domestic affairs of the occupied countries, they were no more able to do so than their Western counterparts. As Communists they could hardly administer the countries they controlled "in such a way as to allow capitalist business to function as usual and non-Communist parties, whose leaders did not even conceal their hatred and contempt of the Communist conquerors, to carry on their activities without hindrance." [30] These anticapitalist tendencies of course provoked their own reaction among the Western powers, who saw in them an attempt by Stalin to go beyond the Yalta agreements and to Communize the entire region.

The inseparability of national from class elements in Soviet policy in Eastern Europe was perhaps most clearly evident in a process which provided the key to the subsequent and relatively peaceful social transformation of the area (for in no East European country before 1956 was there anything remotely approaching the violent resistance encountered by the British-sponsored restoration in Greece). Under the terms of the Allied agreements, the governments of Eastern Europe were obligated to purge their bureaucracies of Nazis, fascists, militarists and all those who had worked against Russia in the conflict. These purges were directed by Communists who, with Soviet assistance, had attained control of the Departments of Interior and Defense in each of the East European regimes. Since the old ruling classes had consisted mainly of antidemocratic elements which had manifested a pro-German or at least an anti-Russian attitude in the war, it was possible without grossly violating the terms of the agreements to deprive them of their organizational base and to render them "politically impotent." [31] As the intermediate groupings lacked cohesion and were extremely weak, these purges prepared the ground for the ascendance of the Communist parties and the eventual transformation of East European society.

For such a development to occur, that is, for the Communist parties actually to be given the signal to take power, it was necessary first that the Kremlin be induced to abandon its policy of coexistence and "self-containment," and thus be

---

[30] Deutscher, *Russia After Stalin*, p. 84.
[31] Deutscher, *Stalin*, p. 519.

prepared to invite open confrontation with the West. What impelled the Kremlin to seek security in "revolution" in Eastern Europe after the war, rather than in alliance and cooperation with the Western powers, was the Western reversal over the Yalta spheres-of-influence understanding, the effective collapse of the wartime coalition, the toleration and support by the Western powers for fascist forces and regimes, the rightward shift in U.S. policy and the early launching of the global anti-Communist crusade.

Never really reconciled to a Russian sphere in Eastern Europe, enjoying a position of unprecedented military and economic superiority, confident, further, that war-devastated "Russia is really afraid of our power," [32] Washington embarked, as early as 1945, on a program to expel Russian influence from its East European sphere, to revive German, and later Japanese, military power, and in fact to mount the third major capitalist offensive against the Soviet regime in a generation. Whether the offensive, which began politically and economically, would develop into a military thrust as some top officials were urging, was hardly a question to which the Soviet General Staff was likely to be indifferent. At the time, Washington was feverishly developing the atomic weapon, securing air and naval bases around the perimeter of the Soviet Union and alerting the populations of the West to an alleged military menace emanating from Moscow, which it must have known simply on logistical grounds to have been nonexistent.

It was in this threatening situation, which reached a decisive turning point with Truman's "Doctrine" speech in March 1947, that the Kremlin's attitude toward Eastern Europe underwent a profound change.[33] Keenly aware of the

[32] Ambassador to Russia Harriman to Secretary of War Stimson, May 10, 1945. Cited in Alperovitz, *Atomic Diplomacy: Hiroshima and Potsdam* (New York: Simon and Schuster, 1965), p. 256.
[33] There was also a partial left shift in its general international policy. A Communist information agency (Cominform) was established to replace the dissolved Comintern. The new body, how-

military importance of Eastern Europe for the defense of the Soviet Union, impressed by the perhaps insurmountable difficulties of taking Russia, alone, through a second forced ascent, Moscow rapidly extended its control in the buffer area and took steps to integrate the East European social, political and economic structures into the Soviet system (recognizing thereby the failure of its autarchical economic policy and the cherished doctrine of Russian self-sufficiency).

This early postwar reversal of Soviet policy was not unprecedented. In 1939 Stalin had entered the Baltic states (whose governments had been inclined toward Berlin rather than Moscow) in order to establish military bases and secure his threatened defenses. A year later, in a situation of heightened danger following the fall of France and the British retreat at Dunkirk, he staged "revolutions" in each of these countries (overthrowing their governments and socializing their economies) and incorporated them into the Soviet Union.[34]

Thirty-five years before, in his original tract on permanent revolution, Trotsky had written: "If the Russian proletariat, having temporarily obtained power, does not on its own initiative carry the revolution onto European soil, it will be *compelled* to do so by the forces of European feudal-bourgeois reaction." [35] (Emphasis in original.) Of course, Trotsky did not expect the revolution to be carried abroad on

---

ever, included only the East European parties and the large French and Italian CPs, and this (and its official status as an "information" agency) reflected the defensive nature of the new militant line adopted by the CPs in the ensuing period and the total subordination of that line to short-term Soviet interests.

[34] The act of incorporation or more accurately reincorporation, since the Baltic states had been severed from the Russian empire through the punitive peace at Brest-Litovsk, distinguished this expansion from the postwar course of events in Eastern Europe, and, of course, in its motivation contained a strong element of Great Russian chauvinism.

[35] *Results and Prospects*, 1906 (printed in *Permanent Revolution*, p. 240).

the points of the Red Army's bayonets, and indeed emphatically opposed "revolution by conquest" when the issue arose with respect to Tukhachevsky's march on Warsaw in 1920. Nor did Stalin, for that matter, occupy the Soviet borderlands in 1940 or 1945 for revolutionary purposes. But the logic of permanent revolution, the permanence of capitalist aggression against the socialist revolution and its bases, and the permanence of the revolutionary reaction (even in this distorted form) as its only viable defense asserted itself dramatically in the events of 1940 as in the early cold war period. By 1949, with NATO in formation and Eastern Europe fully Sovietized, the revolution once again, in spite of Stalin's best efforts and most devious methods, had been compelled to carry itself abroad.

V

A NEW REVOLUTIONARY

EPOCH

10. International Revolution

> When we say Nation we do not mean Nation of all Cubans, but the Nation of the Cuban Revolution. And when we say Cuban Revolution, we are talking about Latin American Revolution. And when we say Latin American Revolution, we are talking about Revolution on a universal scale: the Revolution of Africa, Asia and Europe.
>
> —Fidel Castro

> Our every action is a battle cry against imperialism, ... Wherever death may surprise us, let it be welcome, provided that this, our battle cry, may have reached some receptive ear and another hand may be extended to wield our weapons. . . .
>
> —Che Guevara

The enforced ending of the isolation of the Russian Revolution in the early postwar period ushered in a new era of global revolutionary development, altering in profound respects the old patterns, while recapitulating them in many ways as well. At first, indeed, the repetition of the old may even have been a more prominent feature of these events than any new development. Thus, the manner in which the revolutions were imposed by Soviet policy on the East European region, with the significant exception of Yugoslavia and to some extent Bulgaria,[1] did not really break the national shell of the revolution, but in effect confirmed it.

---

[1] Czechoslovakia may also be considered a partial exception, but a very partial one.

This reinforcement of old patterns was expressed not only in the origins of the revolutions, which lay primarily in the national interests of the Soviet state and the exigencies of its defense, but also in their bureaucratic-military form, which reproduced many of the most characteristic features and institutions of the Stalinist phase of Soviet development, including the police regime, the political purges and the cultural and party monoliths. In part, this repetition was merely a reflection of the actual domination of the East European development by the Soviet Union and its agencies. There were also, however, internal social bases for the similarity, the East European region being generally (but with certain exceptions) the most underdeveloped and backward in Europe, and most closely approximating the prerevolutionary conditions of the Czarist empire. Moreover, just as the most repressive phase of the Russian development coincided with an external threat in the form of the rise of fascism in Europe and Asia and the emergence of an anti-Comintern axis, the worst period in Eastern Europe was even more directly related to a serious war danger from the West,[2] the formation of an anti-Communist military alliance[3] and the rise of McCarthyism in the United States.

As a result of these factors, the expansion of the Soviet system into Eastern Europe concentrated many of the most negative features of the preceding experience, so that the most westward advance of the revolution showed once again

---

[2] In addition to the encirclement of Russia with strategic air bases, the rearmament of Germany and Japan and the formation of NATO, there were at this time the invasion of North Korea by U.S. forces—which strategically speaking, was very different from North Korea's advance into South Korea—the open threats against China and the massive U.S. material aid to the French forces in Vietnam. Russia at this time, of course, was without means of nuclear retaliation.

[3] That is, NATO. The Warsaw Pact was formed as a counter-alliance in 1955, only after the integration of West Germany into the North Atlantic Treaty Organization.

the revolution's most backward and repressive face. This served not only to prime the anti-Communist, antirevolutionary reaction in the West, but also to obscure the newly emerging alignment of capitalist and feudal-military forces, allowing the West to assume the role of defender of freedom and national self-determination in Eastern Europe at the same time as it was coming into league with fascism in Portugal and Spain, and suppressing nationalist revolution in Africa and Asia. This confusion was compounded, moreover, by the Communists' designation of the East European satellite regimes as "peoples' democracies" (with rigged 99 percent electoral majorities). Designed to recognize the strength and significance of the democratic anti-fascist struggle, which the West had now abandoned, this had the effect merely of discrediting the struggle, and thereby echoed the previous fate of the socialist ideal in its identification with the practice of primitive accumulation in Stalinist Russia.

Whereas Eastern Europe symbolized the most repressive aspects of the Russian Revolution in the early period of the cold war, within less than a decade it came to represent the most liberal area of the Soviet bloc. The very suddenness of this reversal reflected the "unnatural" basis of the East European development, its primary determination by the external factor of the East-West struggle, and the related policies of the Soviet state. It was, in fact, internal developments in the Soviet Union and the altered power relation between Russia and the West that paved the way for this reversal in the satellites. For whereas the period of severe repression, from 1949 to 1953, had been one of intense military rearmament and Stalinist construction (or "war communism") in Eastern Europe, the end of this period saw important changes in the military and economic position of Russia and a consequent political relaxation throughout the Soviet bloc.

From 1945 to 1952, as a result of the tremendous postwar reconstruction and industrialization program, the Soviet Union had moved from a position of fourth or fifth among the industrial powers to an undisputed second place.[4] While Eastern Europe's ascent was far less spectacular (not least because the Russians drained the East European economies of billions in "reparations" and extracted an economic surplus through "joint-stock companies" and various other forms of exploitation), it was nonetheless impressive in terms of the social and political impasse of the prewar period throughout most of this region, and also by absolute contrast with comparable areas in the Western sphere, such as Spain, Portugal and Greece.

To this industrial power were added the military factors of the atomic bomb (1949), the hydrogen bomb (1952) and the Chinese Revolution, all of which served to ease the pressures on the Soviet regime, to lessen the threat of preventive nuclear attack and to prepare the ground for a partial de-Stalinization.

The actual course of de-Stalinization in Russia, which proceeded as a controlled reform from above, proved to be very different from its course in Eastern Europe, however, where the relaxation of controls precipitated a violent revolt from below. In Poznan and Warsaw, in Berlin and Budapest, revolutionary nationalism bound anti-Stalinist and anti-Communist currents into a united force, producing upheavals which shook the entire Soviet world, and ensured the initial de-Stalinization measures would be permanent and irreversible against all conservative pressures.[5] The nationalist wellsprings of these upheavals against Russian domination, particularly within the Communist parties which provided their leadership, had, of course, been manifest earlier. In 1948, the

---

[4] Isaac Deutscher, "Mid-Century Russia," in *Heretics and Renegades* (London: Hamilton, 1955), p. 1.
[5] These pressures were very strong in 1956 and were represented by the Molotov-Kagonovich group in the Russian leadership. It was the specific resistance of the East European Communist parties that prevented the re-Stalinization which this group was advocating.

Yugoslav party, which had led a really indigenous revolution, as a struggle for national liberation against the Nazis, had struck out on its own independent course, rather than surrender to a new Russian domination. In the wake of this revolt, the Yugoslavs were expelled from the Communist bloc and branded "fascists," while tens of thousands of East European Communists were purged from their respective parties for "national deviationism" and "Titoism." [6] No East European Communist leader besides Tito had the internal support to permit him to stand alone between the two military camps in this period of intense East-West hostility, but the aftermath, a few years later, showed that while the repressions had temporarily suppressed the opposition in Eastern Europe they had not, as in Russia itself, subdued it. Similarly, though Russian tanks crushed and defeated the revolution when it came in Hungary, the Russian party had to yield shortly to many of the revolution's demands.

As a result of this renewed national resistance in Eastern Europe, the original Yugoslav claim for self-determination and equality of treatment within the Communist bloc and for the right to a "Yugoslav road to socialism" was echoed by the other national parties (and by the parties in the West). Thus, the very process of cracking the nationalist shell of the Russian Revolution was a process by which the monolith of international Communism was also shaken. For this monolith was nothing but the expression of the domination of the Russian party and its forms over the international Communist movement.[7]

Just as the nationalist shell of the revolution was only partially broken by developments in Eastern Europe, however, and just as de-Stalinization was but a partially realized internal

---

[6] These were not the first of Stalin's purges of East European Communists for their intractability. In the thirties, large sections of the East European Communist leaderships perished including the entire Central Committee of the Polish CP.

[7] See above, pp. 142 ff.

reform, so decentralization and democratization in the international sphere was half-hearted and incomplete as well. Limits were placed on Soviet hegemony in the Communist camp, but the fact of that hegemony remained. Indeed, the real challenge to Moscow's dominance did not (and could not) come from the satellites of the West. Once again, rather, the revolutionary movement was compelled to look toward the backward[8] East for a renewed impulse forward.

For in the East, as in the West, the isolation of the Russian Revolution had been dramatically ended by a revolutionary reaction to the imperialist expansions and aggressions of the Second World War and its aftermath. Unlike its counterparts in Russia's western borderlands, however, the Chinese Revolution was not bureaucratically organized from above in the shadow of the Red Army. The Chinese party rode to power on a tremendous upsurge from below, which

---

[8] As should be evident from previous discussion of the "combined" as well as "uneven" character of world development, this "backwardness" cannot be regarded in a one-dimensional way. Otherwise, the revolution itself, with its profoundly progressive features, even in terms of "advanced" Western development, could not be understood: "The historical dialectic knows neither naked backwardness nor chemically pure progressiveness. . . . The present-day history of mankind is full of 'paradoxes,' not so colossal as the arising of a proletarian dictatorship in a backward country, but of a similar historic type. The fact that the students and workers of backward China are eagerly assimilating the doctrine of materialism, while the labour leaders of civilised England believe in the magic potency of churchly incantations proves beyond a doubt that in certain spheres China has outstripped England. But the contempt of the Chinese workers for the mediaeval dull-wittedness of MacDonald, does not permit the inference that in her general development China is higher than Great Britain. The economic and cultural superiority of the latter can be expressed in exact figures. The impressiveness of these figures does not, however, preclude the possibility that the workers of China may win power before the workers of Gt. Britain."—Trotsky, *The History of the Russian Revolution*, III, 1220, Appendix 2.

had been mobilized over decades, in a struggle for national liberation. It was a revolution as important and profound as the Russian October, and wholly unprecedented as to its popular sweep.

The national challenge of Chinese Communism was incomparably greater than that of Eastern Europe not only because of the sweep and strength of the revolution as such, moreover, but because this challenge to Moscow was implicit in the very origins of Maoism and the whole history of its development. For Maoism had been born out of the Moscow-guided defeats of the late twenties, had established itself as a distinctive strategy in opposition to those party leaders who had continued after these defeats to promote Stalin's revised ultra-left line, and had triumphed in 1949 against the explicit advice of Stalin not to attempt to seize power but once again to seek a modus vivendi with the Kuomintang.

Like the East Europeans the Chinese were made to feel the oppressive hand of Russian chauvinism as Moscow set about in the postwar period to secure old Czarist rights and new concessions for itself in Manchuria, and then to strip this industrial heartland of its most advanced equipment. In 1950, after the Chinese Revolution, the Russians agreed to relinquish these rights within three years and return the equipment, but they also secured new privileges in the form of "joint-stock companies" for the exploitation of Chinese resources (oil and nonferrous metals) which, as events later showed, the Chinese themselves regarded as a mode of economic imperialism.

Despite this background, and despite the fact that even in the thirties the Chinese were openly laying claim to a distinctive revolutionary experience, and in 1946 to having developed a specifically Chinese path that would influence the coming revolution throughout Asia, the iron unity of the Sino-Soviet alliance was maintained. As late as November 17, 1957, Mao declared in Moscow: "The Socialist camp must have a head, and this head is the U.S.S.R. . . . The Communist and workers' parties of all countries must have a head and that head is the Communist Party of the Soviet Union." [9]

This statement of "unity," however, far from reflecting the realization of a community of socialist states based on the internationalist principle of equality, only underlined, of course, the failure to achieve such a community. Similarly, the subsequent split between China and Russia, like the preceding East European revolts, was but a more vivid expression of the same nationalist limitations of the socialist revolution in its new multi-national setting.

These limitations were, first of all, rooted in the legacy of Russia's own nationalist development, the emergence of socialism in one isolated backward country. The resurgent nationalism of Eastern Europe, and to a large extent that of China as well, was thus but a defensive reaction to Soviet chauvinism and domination, while the national egoism of China's bid for leadership and the propagation of its own path as *the* model to be emulated merely mirrored the Russian precedent. But beyond the impact of Russia's national communism in strengthening the nationalist bias of these revolutionary developments, there were the same social and historical factors, the legacy of Western domination, and the consequent struggle for national liberation, the proximity of the revolutions' emergence to the emergence of the nations as such, and to their integration from the particularistic divisions of the precapitalist, preindustrial past.[10] The dis-

---

[9] Compare Mao's remarks in October 1938: "A Communist is a Marxist internationalist, but Marxism must take on a national form before it can be applied. . . . the Sinification of Marxism—that is to say, making certain that in all of its manifestations it is imbued with Chinese peculiarities, using it according to these peculiarities —becomes a problem that must be understood and solved by the whole Party. . . . We must put an end to writing eight-legged essays on foreign models. . . ."—Schram, *op. cit.*, pp. 113 f.

[10] In China and Yugoslavia, for example, the disintegrative tendencies are still quite significant. On the former, for example, see Franz Schurmann, "Party-Government," in Schurmann and Or-

lodgement caused by industrialization created a need for the continuity and stabilizing framework provided by the nation-state; the persisting inequality and stratification,[11] for the cohesion produced by the nationalist program. A further important source of the nationalist emphasis and national tensions in the Communist bloc lay in the profoundly uneven development of the different national sectors[12]—for example, between China and Russia, the former having begun its socialist development at a much lower economic level than Russia had attained even by 1913.

Finally, there was the immense role played by the centralized, monolithic and abnormally expanded state organization in all these countries. For, as the organ of external defense (its burdens intensified by the calculated policies of the hostile capitalist powers[13]), as the organ of internal control (strained and extended by the conflicts arising out of the conquest of power and the hardships imposed by rapid industrial ascent), and as the primary accumulator of capital, the state apparatus in each of these primitive socialisms was vastly enlarged and showed no signs of contracting or "withering" as in the classical Marxist prescription. Consequently, the official bureaucracy, with its inevitably state-centered (nationalist and conservative) orientation, unrelieved even by the leavening process of a multi-party system, was for each of them (despite very important differences between China and the rest) the exclusive and unchecked formulator of national policy.[14]

---

ville Schell, eds., *Communist China* (New York: Vintage Books, 1967).

[11] In China, inequalities were considerably less marked than in the other Eastern bloc states.

[12] Unevenness also existed between "national" sectors within a single state, such as in Yugoslavia.

[13] See above, p. 63n.

[14] The Chinese party, because of its historical development as the leadership of a broadly based revolutionary movement, and because of its continuing attempts to reestablish connection with the

However, while all these historically conditioned factors in any case would have imposed severe limits on the possibility of achieving an international socialist community for a long time to come, they did not in themselves serve to explain the open split between Moscow and Peking, which followed nearly a decade of unity[15] *under these same conditions.* Indeed, in the light of the divisive factors already mentioned, it is this very unity that would seem first to require explanation.

For such an explanation it is necessary to look beyond the Communist bloc itself, which does not exist in a vacuum but in the context of an overwhelmingly more powerful and hostile capitalist world system. Thus, even a decade and a half after the victory of the Chinese Revolution the dominant Western powers in this system, and particularly the United States, could be seen to command such an advantage in economic,[16] military and political power as to exercise a determinant influence on relations with and even inside the Eastern camp. The exclusion of China from the United Nations and from world trade, the encirclement of the mainland by military bases and naval fleets, and the bombing of territories on the Chinese border were merely the most visible aspects, for example, of the overwhelming U.S. dominance vis-à-vis Peking.

---

popular base (the various rectification campaigns, the Cultural Revolution, etc.) must be differentiated from the much more conservative and elitist Soviet and East European bureaucracies. However, in China as in Russia, the party is monolithic and on major issues there is no basis for organized opposition. Even during the Cultural Revolution there was but one party line, though it was advanced by more than one subsequently discredited leadership.
[15] The Chinese date the serious differences from 1956; divisions were first manifest in 1958, and first acknowledged only in 1963.
[16] "The most meaningful index of economic power is labor productivity, rather than aggregate output. As late as the mid-sixties Russian output per man-hour was estimated at only 40% that of the American (in the 1920's it had been but a tenth)."—Deutscher, *The Unfinished Revolution,* p. 49.

In the early cold war period this dominance was, of course, even more extensive, and the kind of military, economic and political superiority with which Washington was able to face China in the mid-sixties in Asia it was able to face Russia with in Europe as well. It was not surprising, therefore, that despite Soviet coolness to the Chinese revolution, even in its last stages, Mao should announce in 1949 China's decision to "lean" to the Soviet side of the international struggle or that this gesture should be encouraged by Moscow. Alliance with the Soviet Union was necessary, according to Mao, in the light of the whole experience of China's national struggle, of "the forty years' experience of Sun Yat-sen and the twenty-eight years' experience of the Communist Party." For, as events had shown, the world was irrevocably divided between the forces of imperialism and the forces of revolution: there was no "third road." The Chinese Revolution therefore had to lean to the Soviet side *in order to survive*. As Mao put it: "In the epoch in which imperialism exists, it is impossible for a genuine people's revolution to win victory in any country without various forms of help from the international revolutionary forces, and even if victory were won, it could not be consolidated." [17] This had been the lesson of the imperialist interventions in Russia in 1918 and the interventions in China, particularly the American intervention in the postwar period which had been limited partly by domestic American pressures and partly by the conflict with the Soviet Union over Eastern Europe, but whose revival remained a threatening possibility.[18]

If the logic of the alliance was persuasive from the Chinese side, it was no less persuasive from the Russian, precisely because of the superiority enjoyed by the United States during this period of its nuclear monopoly and the Soviet Union's arduous postwar reconstruction. Moreover, Russia

---

[17] "On the People's Democratic Dictatorship," June 30, 1949, in *Selected Works*, pp. 415–16.
[18] See above, p. 141.

was, at this time, the object of an American offensive no less threatening than that which faced China; indeed, China was portrayed by Washington as the mere victim of remorseless Russian expansion, the Chinese Revolution being treated by the State Department as a Russian takeover.

As for the necessity of choosing alternative sides in a global struggle, it was the *American* President who had proclaimed in 1947 the division of the world into opposing and irreconcilable camps. Russia's response to this declaration and to the Western offensive which accompanied it, was to play down the line of peaceful coexistence, adopt a posture of ultra-left militancy, accept the two-camp division, and prepare for the expected military onslaught. In the light of subsequent developments, it is interesting to note that it was not Peking, but Moscow, as the main target of the American threat, which at this time took the most uncompromising line on so-called third-camp or neutral forces. By contrast, it was the Chinese who sponsored the formation of a front with the third-camp forces of anti-imperialist nationalism, i.e., one including the national bourgeoisies of the colonial and neocolonial countries.

By 1953, the position of the Soviet Union had strengthened considerably vis-à-vis the West, with Russia's development of the atomic and hydrogen bombs, the completion of the first stage of postwar reindustrialization, the death of Stalin, and the signing of a truce in Korea. This change was registered in a renewed emphasis of the doctrine of peaceful coexistence (although even at the height of the preceding period of tension Stalin had stressed the desirability and feasibility of coexistence between the two camps) and renewed overtures to the West to negotiate a European settlement. In 1955, a conference of Afro-Asian countries, including China, met at Bandung and endorsed five basic principles of coexistence. At Geneva in the same year a summit witnessed the first encounter between Soviet and American heads of state since Washington had put an end to such meetings ten years previously.

While Washington shortly reiterated its cold war demand for a reversal of the status quo in Eastern Europe as the precondition for any European settlement, the meeting represented the first major gesture toward Moscow from Washington since Truman had proclaimed the irreconcilable struggle against Communism and the Soviet system. It was in the subsequent development of these gestures toward Moscow (but not Peking) and in their acceptance by the Soviet leaders that a principal source of the emerging split between the Communist powers lay.

Thus, in the critical year 1958, while China and the United States were "eyeball to eyeball" over the Formosa Straits, Washington was inviting Premier Khrushchev to visit the United States, a gesture that Secretary of State Dulles had always opposed because it would be de facto recognition of the status quo in Eastern Europe and indeed the U.S.S.R. itself. This pattern was repeated (with certain irregularities) throughout the subsequent development of Sino-Soviet relations toward the open acknowledgement of a breach in 1963. For, as Moscow continued to develop its economic and nuclear power and its missile capability, the United States was more and more compelled to accept the necessity of coexistence with the Kremlin regime, which meant in practice recognizing the status quo in Eastern Europe.[19] At the same time, U.S. policy toward China remained as implacably hostile as before, as unreconciled to Chinese rights (for example, in

---

[19] Official U.S. accommodation to the Soviet Union and its sphere in Eastern Europe, which coincided with the open acknowledgment of the Sino-Soviet split, was registered in the nuclear test ban (which excluded China from the nuclear club) and in President Kennedy's speech at the American University, June 10, 1963, which recognized Soviet predominance in Eastern Europe and renounced the U.S. program of "liberation" ("We must deal with the world as it is, and not as it might have been had the history of the last eighteen years been different"). The steps of U.S. accommodation are traced in David Horowitz, *The Free World Colossus* (New York: Hill & Wang, 1965), Part III.

Formosa), as determined to impose the maximum tensions and strains on China's regime, and as resolved to deny it the least external respite in its fierce struggle with economic scarcity and cultural backwardness and the immense problems of industrialization. Indeed, the United States even *intensified* its hostility toward China as the latter began to replace Russia in U.S. strategy and cold war rhetoric as the primary menace to America's global "security."

The effect of this shift in U.S. policy was to evoke cooperative responses in Moscow which looked very much like betrayal to Peking, and in Peking a militancy which looked to Moscow like dangerous provocation of American power.[20] In other words, the growing divergence in the orientation of America's overweening power toward the Russian and Chinese regimes—accommodating to one, seriously threatening the very existence of the other—deprived the Communist states of the basis of their previous unity, and eventually provoked a split.

Washington's increased emphasis on a alleged expansionist threat from revolutionary China,[21] while directly related to

---

[20] Peking's militancy was, of course, basically the maintenance of a stance which both powers had adopted previously in response to the cold war crusade directed against both of them from the West. Russia's attitude toward China contrasted with Washington's attitude toward allies like West Germany. Thus, instead of insisting on some comparable relaxation of Washington's campaign against China as a quid pro quo for the détente (e.g., diplomatic recognition, a lifting of trade restrictions), Moscow attempted to include China in the détente by compelling Peking to yield to American terms; for example (if Peking is to be believed), to accept Washington's "Two China" solution for the Formosa problem, a "solution" that would call into question the very validity of the Peking regime. Cf. *The Origin and Development of the Differences Between the Leadership of the CPSU and Ourselves* (Peking, 1963).

[21] This threat, militarily speaking, was in fact as nonexistent as the Russian threat had been in the post-1945 period. As one expert on the Chinese army put it: "China has shown no signs of wishing to

the détente with Moscow (and thus the loss of Russia as an external menace justifying U.S. interventions and global "security" measures), also reflected the shift of capitalist instability from Europe, as in the early cold war period, to the underdeveloped world generally and Asia in particular, with Vietnam as its immediate center. Another source of Washington's policy lay in the fact that China, like Russia of the early postwar years, was still a very weak power despite her successful nuclear tests, and there were definite hopes in Washington of destroying the revolutionary regime (perhaps even by atomic assault) and at the very least of retarding its development and progress. This hostility of course produced a self-justifying reaction, for, as indicated previously by Russian policy (not only in the early cold war, but in the first years of the revolution itself), China's response to intensified pressure could only be a renewed revolutionary militancy, with a view toward developing counter-pressure to break the tightening containment ring.

Just as the previous Russian experience threw light on Washington's policy toward Peking, and Peking's militant response, so it seemed to indicate the course that both were likely to pursue once China attained a self-sustaining industrial development, internal stability and a deterrent intercontinental missile force. For despite China's rhetoric of irreconcilable struggle, her disposition to coexist with those capitalist regimes that were willing to accommodate themselves to her

---

acquire the military capability with which to carry out physical expansion. Its armed forces are ill-equipped to mount any sustained operation beyond Chinese frontiers, and their equipment, training, and deployment suggests an intense pre-occupation with defence. Its navy has no offensive capability to speak of, and that of its air force is inconsiderable. (This assessment is shared by almost every Western expert in the field.)"—John Gittings, "China and the Cold War," *Survey*, January 1966. Gittings is the author of *The Role of the Chinese Army* (London: Oxford University Press, 1967), a study undertaken for the Royal Institute of International Affairs.

presence (e.g., France and Pakistan) was already manifest, and thus her own willingness, like that of Russia previously,[22] to subordinate revolutionary principle to *raison d'état*.

Of course, throughout most of the underdeveloped world, the combination of U.S. dominance and pressure and China's weakness served to maintain Peking's isolation, and therefore induced her to seek security in revolutionary agitation against a hostile status quo. This contrasted profoundly with the Soviet Union's stress on friendly relations with capitalist powers, economic aid for underdeveloped capitalist regimes (and capitalist enterprises),[23] military support for the armies of these regimes whose primary purpose was to maintain the internal propertied status quo, and reformist politics for the Moscow-oriented Communist parties throughout Asia, Africa and Latin America. But in those underdeveloped countries which sought links with China, the Chinese themselves did not hesitate to establish fraternal relations (even as in Pakistan, with a right-wing military dictatorship, based squarely on the landowning and capitalist ruling classes) and to urge the pro-Peking Communists to support the national bourgeoisie in its "struggle" with the imperialist powers.[24]

In Indonesia, these Soviet and Chinese national policies converged tragically. The pro-Peking Communist party allowed itself to be integrated into a bourgeois-dominated nationalist movement and consequently was mercilessly crushed by the ascendant Right in one of the largest massacres of

---

[22] The "necessity" of coexistence thus was already well formulated by Lenin's foreign minister, Chicherin, who said: "There may be differences of opinion as to the duration of the capitalist system, but at present the capitalist system exists, so that a *modus vivendi* must be found in order that our socialist states and the capitalist states may coexist peacefully and in normal relations with one another. This is a necessity in the interest of all."—cited in Carr, *The Bolshevik Revolution*, III, 166.

[23] Cf. Kidron, *Foreign Investments in India*, pp. 113–14.

[24] Cf. K. S. Karol, *China: The Other Communism* (New York: Hill & Wang, 1968), pp. 407 ff.

modern times (with an estimated half million "Communist" victims).[25] The parallel with China (1927) was obvious,[26] except that this time it was the Chinese who had encouraged a Communist party to subordinate its class orientation to a bourgeois nationalist regime which pursued a "progressive" foreign policy in accord with China's own narrowly conceived national interests. (It was, of course, with Russian arms that the reactionary army generals seized state power.[27]) This

---

[25] "The massacres," as a leading expert on Indonesia pointed out, "were primarily rural. To understand them, particularly in Java, it is necessary to go back to 1960, when Sukarno had a law passed on agrarian reform. It was badly applied by functionaries of little zeal. So the peasant unions themselves began to divide the land of Muslim proprietors. . . . The PKI (Communist party) collaborated in Sukarno's government, and these movements served as a challenge to the party which tried to hold them back at the end of 1964, all the more so since at the time [Muslim] parties . . . and the Indonesian Nationalist party threatened to withdraw from the coalition if the PKI did not put a stop to the unilateral division of the land. What was seen next, in the fall of 1965, was the proprietors recuperating their land. So it was a massacre of the landless; it was the poor who were killed, along with their families."—Interview with Professor Wertheim, of the University of Amsterdam, in *Le Monde*, February 18, 1967 (translation in *World Outlook*, Paris, New York, March 24, 1967).

[26] "It is . . . reminiscent of things in China in 1927 after the Shanghai affair. There, too, the collaboration between the Communists and the Kuomintang, established under Sun Yat-sen, was broken by the military chiefs like Chiang Kai-shek, who unleashed a savage repression against the left."—*ibid*. For a critique of the PKI's collaborationist policies prior to the coup, see "Lessons from the Setback in Indonesia," *Marxism Today* (London, September, 1967).

[27] Indeed, the Kremlin continued its aid to Indonesia even after the coup, publicly maintaining that under the new counterrevolutionary dictatorship, Indonesia was "continuing her anti-imperialist and anti-colonialist policy" (to quote Ambassador Sytenko, September 18, 1966). "Soviet-Indonesian collaboration," as the Moscow bureau of the Soviet press agency explained to puzzled Italian Communists in the year after the coup, "is first of all to

triumph of the Right and the sudden destruction of the largest Communist party in the non-Communist world only served to illustrate once more, however, the fatal shortsightedness on the part of the Communist states—even from a purely national point of view—of basing their policies on the (non-socialist) status quo in an era of permanent revolutionary instability and change.

The dynamic character of the international revolution also rendered the Soviet program of seeking an entente with the dominant conservative power in the world on the basis of the existing status quo as ultimately self-defeating as before. For, despite the evident desire of the Soviet leaders to come to terms with the United States and to participate in a global condominium, and despite the very real accommodation imposed on Washington with respect to Eastern Europe by Soviet nuclear prowess, this accommodation could not be extended generally (e.g., at the time, to Cuba, China and Vietnam),[28] nor could the basic structural antagonism between the two powers be overcome. For as long as the Soviet Union maintained its socialist ideology and its socialized economic base, Soviet development and progress would continue to represent a threat to existing order in all capitalist countries. And as long as this antagonism was present, even in potential, the Soviet Union's *national* interest would tend to lie in supporting socialist revolutions, just as surely as the United States' "national" interest would lie in opposing them.

If the world social status quo were stable, there would be

---

the advantage of the world in evolution. It contributes to the development of the world revolutionary process." (!)—*Avanti*, December 17, 1966. Both quotations are cited in *World Outlook* (Paris, New York), February 17, 1967.

[28] One source of Moscow's inability to impose a general coexistence policy on Washington lay in the disparity of power between the two states. As Sartre expressed it: "Today we must conceive our struggle in the perspective of a durable American hegemony. The world is not dominated by two great powers, but by one only. And peaceful coexistence, despite its very positive aspects, serves the United States."—*Liberation*, January 1967.

no inherent reason why this antagonism should not remain latent. The immense preponderance of U.S. power put enormous pressures on the Soviet leadership to avoid confrontation and minimize conflict, and therefore to acquiesce in the U.S.-dominated international order. But it is just this assumption of underlying stability in the world capitalist system (and hence in international alignments) that cannot be made. For, independently of Soviet will or action, the global nationalist and socialist revolutions raise a continuous and permanent challenge to the world stake and expansionist aims of the dominant capitalist powers.

To this conflict the Soviet Union cannot remain an indifferent bystander. Surrounded by U.S.-sponsored military alliances and embodying a social system and philosophy that is made the object of intense ideological hatred by the capitalist ruling classes in the West,[29] the Soviet leadership sooner or later must attempt to seize the opportunities with which the struggle presents it. It must strive to contain and weaken the threat from the capitalist powers, and therefore to lend support—however ambiguous and conditional—to power that is antagonistic to the West, that is, to revolutionary forces and states. (The support is ambiguous because, as we have seen, the Kremlin will seek to harness these revolutionary forces to its own strategy of coexistence, to compel them to surrender their revolutionary initiative and become mere pressure groups within the status quo. On the other hand, once a revolutionary movement attains *actual* state power, which it can do only by going against the grain of Soviet policy, the relation of forces changes; then, Soviet aid, for basically national reasons, is likely to be forthcoming, and—in the case of underdeveloped revolutionary states—a crucial factor.[30])

---

[29] The degree of this hostility may be subject to periodic variations, bearing a strong relation to the apparent internal health of the capitalist societies and the revolutionary "threat" posed by their own working classes.

[30] For insight into the paramount importance of Soviet economic support for Cuba (mainly in the form of trade), see Boorstein,

Conversely, it is impossible for the Western capitalist powers themselves to pursue their own containment of revolutionary challenges (both domestic and foreign) without invoking the specter of International Communism, and therefore without linking these revolutions to the Communist bloc generally and to Moscow in particular. For it is only by *nationalist* appeals that ruling classes in post-monarchical societies can rally the conservative forces of "unity" against the forces of radical division and revolutionary change.

Therefore, though a given international equilibrium may give rise to a convergence of interests and a basis for temporary collaboration between the rulers of capitalist and Soviet bloc states, the pressures of permanent revolution continually undermine the ground of cooperation, and force the confrontation between the two camps which even ascendant forces within them seek to prevent.

These general observations are borne out by the dangerous confrontation between the United States and Russia over the revolution in Cuba, the first socialist revolution to achieve power under the leadership of forces outside the Communist International. For, just as the United States was driven into opposition to the regime when its nationalist revolution challenged U.S. economic and political domination of the island, so the Russians were compelled to support the revolution by the very fact of its opposition to the United States.

Even more revealing than this conflict which reached its climax with the missile crisis of 1962 was the failure of the détente following that crisis. Initiated by the signing of the test-ban treaty in 1963, the détente failed to progress significantly during the next few years principally because of U.S. military interventions to contain revolution in Vietnam, but also because of its interventions in Latin America and Africa. For Washington's open disregard for international law

---

The Economic Transformation of Cuba (New York: Monthly Review Press, 1968). Chap. 6.

and international norms, and the escalation of its military program and activities, naturally constituted grave developments from the point of view of Soviet security, and world peace, and consequently deprived the détente of its substance. The counterrevolutionary nature of these interventions, with their accompanying invocations of the international Communist menace, served to revive the antagonisms and atmosphere of the early cold war period, and therefore to present themselves as a threat—again on a strictly national basis—even to the most cynical and conservative officials of the European Communist states.[31]

In sum, the class framework of international politics—the reality of imperialist expansion and revolutionary resistance, the polarization of world social forces over the control of production and natural resources and the distribution of material wealth—prevented the realization of a Moscow-Washington entente; it forged a degree of solidarity between Communist states and revolutionary parties that would otherwise have been impossible in the post-Stalin era.

Moreover, while temporarily weakening the military defenses of the Communist bloc against imperialism and making possible the U.S. aggression against North Vietnam, the split also prepared the way for a contrary development, by allowing space for new revolutionary centers to appear and by making possible the creation of new sources of revolutionary consciousness and strength.

---

[31] For example, "an Eastern European diplomat" told U.S. Senator Fulbright "that he regarded the Vietnamese war as remote to the concerns of his own country except when he read statements in the American press celebrating the number of 'communists' killed in a particular week or battle. Then, he said, he was reminded that America considered itself to be at war not merely with some Vietnamese rebels but with communism in general, and that America, therefore, must be considered hostile to all communists, including himself, and all communist countries, including his own."—J. W. Fulbright, *The Arrogance of Power* (London: Jonathan Cape, 1967), pp. 120–21.

The most important of these new centers was undoubtedly revolutionary Cuba which, partly because of its prerevolutionary development, partly the material support it received
from Russia (relative to its small size) and partly the exceptional quality of its leadership,[32] was ideologically and in many
other crucial respects the most advanced revolution to date.
This ideological maturity was reflected, among other things,
in Cuba's position on the Sino-Soviet split.

In a speech on October 3, 1965 Castro asserted the right
of the Cuban party to self-determination. Cuba's policy
would be to promote the unity of the revolutionary camp, he
declared, but the Cuban party would reserve the right "to
educate and orient" her own revolutionary masses. "*No other
Party* would have that right in Cuba." (Emphasis in original.)
Castro not only served notice that Cuba would not submit to
the orthodoxy of Peking or Moscow, moreover, but challenged
the very notion of an international orthodoxy for Marxist
parties: "We might disagree on any point with any party.
Due to the heterogeneity of this contemporary world, under
such diverse circumstances, made up of countries with the
most dissimilar situations and most unequal levels of material,
technical and cultural development, it is impossible to conceive of Marxism as something like a church, like a religious
doctrine, with its Pope and Ecumenical Council." "The Pa-
pacy is a medieval institution, and the infallibility it claims is
totally alien to Marxist thought. . . ."[33]

Previously, in a major speech on March 13, Castro had
thrown down a direct challenge to Moscow and Peking, calling on them to end their dispute and unite forces in the face
of U.S. aggression in Vietnam. Frankly stating Cuba's own
national interest in bloc unity, Castro scored Russia and China

---

[32] This, in turn, could be traced to the nature of the Cuban revolution, the relative ease of its success, the absence of a long, bitter
civil war, the non-Stalinist, non-Communist character of the Cuban
revolutionary movement.

[33] Speech of September 30, 1966.

for their division before the enemy: "Who doubts that to face the enemy with a united front would make them hesitate . . . before launching their adventurous attacks and their barefaced intervention in [Vietnam]?" Cuba recognized the danger of this division not only because as a small country like Vietnam she depended on the strength of the entire bloc to shield her from U.S. aggression,[34] but also because as a small country, Cuba did "not aspire to become the navel of the world, . . . the revolutionary center of the world." [35]

While not actually seeking to lay down a *global* revolutionary line, Cuba was in fact becoming, by the mid-sixties, a third revolutionary center for sections of the underdeveloped world, and for Latin America in particular.[36] This development marked a qualitatively new stage in the internationalization of the socialist revolution, coinciding with an internal leftward shift in the Cuban revolution itself (manifested by a concerted attack on bureaucratism[37] and an emphasis on moral rather than material incentives in the field of production). Cuba's new external policy laid stress on the principle of international solidarity and on the proposition that armed guerrilla forces, rather than urban-based Communist parties, must form the nucleus of revolution in Latin America.[38] While

---

[34] On many occasions, however, Castro pointedly affirmed the determination of the Cubans to go it alone if necessary, rather than surrender the integrity or gains of their revolution.

[35] "Division in the Face of the Enemy was Never a Revolutionary or Intelligent Strategy"—Speech of March 13, 1965.

[36] In a formal sense, this bid for leadership was made with the convocation of the Tri-Continental Conference of Afro-Asian and Latin American Solidarity in Havana in January 1966 and the First Conference of the Latin American Organization of Solidarity (OLAS) in Havana in July–August 1967.

[37] For the theoretical principles underlying this campaign, see the lengthy article "The Struggle Against Bureaucracy: A Decisive Task," in *Granma* (English language edition) March 5, 1967.

[38] For an authoritative account of this strategy, see Regis Debray, *Revolution in the Revolution?* (New York: Monthly Review Press, 1967).

this strategy stemmed in part from a consideration of the tactical problems of guerrilla warfare and in part from a well-founded disbelief in the viability of electoral politics in Latin America, it also represented an unprecedented attempt to liberate the Latin American revolutionary movement from the bureaucratic grips of the pro-Soviet Communist parties and their reformist political orientation.

Nowhere was this intent more evident than in Castro's slashing attack on the leadership of the Venezuelan Communist party, which had attempted first to subordinate its own guerrilla campaign to the electoral struggle and then to liquidate the armed struggle altogether. Denouncing these policies as capitulationist and reformist while backing the dissident Communist insurgents, Castro declared that the Cuban party would regard as Communists only those dedicated fighters who really possessed a "revolutionary spirit": "The international communist movement, to our way of thinking, is not a church . . . that obliges us to hallow any weakness, . . . to follow the policy of a mutual admiration society with all kinds of reformists and pseudo-revolutionaries. . . . To us the international communist movement is in the first place just that, a movement of communists, of revolutionary fighters. And those who are not revolutionary fighters cannot be called communists." [39]

As we have seen, the reformist tendency among the parties of the Communist International was rooted in their identification and links with the Soviet nation-state and with the priority given by the Kremlin to coexistence with the capitalist West. Since the nuclear showdown with Washington during the Cuban missile crisis, Soviet policy in Latin America (the United States' most sensitive external domain) had been even more coexistence-oriented than elsewhere. Indeed, while the United States refused recognition to Cuba, maintained a tight economic blockade of the island and did everything in

[39] Speech of March 13, 1967.

its power short of invasion to destroy the Cuban regime, the Soviet Union not only recognized and traded with the Latin dependencies of the United States but even sent them technical and economic aid. It was no accident, therefore, that Castro coupled his attacks on the reformist leaderships of the Latin American parties,[40] with trenchant criticism of Soviet aid to the Latin government oligarchies:

> No one can imagine to what lengths the imperialists go to extend their economic blockade against our country. And all those governments are accomplices; . . . And if that is true, . . . and if internationalism exists, if solidarity is a word that is worthy of respect, the least we can expect of any State of the socialist camp is that it refrain from giving any financial or technical aid to those regimes.[41]

The vigor with which the Cuban leadership pressed its program of revolutionary internationalism clearly reflected the real needs of the Cuban revolution, rather than any romantic adventurism as some of their critics charged. Diplomatically isolated and cut off from its natural markets by the U.S. blockade, subjected to incessant sabotage raids and constantly menaced by a possible military invasion, Cuba naturally tended to see in the advance of revolution in Latin America its principal hope of support and *national* survival. Moreover, the very health and development of the revolution were also at stake. A small country, isolated and threatened by one great power and dependent for energy supplies and basic markets on another, Cuba could not afford to permit an organized political opposition to form without seriously jeopardizing her national sovereignty.[42] This situation, which by

---

[40] Several Latin American Communist parties, it should be noted, sided with Castro in his conflict with the urban leadership of the Venezuelan CP.

[41] Closing speech at the First Conference of the Latin American Organization of Solidarity (OLAS), August 10, 1967.

[42] Significantly, the first big "purge" in the Cuban revolution was of a pro-Soviet faction in the Cuban party, headed by Anibal Escalante, and charged with attempting to get the Soviet Union

its very nature the Cubans could not solve on a purely national basis, posed grave dangers for the revolution and its future. "We feel ourselves an inseparable part of this continent which is destined to play a decisive role in the world," declared the Secretary of the Cuban Communist Party in August 1966. "We consider the victories of Latin American revolutions as our own. . . ." [43]

Just as Washington's aggressive counterrevolutionary policy stimulated the development of Cuban internationalism, so it spurred the growth of a similar outlook and concern among the Latin American revolutionary movements. The very nature of U.S. hegemony in the hemisphere and the virtually exclusive character of its dominion forged bonds between the forces of revolutionary resistance. Following the triumph of the Cuban revolution, the integration of the continental counterrevolution[44] under Washington's lead accelerated the internationalization process. "Definitive liberation from the imperialist yoke can only be conceived as continent-wide," declared a typical manifesto, as early as 1960. "The work of liberation [must] surpass frontiers. Imperialism operates on an international plane to stamp out this struggle; it compels all the governments of the continent to throw themselves into fratricidal struggle. The social revolution has to have an international character, . . ." [45]

---

to use its economic power over Cuba as a lever in the internal policy disputes of this faction with the Cuban party leadership.
[43] Cited in "The Latin American Revolution: A New Phase," *Monthly Review*, February 1967.
[44] Most notably in the attempt to form an Inter-American Defense Force, but less openly in a whole variety of well-known measures.
[45] From the Peruvian MIR "Manifesto to the Nation," November 1960. Cf. the following statement by Luben Petkoff, second in command of the Venezuelan FALN: "We do not see the liberation of Venezuela as the liberation of our fatherland, as the liberation of the land in which we were born. No, when we speak of the liberation of Venezuela we mean the liberation of all Latin

While stressing the international framework of the confrontation, however, the revolutionary movements did not ignore the national dimension of the struggle. Liberation would only "become reality in and through the *national and popular revolution:* national because it rises up against foreign imperialist domination, economically and politically; popular because it will be a revolution by the exploited classes, for the exploited classes." [46] Indeed, it was not the revolutionary program but the interventionist policies of the United States that had dealt the concept of national sovereignty an all but mortal blow. So necessary was U.S. intervention to the preservation of the status quo in these, its external domains, that Washington felt compelled to come very close to proclaiming the obsolescence of the national principle. Thus, in the wake of the intervention by thirty thousand marines to halt the Dominican Revolution of April 1965, President Johnson declared: "Out of the Dominican crucible, the 20 American nations must now forge a stronger shield against disaster. . . . In today's world with the enemies of freedom talking about wars of national liberation, the old distinction between civil war and international war has already lost much of its meaning." [47]

This, of course, was only a particularly brazen attempt to justify a policy of intervention against social and national revolutions that had been pursued throughout the cold war period and justified in similar, if less naked, terms. The difference —and it was an important one—was precisely in the self-

---

America; we do not recognize frontiers in Latin America. Our frontiers are ideological frontiers. We interpret international solidarity in a truly revolutionary way, and we are therefore committed to fight . . . against imperialism until it no longer exists. . . ."—cited in "The Latin American Revolution: A New Phase," *Monthly Review,* February 1967.

[46] Statement by the MIR—*ibid.*

[47] U.S. Senate Congressional Record, *Proceedings and Debates of the Eighty-ninth Congress,* First Session, June 1, 1965, pp. 11697–8.

exposure which Washington was compelled to make. For although there was an attempt to single out fifty-three Communists (!) in the Dominican revolutionary forces, it was not really possible to link the revolution (hence the intervention) to the hand of Moscow or Peking.[48] This reflected the momentous fact that for the first time since the formation of the Comintern there existed diverse national revolutionary centers not under Moscow's influence or control that were ready to challenge the world system of imperialism, and to carry forward the revolutionary struggle on a truly international scale.

---

[48] Cuba would not provide a very convincing scapegoat for the U.S. intervention because it is a small country, surrounded by U.S.-controlled waters, and in any case the revolutionary strategy advocated by the Cuban leaders called for a revolutionary movement in which the struggle is not centrally controlled, but rather is directed from the guerrilla *focos* themselves.

11. The Epoch and Its Crisis

No nation can be free if it oppresses other nations.

—Marx

By the end of the second decade of cold war, developments within both world camps were ushering in a new era of relations between imperialism and revolution. The chief characteristic of this new period, distinguishing it from the preceding one of confrontation between national power blocs, was the increasingly clear polarization between international class forces—between the world socialist revolution on the one side and the imperialist-dominated bourgeois *counter*revolution on the other.

This polarization was partly a result of the post-independence radicalization of nationalist movements in the underdeveloped world, their adoption of "class" programs linking economic exploitation with national dependence, and socialist revolution with national liberation.[1] In part, it reflected the advances made within the socialist camp itself, and in part, it represented a final conservative shift in the orientation of the leading bourgeois power, the United States, which had consolidated and completed its ascendancy in the postwar period.

In one sense, the liberalization within the Soviet bloc and the newly apparent conservatism of bourgeois power were closely related. Thus, the recent developments within the So-

---

[1] Cf., for example, the resolutions of the First "Tri-Continental" Conference held in Havana in January 1966.

viet camp and the emergence of new revolutionary centers of power had the effect not only of releasing the revolution from its national Russian confines, and of accelerating social-ist development in the direction of its democratic and interna-tionalist ideals, but also of lifting the veil on the bankruptcy of the bourgeois revolution in the coming epoch.

For whereas the democratic rhetoric of the "free world" camp had previously been given resonance by Soviet domina-tion and exploitation of the East European countries within its "security" zone, the partial self-liberation of these coun-tries in the mid-fifties and the immobility of the NATO powers during the East European revolts deprived this cause of much of its substance.[2] As a result the international con-frontation between exploited and exploiting classes was seen to run that much more clearly from East to West, from the ris-ing revolutions in the underdeveloped world to the colonial and neo-colonial powers of the NATO alliance. The basic character of the postwar conflict was increasingly recognized, even by the Western peoples, to be reflected in the fact that these same NATO powers had killed more than four million inhabitants (mostly peasants) of the underdeveloped world in counterrevolutionary actions in the first two postwar decades,[3] and that in the third decade these actions were continuing as strongly as ever.

---

[2] The invasion of Czechoslovakia in August 1968, and the subse-quent proclamation of the so-called "Brezhnev Doctrine," showed how severe the limits of this "liberation" were. The seeds of self-determination were irrevocably sown in the Communist move-ments of the bloc states, however, and the resistance to national oppression by Russia and to the political dictatorships within the bloc was bound to grow in the future.

[3] In the suppression of national rebellions in Madagascar, Kenya, the Congo and elsewhere in Africa, more than a hundred thou-sand; in the civil war and intervention in Korea, between one and two million; in the Algerian war of national liberation, one mil-lion; in the Vietnamese war of national liberation against the French, one million, and against the Americans well over a mil-lion; and untold thousands in interventions in China, Cuba, Guate-mala, Santo Domingo, Egypt, Aden, Oman, British Guiana, Indo-nesia, Malaya and elsewhere.

To be sure, the continuing confinement of the socialist revolution to the economically and culturally backward regions, the maintenance of the single-party monolith in the Soviet Union and the Communist bloc generally, and the unbroken Russian domination of the East European states still reserved to the advanced bourgeois democracies—at least in some eyes—a semblance of that progressiveness which had hitherto prevented the historical polarization from attaining completeness. Nonetheless, developments within the capitalist camp itself were rapidly combining with the changes in the East to reveal the tenuousness of the bourgeois commitment to bourgeois ideals and the primacy of its commitment to bourgeois power and survival—and thus were serving to accelerate and deepen the historical trend.

Previously, the basic conservatism of the capitalist West had been somewhat obscured both by the unfinished struggle between feudal-fascist and liberal-imperialist powers and by Washington's ambiguous opposition to the vestiges of European colonialism. The defeat of the Nazi Axis, however, the decolonization of most of the old empires, the emergence of the United States to undisputed global predominance and the general adoption of its own *neo*-colonial system by the other imperial powers all served to bring about a change in the balance of international forces. Where, since the turn of the century the United States had appeared in the guise of a liberalizing force among the dominant world powers in the new framework created by these developments, this most advanced, most democratic and most powerful of the capitalist states stood revealed more and more unambiguously as the conservative guardian of the international status quo.

Symbolic of this change and transformation was Washington's support for the fascist coup in Greece in April 1967.[4]

---

[4] According to reliable accounts appearing at the time of the coup, the plan for the military takeover had been drawn up with the help of the Greek army's American NATO advisers as a precaution against a liberal success in the forthcoming elections. U.S. and

As a result of the recent U.S. détente with Moscow and the centrifugal developments in the world Communist movement, this coup appeared in a very different light from the previous U.S. intervention in behalf of Greek reaction and monarchism in 1947. For in the changed international context, the coup could not be portrayed, with the slightest degree of plausibility, as a necessary if deplorable defense against Russian expansionism. Rather it openly revealed itself as a classic fascist attempt to close the liberal door to potential *internal* socialist and Communist revolution. The United States' tacit but crucial support for the coup—against those same "liberal" forces that had fought the Communists in 1947 —without the traditional justification of containing an external expansionism, expressed eloquently the changes which the new correlation of international forces had wrought.

America's readiness to abandon the bourgeois-democratic revolution in order to preserve the propertied status quo was even more decisively indicated by the failure of the Alliance for Progress, which Washington had initiated in 1961 to spur the "democratic revolution" in Latin America as an alternative to Cuban socialism. For not only were most of the existing dictatorships of the continent included by Washington in its self-proclaimed "alliance of free governments," but U.S. support was given in the ensuing years to every military coup (without exception) against the remaining consti-

---

monarchical fears of the liberals' incipient nationalism and republicanism motivated the precaution. The coup itself, however, was prematurely triggered by junior officers with an even more rightist bent than the court and its U.S. backers, and this accounted for a certain uneasiness which they manifested toward the regime, which, however, could not maintain itself for even a short time without U.S. aid and tacit approval. While the State Department pressed the regime to provide a democratic façade for its repressive measures against the Left, it shrank from any ultimatum. As the Manchester *Guardian* (September 11, 1967) reported five months after the coup: "No one in Athens believes that Washington is prepared to force the collapse of the regime since it fears the chaos that might follow."

tutional regimes.[5] The conservative outlook underlying this policy was well exemplified by a U.S. Embassy official explaining U.S. support for the brutal dictatorship in Paraguay, one of the most desperately poor and exploited countries in Latin America. "In the last analysis," commented the official, "our policy is one of *survival*. Thus a sure anti-Communist, no matter how despicable, is better than a reformer, no matter how honest, who might turn against us." [6] (Emphasis added.)

Not surprisingly, before the end of the first five years of the Alliance, Washington had openly abandoned what it had never really in practice been ready to maintain, namely, its support for bourgeois social reform and political democracy and its commitment to a policy of nonintervention in Latin American countries, at least at the overt military level. Henceforth, in pursuit of its real objectives as imperial guardian, Washington was to put far less stock in what were in the end only tactical concessions to democratic sentiment. These objectives were: internal political and economic stabilization in the satellite countries, coordinated intervention and counterrevolution to preserve the hemispheric status quo.

The failure of the ambitious Alliance program of eco-

---

[5] Under the "liberal" Kennedy administration alone, this included coups in El Salvador, Argentina, Peru, Guatemala and Ecuador.

[6] "Less than one-quarter of the population of Paraguay owns three-quarters of the land; at least 80% and probably more than 90% of the population is illiterate; 50% of the state budget is military (soldiers outnumber productive workers two to one) and the political situation under the Stroessner dictatorship is so bad that an estimated one-third of the population is in exile. Yet in the first year and a half of the Alliance under Kennedy, Paraguay received $15.9 million making it one of the most favored Alliance countries (in per capita terms)." The above remark was made to reporter John Gerassi when he confronted an embassy official with a statement by exiled Liberal party President Carlos Pastore to the effect that "If all U.S. aid to Stroessner stopped today, democracy might still be salvageable tomorrow."—John Gerassi, *The Great Fear in Latin America* (New York: Macmillan, 1963), p. 127.

nomic, social and political reform within Washington's proto-type neo-colonial system testified eloquently to the futility of the hope of progress for the dependent nations within the capitalist orbit in the present historical epoch, the utter uto-pianism of attempting to resurrect the corpse of the bour-geois revolution with the aid of the bourgeois imperialist powers.

The depth of U.S. commitment to the status quo, how-ever, was nowhere more poignantly manifested than in Wash-ington's massive military intervention in Vietnam. While not entirely unique among U.S. actions in the cold war dec-ades, this savage aggression showed more vividly than any-thing previously the lengths to which Washington was pre-pared to go to defeat a social revolution that threatened to breach its international system. Wholly indifferent to the claims of national sovereignty and the rights of self-determina-tion, Washington showed itself willing to wage a war of un-paralleled ferocity, even to the point of obliterating a poor and underdeveloped society, rather than allow its people to pursue their independent course.

This virtually unprecedented assault by the world's greatest industrial power on a small and impoverished peasant country impressed for the first time on the consciousness of millions the real character of U.S. imperialism, which had previously been concealed by its geographical isolation and the background role which it had been able to play during the twilight years of European power. Thus, as Trotsky noted long ago, "American imperialism is in essence ruthlessly rude, predatory in the full sense of the word, and criminal. But owing to the special conditions of American development, it has the possibility of draping itself in the toga of pacifism." [7]

By the middle of the second decade of cold war, these special conditions no longer continued to prevail. In the wanton destruction of Vietnam, the brutality of American

---

[7] *The Age of Permanent Revolution*, p. 210.

imperialism and its triumph over America's liberal ideals were starkly revealed: "Every bomb that falls on helpless peasants destroys the clearest claim upon humanity's allegiance that Western democracy once could make: that it was no terrorist society, that for all its defects it was a way of solving problems peacefully, and for that reason well worth defending. At bottom, this was perhaps always an allusion. Now, at any rate, each day's headlines shatter it." [8] "There is a growing belief," reported Walter Lippmann after a tour of Europe in 1967, "that Johnson's America is no longer the historic America, that it is a bastard empire which relies on superior force to achieve its purposes, and is no longer providing an example of the wisdom and humanity of a free society. There is, to be sure, envy, fear, rivalry in the worldwide anti-Johnsonism. But the inner core of this sentiment is a feeling of betrayal and abandonment. It is a feeling that the American promise has been betrayed and abandoned." [9]

It might be contended, however, that the Vietnam war represents merely a dreadful episode, rather than the magnified expression of a real historical trend, that the polarization which is visible in this conflict and in other areas represents only a temporary sharpening of the class struggle, rather than a long-term development and prospect. Such a hypothesis would carry more conviction if it were not for the cumulative historical experience of counterrevolutionary interventions by the imperialist powers and their inevitable continuing commitment to the social status quo.[10] Moreover, it can be seen that underlying this historical experience and this commitment are powerful structural forces operating at the heart of the present epoch which will, in the long run, intensify the

---

[8] Barrington Moore, Jr., "Why We Fear Peasants in Revolt," *The Nation*, September 26, 1966.

[9] Walter Lippmann, "The American Promise," *Newsweek*, October 9, 1967.

[10] Cf. Charles A. Beard, *The Economic Basis of Politics* (New York: Vintage Books, 1967), pp. 246–47.

developing conflict and force the confrontation between the socialist world revolution and the imperialist-dominated bourgeois counterrevolution.

· · ·

The unprecedented expansionist drive of U.S. imperialism in the postwar period is undoubtedly the most important of these forces. Usually expressed in political terms as marking the end of U.S. "isolationism" and measured militarily in the acquisition of thousands of bases across the globe, this expansion has been supported economically by an equally impressive and in the long run even more significant program of overseas financial and industrial investment.

U.S. direct foreign investments alone increased more than sevenfold between 1946 and 1966—from $7.2 billion to $54.6 billion.[11] By 1964, sales of U.S. goods abroad had tripled since 1950, and the size of the foreign market for U.S.-owned firms in 1965 was equal to approximately 40 percent of the domestic U.S. output of farms, factories and mines. Indeed, U.S. firms abroad constituted the third largest economic unit after the U.S. and Soviet domestic economies.

Not only was U.S. overseas investment expanding on an unprecedented scale in the postwar period, it was becoming more and more vital to the prosperity of the domestic economy itself. Thus, in 1964, in the crucial capital-goods sector, the combined support given by exports and military-investment demand (an obviously related factor) ranged

---

[11] Joseph D. Phillips, "Economic Effects of the Cold War," in *The Corporations and the Cold War*. By contrast, the direct investments of U.S. corporations *declined* slightly in the preceding seventeen years, from $7.5 billion in 1929 to $7.2 billion in 1946. Cf. Baran and Sweezy, "Notes on the Theory of Imperialism," in *Problems of Economic Dynamics and Planning* (New York: Pergamon Press, 1965). Indicative of this expansion was the fact that the largest U.S. bank, the Bank of America, which had only one overseas branch in 1945, had eighty-five two decades later.

from 20 percent to 50 percent of total output.[12] U.S. leaders
guiding this postwar overseas expansion were, of course, not
ignorant of its important role vis-à-vis the domestic economy.
In fact, in approaching the postwar period they had put
this consideration at the very center of their calculations. For,
like their predecessors, U.S. leaders during the Great Depression saw the solution to the domestic economic problem not
in terms of internal structural changes, but in terms of staking
out ever new, externally situated frontiers.

Mincing no words in describing the grave implications of
the economic crisis, Undersecretary of State Dean Acheson
had told a Congressional audience in November 1944, on the
very eve of the postwar expansion: "We cannot go through
another ten years like the ten years at the end of the twenties
and the beginning of the thirties without having the most far-
reaching consequences upon our economic and social systems.
. . . We have got to see that what the country produces is
used and sold under financial arrangements which make its
production possible."

Analyzing the options available, in a fashion wholly
orthodox for Washington and the leadership of America's corporate ruling class, Acheson held that so long as the United
States maintained a capitalist economic system domestic markets would not suffice to absorb production on a profitable-
enough basis to keep up the level of output and employment.
"Under a different system," Acheson observed, "you could
use the entire production of the country in the United
States." However, to introduce such a system, namely, socialism, "would completely change our Constitution, our relation
to property, human liberty, our very conception of law. And
nobody contemplates that. Therefore, you must look to the
other markets and those markets are abroad." [13]

---

[12] All the above figures from Harry Magdoff, *Economic Aspects
of U.S. Imperialism*, pamphlet (New York: Monthly Review
Press, 1966).

[13] Cited in Williams, *The Tragedy of American Diplomacy* (New

Acheson's remarks, which only expressed a consensus among the U.S. leadership at the time, reflect the consistency of the ideology of U.S. imperialism. In the calculations of U.S. leaders—from William McKinley to Franklin Roosevelt, from Woodrow Wilson to John F. Kennedy and Lyndon Johnson—the preservation of American prosperity and institutions and of "the American way of life" has been predicated on the preservation and extension of U.S. control of foreign markets, and thus the inevitable expansion of U.S. power overseas. Viewed in this perspective, the cold war can be seen as the U.S. ruling class evidently sees it, namely, as a war for the American frontier.

Of course, "frontier" in this usage is not to be understood in a territorial sense but in terms of a set of political institutions and ideological attitudes based, as they can only be based in this conception, on an international "free enterprise" economic system open to penetration and domination by United States capital. The security of these institutions at home is firmly believed to be dependent on the preservation and expansion of their outposts overseas—in short, of the United States' extra-geographical frontier, the "free world."

At this point it may be suggested, however, that this traditional expansionist outlook of the American ruling class is mainly based on a Hobsonian misconception of capitalist economics,[14] and hence is bound to change and lead to a redirection of American energies from the enterprise of expansion and control in external frontiers to a much needed program of social reconstruction and rehabilitation at home. For with

---

York: Delta, 1962), pp. 148, 169. See especially Chapter 6, "The Nightmare of Depression and the Vision of Omnipotence," for estimates similar to Acheson's. See also Lloyd C. Gardner, "New Deal, New Frontier and the Cold War," and David Eakins, "Business Planners and the Development of American Postwar Economic Policy," in Horowitz (ed.), *The Corporations and the Cold War*.

[14] See above, pp. 36 f. and p. 37, Note 15.

the development and acceptance of Keynesian doctrine, it is apparent that capitalist governments can, by their own action, raise the level of effective domestic demand, and thus, presumably, mitigate the necessity of an expansionist economics and politics.

However, even if insufficient demand at the national level were the fundamental cause of America's overseas expansion, there would be little historical basis for expecting such a revision of national priorities through the application of the Keynesian remedies. For it was precisely the two postwar decades which witnessed the increasing acceptance of the Keynesian analysis and techniques that at the same time marked the unprecedented expansion of U.S. foreign investment. Moreover, as previously noted, such expansion of the federal budget as did take place was primarily directed toward military investment (more than $904 billion since 1946, or 57 percent of the total).[15] In fact, since 1929 there has been relatively no change in the level of federal nonmilitary expenditures as a fraction of GNP.[16] In other words, given the class structure of U.S. monopoly capitalism with its intense resistance to redistributive measures and to any allocation of resources which runs against or circumvents the channels of the existing market,[17] the only way demand can be significantly raised is by creating and supplying a huge military machine. Far from making possible a disengagement from the external frontier, Keynesian policy in practice has created a new and immensely powerful bureaucracy, which, with its corporate allies, has a vital and increasing stake in the maintenance and expansion of that overseas empire.

In other words, the net effect of the application of the Keynesian prescriptions has been to intensify the expansionist bias in American policy rather than lessen it. However, even

---

[15] J. W. Fulbright, "The Great Society is a Sick Society," *The New York Times*, August 20, 1967.

[16] Hansen, *op. cit.*, p. 30.

[17] Magdoff, *op. cit.*, p. 18.

if federal outlays could be allocated to meet domestic needs at a level adequate to sustain demand—despite all historical experience to the contrary—this still would not arrest the outward pressure of American imperialism. For the fundamental pressure behind imperialist expansion is not the overall level of demand (though it is influenced by that level) but the pressure of the system itself: the competitive struggle for the control of markets, or, as Lenin put it, for the completion of monopoly not only at home but internationally as well.[18]

Properly viewed, imperialism is a "class" phenomenon, with its dynamic center at the corporate level (in the framework of the existing market).[19] The global extension of the U.S. petroleum industry, for example, has less to do with domestic profit margins (though these certainly play a role)[20] than with the global dispersion of the resource itself, and the necessity of controlling the sources of supply in order to maintain monopolistic prices for the finished product (not only abroad but at home as well).[21]

---

[18] See above, p. 32.

[19] "At the outset it must be stressed that the familiar national aggregates—GNP, national income, employment, etc.—are almost entirely irrelevant to the explanation of imperialist behavior. In capitalist societies, these are *ex post* calculations which play little if any causal role. Nor does it make any difference whether the 'costs' of imperialism (in terms of military outlays, losses in wars, aid to client states, and the like) are greater or less than the 'returns,' for the simple reason that the costs are borne by the public at large while the returns accrue to that small, but usually dominant, section of the capitalist class which has extensive international interests. If these two points are kept firmly in mind, it will be seen that all liberal and Social Democratic efforts to refute Marxian—or for that matter any other predominantly economic—theories of imperialism on the ground that in some sense or other it 'doesn't pay' have no claim to scientific standing."—Baran and Sweezy, "Notes on the Theory of Imperialism."

[20] For example, while only 20 percent of Standard Oil's assets were located in Latin America, 40 percent of its profits in 1958 were made in that area (*ibid.*).

[21] Magdoff, *op. cit.* On the vital importance of controlling raw

The postwar overseas expansion was stimulated by a combination of factors: these included a domestic profit squeeze, a new wave of corporate mergers; fears of a reconversion crisis and the consequent availability of U.S. government financing; economic nationalism in the underdeveloped world;[22] and the continuing push of the productive forces against national frontiers. To develop commercially the new technologies (many of which received an immense stimulus from the war) required large investments of capital and hence mass markets over which to spread unit costs. At the same time, modern communications and mass media standardized tastes in different countries, while resurgent economic nationalism, often coupled with foreign-currency shortages, induced governments to ensure that international goods which they bought were manufactured on their own soil.

In the course of these developments a new corporate form emerged—the "multinational" or *international* corporation. Carrying out both manufacturing and marketing operations in literally dozens of countries, such corporations, as distinct from even their giant predecessors, no longer merely look to foreign sources for an important share of sales, profits and growth but rather seek "to apply company resources on a global scale to realize business opportunities anywhere in the world." [23] In other words, once placed in "external" markets, international corporations seek to expand their control of these markets as such, for they are locked in mortal struggle with similar giants for control of markets at an *international*

---

material sources, see Nelson Rockefeller, "A New Approach to International Security" (speech before the Congress in support of the Mutual Security Act, 1951).

[22] See below, p. 243.

[23] Usually this change in outlook has been found to take place when direct foreign investment as a proportion of a company's total assets passes the 20 percent mark. Gilbert H. Clee, "Investing Overseas," in *The United States*, supplement of *The Financial Times*, April 12, 1965. Clee is director of McKinsey & Co., a leading management consultant firm advising international corporations.

level. The predominance of U.S. international corporations within the American political economy, based not least on the fact that *its* prosperity depends on their own, will assure them the necessary leverage over foreign policy to support their operations.[24]

Thus, it is irrelevant that total exports or aggregate "super-profits" from foreign holdings may form only a small fraction of GNP for the expansionist power,[25] though this is often raised to challenge the importance of economic motives and power in the structure of U.S. expansionism. What is significant is the role of the foreign holdings of the giant U.S. corporations in *their* operations, and their own preponderant role in the U.S. domestic economy and polity. The evidence shows that both are overwhelmingly great. In 1964, for example, foreign sources of earnings accounted for about *one quarter* of *all* domestic nonfinancial corporate profits. As for concentration, the hundred largest U.S. corporations, or less than 0.1 percent of all U.S. corporations, owned 55 percent of total net capital assets, and it was among these that the giants of the international field were to be found. Moreover, concentration does not stop at the national frontier: only forty-five U.S. firms account for almost 60 percent of direct U.S. foreign investment, while 80 percent is held by a hundred and sixty-three firms.[26] Furthermore, it is estimated, on the basis

---

[24] The giant corporations and international investment banks also exercise direct influence on U.S. foreign policy in a variety of ways; cf. G. William Domhoff, *Who Rules America?* (Englewood Cliffs, N.J.: Prentice-Hall, 1967), and "Who Makes American Foreign Policy?" in Horowitz (ed.), *The Corporations and the Cold War*. Robert Engler's *The Politics of Oil* (New York: Macmillan, 1961) indicates the immense influence and overt control exercised by a single international industry.

[25] Cf. also Note 19, above.

[26] Figures from Magdoff, *op. cit.*, and *Economic Concentration*, Hearings Before the Subcommittee on Antitrust and Monopoly of the Committee on the Judiciary, United States Senate, Eighty-eighth Congress, Second Session, 1964, Part I, Overall and Conglomerate Aspects, p. 115.

of current growth rates of U.S. overseas companies, that within the next decades some 75 percent of all industrial assets in the "free world" outside the public sector will be controlled by a mere three hundred international firms, of which a hundred and seventy-five will be U.S.-owned.[27]

. . .

The postwar expansion of the U.S. corporate stake in the global economy from a relatively modest $7 billion to more than $50 billion in *direct* investments ($70 billion in *total* private foreign investments) undoubtedly played a major part in the growing conservatism of the U.S. corporate ruling class and in Washington's intensified commitment to the international status quo. To assess the impact of this expansion on the overall polarization of global bourgeois and socialist forces, it is also necessary to gauge its effect in the developed and underdeveloped worlds. In particular, it must be asked whether any section of the global bourgeois forces could be expected to come forward to occupy the vanguard position vacated by the United States when it acceded to its role as chief beneficiary and policeman of the international system of property and privilege. For the bankruptcy of the bourgeoisie as a historical force would be irrevocably sealed if it failed to advance those values with which its rise was associated and which continued in the present to provide its legitimating and validating principles. Conversely, a serious commitment to those values by a section of the international bourgeoisie against the inevitable encroachment of the expanding American empire would lead to a new lease on life for the bourgeois democratic revolution and the capitalist system.

Such a challenge to American expansion and domination appeared to have been raised, at least potentially, in the early

---

[27] Richard J. Barber, "The New Partnership: Big Government and Big Business," *The New Republic*, August 13, 1966.

sixties, by Gaullist France. American investment in Europe had increased from $2 billion in 1950 to a total of over $15 billion a decade and a half later. More than half of this investment, moreover, was in manufacturing and included the fastest growth sectors and most technically advanced industries of the European economy. In France alone, U.S. corporations had come to control almost the whole electronics industry, 90 percent of the production of synthetic rubber, 65 percent of petroleum distribution and 65 percent of farm-machinery production.

The extent of this penetration already indicated the ultimate futility of the Gaullist opposition. It was not merely the U.S. economic foothold that ensured this futility, however, but the balance of international class forces. For potential opposition to U.S. domination had to be tempered by the recognition that the capitalist system could no longer afford a showdown struggle between its leading powers. The European powers' use of their financial strength to reduce the American capital inflow, could not, for example, be carried to the point of precipitating an international monetary crisis without at the same time creating a grave threat to the European ruling classes themselves.[28] As a result of the undiminished, and indeed increasing, strength of the European socialist Left and the presence of an expanding and progressing socialist world camp, any European bourgeoisie would hesitate at the outset to embark on a course of opposition to the United States that would lead to such a point of no return.[29]

Underlying the weakness of the European bourgeoisie and the historic bankruptcy of its cause was the basic fact

---

[28] Cf. the symposium "$ and Gold: Four Articles on Monetary Problems and Crises of the World Capitalist System," *Monthly Review*, December 1966.

[29] This was written before the historic strikes of the French students and workers in May 1968 undermined the position of the franc and demonstrated in stark terms the alternatives open to the Gaullist bourgeoisie.

that, short of an unworkable fascist "solution" (leading to eventual inter-capitalist war), the only possible structural basis for an *independent* European development was a *socialist* one.

Nearly half a century earlier, the Bolshevik theorist Preobrazhensky noted that America had already acquired a dominant role in the world economy, and drew a momentous conclusion: *"American expansion,"* he wrote, *"cannot encounter an unbreakable resistance in any country of the capitalist world so long as the country undergoing attack and pressure remains capitalist."* The reason for this was that American dominance was a function of the commanding superiority of its monopolistic and technically advanced economy in the increasingly integrated world market, and that this very superiority ensured its future triumph in any competition in that market. He wrote: "The very economic structure of the present-day capitalist countries excludes the possibility of serious resistance to American conquest, because the already attained level of the world division of labor, of world exchange, with the existence of the huge and ever-growing economic, technical, and financial superiority of America over all the rest of the world inevitably subjects this world to the value-relations of America. Not a single capitalist country can, without ceasing to be capitalist, break away from the operation of the law of value [i.e., the market] in its changed form. And it is just here that the avalanche of American monopolism falls on it. Resistance is possible only, perhaps, on a political basis, specifically on a military basis, but just because of America's economic superiority this would hardly prove successful. . . ." (And because of the strength of the Left, as well as the deterrent factor of nuclear weapons, would hardly be tried).

"A struggle against American monopolism," concluded Preobrazhensky, "is possible only through changes in the whole structure of the given country, that is, through going over to a socialist economy," which would permit the total

mobilization of economic resources, "and would not allow
American capitalism to get hold of one branch of industry
after another, subjecting them to American trusts or banks, as
is happening with the 'natural' contact between present-day
American capitalism and the capitalism of other capitalist
countries. . . . For Europe of today the old freedom of
competition is impossible *in any sense*. Europe must choose
between capitalist monopoly, externally bound to the monopolism of the United States, and internal socialist monopoly, which would make independence possible." [30] (Emphasis
in original.)

Notwithstanding the prematurity of Preobrazhensky's
posing of the problem, it is evident that in the postwar decades the very choice which he outlined has been firmly placed
on the historical agenda.

. . .

That which applies in the realm of economic power to the
bourgeoisies of the developed capitalist countries, moreover,
applies with immeasurably greater force to those of the
underdeveloped world. Yet, it is precisely this section of the
global bourgeoisie that in the postwar independence struggles
provided one of the few instances of bourgeois revolutionary leadership since 1848. Even though ultimately no effort
to achieve economic independence in the underdeveloped
world can be successful except on a socialist basis, it is still
important to consider what the alignment of such a class
would tend to be in the next stages of the historical process.

In fact, the very conquest of political sovereignty, taken
together with the triumph of the Russian, Chinese and Cuban
revolutions tends, as has in fact already been noted, to sap the
revolutionary will of the national bourgeoisie in the under-

---

[30] *The New Economics* (New York: Oxford University Press,
1965), pp. 157–59.

developed world, as the social and economic questions are approached.[31] To these conservatizing influences can be added yet another factor in the new postwar patterns of imperialist investment. These patterns were pioneered by the United States in its neo-colonial system in Latin America, and are associated in the postwar period with the emergence of the international corporation.

Under classic imperialism, investment was largely in extractive industries, and indigenous manufacturing industry was suppressed, while direct control of the state was used to enforce this basic pattern. There was, therefore, an inherent conflict between the development requirements of an indigenous bourgeoisie and the policies of the imperial power, so that the potential growth of the former came to hinge on freedom from foreign rule.

The post-colonial pattern has been significantly different. As a result of the nationalist protectionism of the new formally independent governments, the international corporation has come under pressure to defend its markets by setting up manufacturing industries[32] inside the freshly erected tariff walls in the underdeveloped regions. This has been one of the crucial factors in the postwar economic expansion,[33] and has

---

[31] There are exceptional cases, especially in the short-run period, but the long-run tendency seems clear enough.

[32] As Boorstein and others note, however, "a large proportion of these plants are little more than disguised . . . export operations bringing in goods for the local upper classes. Throughout Latin America, there are outpost plants for turning out soaps, detergents, toiletries, bottles and cans, paint, rayon, automobile tires, and so on, from imported materials."—*The Economic Transformation of Cuba*, p. 232.

[33] For example, Kidron, *Foreign Investments in India*, pp. 253 ff. Cf. the remarks of Henry Ford to the effect that "Ford of Britain is the only one of our manufacturing and assembly operations outside the U.S. that was not established, at least in part, in response to trade barriers designed to protect and stimulate local manufacture or assembly of motor vehicles."—*The Sunday Times*, May 14, 1967. Ford has operations in 29 countries.

resulted in a new partnership between the national bour-geoisie and the foreign corporations.[34]

The national bourgeoisie is now needed by foreign capi-tal to mediate with the local environment and the national state, over which the metropolitan power no longer exercises overt control. In return, national capital is allowed a share in the new manufacturing and marketing industries which can amount to as much as 51 percent or more (the so-called "Chileanization," "Indianization," etc., of the economy). In fact, however, the technical and economic superiority of the metropolitan-based corporations still ensures their effective control of these satellite industries, even in the absence of majority shares.[35] Moreover, the conflict between the policies of these monopolistic international firms and the require-ments of national development remain basically as intense and unresolvable as before.[36] Consequently, while political decolo-nization and neo-colonial investment tend to divest the na-tional bourgeoisie of the last remnant of its revolutionary character, real domination of the satellite country (which also takes place through its overall financial, economic and mili-tary dependence on the metropolis) continues, and the neo-colony remains caught in the vise of economic stagnation and underdevelopment.

Sooner or later, this post-independence impasse compels

---

[34] Michael Kidron, "International Capitalism," *International So-cialism*, Spring 1965.

[35] On the new sophisticated methods of control, compare Kidron, *Foreign Investments in India*, pp. 285 f.; Hamza Alavi, "Imperial-ism Old and New," in *The Socialist Register 1964* (New York: Monthly Review Press); and "Indian Capitalism and Foreign Im-perialism" (a review essay on Kidron's book), *New Left Review*, May–June 1966.

[36] On the conflict between the policies of the international cor-porations and national development needs in the satellites, com-pare the previously cited works by Baran, Boorstein, Kidron, A. Gunder Frank and others.

recognition of the fact that formal political independence does not really free the satellite country to pursue its national development and consequently that "the interests of the national liberation movement are intimately connected with the needs of social revolution." [37] It is no accident that this was first recognized by the revolutionary movements in Latin America which achieved formal political independence more than a hundred and fifty years ago, and where the Castroist revolution in Cuba has provided the basis for a concerted challenge to the tenets of Stalinism among the international revolutionary forces. In the shaping of this recognition, the Cuban Revolution and the intimately related and abortive Alliance for Progress were pivotal events.

The Cuban Revolution began as an attempt to solve the problems of national development within a bourgeois democratic framework,[38] but quickly found the backbone of the opposition to its reforms (particularly the land reform) to be U.S. corporate interests and, behind them, the U.S. government. In order to carry out the program of bourgeois re-

---

[37] "The Nations of Asia, Africa and Latin America which have won their political independence are realising that formal sovereignty is not enough to ensure full liberation; to obtain this it is vital to eliminate all the causes of imperialist oppression and exploitation and to carry out profound transformations in the social and economic structure. . . . Economic liberation must be added to political liberation."—"General Declaration" of the Tri-Continental Conference (Havana, January 1966), in *International Socialist Journal*, January 1966. Cf. Frantz Fanon, *The Wretched of the Earth* (New York: Grove Press, 1966), Chap. 3.

[38] That is, the *program* advanced by the revolutionary coalition (which included middle-class forces) was bourgeois-democratic. The composition of the revolutionary faction which Castro headed and which was the main force of the revolution was itself composed of *non*-middle-class elements. Cf. Hugh Thomas, "Middle Class Politics and the Cuban Revolution," in Claudio Veliz (ed.), *The Politics of Conformity in Latin America* (New York: Oxford University Press, 1967).

forms, therefore, it became necessary to wage a struggle for *national* liberation.[39]

However, partly because the national bourgeoisie refused to support a head-on collision with the United States and—putting its class interests before its national allegiance—left the revolutionary coalition to go over to the counterrevolution, and partly because to concentrate economic power in the hands of the state was the only possible way to wage such a struggle, the Cubans soon discovered that to be successful, the nationalist revolution must be socialist.[40]

The inability of the Cuban bourgeoisie to carry through a bourgeois nationalist revolution or—what amounts to the same thing—the impossibility of carrying out a bourgeois revolution on the basis of the capitalist, neo-colonial production relationships in Cuba was shown to be a phenomenon of hemispheric significance by the subsequent failure of the Alliance for Progress. For in this Alliance, Washington at-

---

[39] The transition from one level of struggle to the next was reflected in the transformation of the revolution's slogan from *Libertad o muerte!* to *Patria o muerte!* (country or death).

[40] Castro proclaimed the revolution to be socialist directly following the U.S.-sponsored invasion of April 1961. The fact that the social revolution in Cuba was rapid, relatively peaceful and defended by the vast majority of the Cuban people indicated that "a social revolution of a specifically socialist character was not merely an ideological product," as some critics have suggested, "but a realistic and authentic response to social reality."—James O'Connor, "On Cuban Political Economy," *Political Science Quarterly*, June 1964. O'Connor suggests that the socialization of the monopolistic and stagnant Cuban economy was "necessary for the island's further economic and social development," and in that sense "inevitable." Cf. also O'Connor, "Industrial Organization in the Old and New Cubas," *Science and Society*, Spring 1966, and Edward Boorstein, *The Economic Transformation of Cuba*, p. 140. Boorstein, who was an economist in the Ministry of Foreign Commerce in Cuba, also points out the necessity for economic planning once Cuba became dependent, as a result of the U.S. blockade, on trade with the planned economies of the Soviet bloc.

tempted to put its financial and political resources behind a bourgeois-democratic program of social and economic reform. "Those who possess wealth and power in poor nations," declared President Kennedy, "must accept their own responsibilities. They must lead the fight for those basic reforms which alone can preserve the fabric of their own societies." [41] This program, however, came up against the hard reality that the bourgeoisie was not prepared, in the first place, to relinquish its own privileges, and in the second, to jeopardize its economically and socially dominant position by playing with revolutionary—even "moderate" revolutionary —fire. Even more important, any attempt to carry through really basic reforms fundamentally conflicted with U.S. corporate interests and the U.S. corporate system in Latin America.[42]

In fact, just as a radical bourgeois government, bent on reform, had been overthrown by U.S. agents in Guatemala in pre-Alliance days (1954), so similar Alliance governments were toppled by military coups engineered or supported by the United States, including those in the Dominican Republic (1963) and Brazil (1965). A land reform in Honduras which touched the interests of the U.S.-owned United Fruit Com-

---

[41] Note the formula: "Those who hold wealth and power . . . must lead the fight for . . . basic reforms." And these people call Lenin an elitist!

[42] The dangers were underscored by the editors of *Business Week* (July 5, 1961) at the time: "A U.S. policy of sponsoring revolutionary change in the underdeveloped countries could well undermine the position of U.S. private investment in many areas." However, steps were taken by the U.S. business community from its strategic positions inside and outside the federal government to ensure that the very formulation of the program would minimize any threats to its interests. Thus, for example, resources of the Alliance Fund could not be used to buy agricultural land (i.e., for reform), and the emphasis as in all U.S. aid programs was to be on the encouragement of private enterprise and foreign investment. Cf. Gerassi, *op. cit.*, pp. 266–67; also Horowitz, *The Free World Colossus*, Chap. 13.

pany was frustrated by the U. S. Congress, while in 1965 a revolution to restore the deposed Alliance government in Dominica was crushed by 30,000 U.S. marines. The failure of the Alliance in practice (the program of reforms was abandoned, the minimum growth goals were not even approached) demonstrated that there was no U.S.-backed "democratic" alternative to Castroist revolution: to be successful, the nationalist revolution must be socialist.

This did not mean that the coming Latin American revolution would necessarily be fought under socialist rather than nationalist and bourgeois-democratic banners. It meant, rather, that democracy and self-determination, even in their limited bourgeois forms, could no longer be realized in Latin America under bourgeois conditions of production, i.e., without breaking out of the United States' "free world" system, the system of international capital.[43] Such is the concrete meaning of the "historic bankruptcy" of the bourgeois-democratic revolution in the underdeveloped world in the present epoch.

• • •

Nowhere, however, was the imperialist decay and failure of the capitalist system more significantly manifested, or the question of its future more fatefully posed, than in the crises besetting its transfigured dominant power. In 1945 the United States had provided inspiration to a demoralized and discred-

[43] ". . . the necessity, and indeed the inevitability, of socialist revolution, not in some vague future but as the next historical stage in Latin America is rooted in the underdeveloped, imperialist-enforced reality of that region. This is not to say that socialist revolution is coming in Latin America tomorrow or next year: great historical changes do not happen that way. It is simply to say that no other kind of revolution is possible in Latin America and that sooner or later all serious revolutionaries are going to have to come to terms with that fact."—Huberman and Sweezy, commentary on the Tri-Continental Conference, *Monthly Review*, April 1966.

ited bourgeois world, which had seen in America's New Deal welfarism, liberal politics and egalitarian outlook the promise of a better capitalist future. (The fact that this "egalitarianism" excluded black people was as expressive of the character of America's bourgeois-imperialist social order as was the acceptance of American racism by the liberals of Europe characteristic of their own imperial role and outlook.)

Little more than two decades later, the bitter disillusionment with America's performance and the widespread sense of betrayed hope in the American future were recognized and reflected upon even by the system's committed adherents. "At the present," declared the chairman of the U. S. Senate Foreign Relations Committee in the summer of 1967, "much of the world is repelled by America and what America seems to stand for. Both in our foreign affairs and in our domestic life we convey an image of violence, . . . Abroad we are engaged in a savage and unsuccessful war against poor people in a small backward nation. At home—largely because of the neglect resulting from 25 years of preoccupation with foreign involvement—our cities are exploding in violent protest against generations of social injustice. America, which only a few years ago seemed to the world to be a model of democracy and social justice, has become a symbol of violence and undisciplined power." [44]

As befitted the remarks of a partisan, the statement retained a residue of undaunted optimism. The great unchecked domestic crises in race relations, urban development, education and the general pollution of the human environment are blamed not on a system of irrational and inequitable resource allocation based on the private accumulation of social capital but on "foreign involvement." This is indeed to misunderstand the essence of the system. For the unchecked concentration of financial and corporate power and its expansion

---

[44] J. W. Fulbright, "The Great Society Is a Sick Society," *The New York Times*, August 20, 1967.

beyond local and national boundaries are the very corner-
stone of "free enterprise" capitalism. The system is not
merely *involved* in global markets and politics; it *is* global.
Even if it were possible to take the social decision to surrender markets abroad while retaining capitalist relations at
home, such a decision would merely be to choose the existence of a colonial satellite in place of that of an imperial
power. Within capitalism there is no way to avoid the toils of
imperialist rivalry and competition, no way to elude the political and military conflicts which the imperialist struggle entails.

Moreover, the assumption that it is possible within capitalism to reallocate resources domestically according to social
rather than market criteria and on a scale adequate to meet
the cumulative social crisis has no foundation in reality. For it
is belied by the whole historical experience of capitalist societies and runs counter to the logic of the system itself. Historically, the capitalist state, whether under the formal rule
of social democratic radicals or tory conservatives, has never
marshaled the funds necessary to even begin a genuine social
reconstruction. War and preparation for war have proved the
only vast expenditure programs (proportionate to calculated
need) that capitalist states have been willing or able to undertake.[45]

As an indication of the larger pattern of fiscal priorities,
just before the Vietnam escalation and the subsequent increase of annual government outlays on the war from less
than $500 million to more than $30 *billion*, pleas to expand the
government's poverty program were rejected on the grounds
that no money was available for such an expansion. In the
preceding Keynes-oriented Kennedy administration, which
expanded the military budget by 20 percent in its first two

---

[45] One other important government program, particularly in the
United States, has been highway construction, which, for obvious
reasons, is an acceptable government expenditure to the corporate
interests.

years, plans to stimulate the flagging economy by increased social expenditure were similarly rejected, under intense corporate pressure, in favor of a tax cut.[46] (This tax cut, moreover, had the net effect of redistributing income to the wealthier classes.) For the vital interests of the corporations require that nondefense government expenditure on social welfare be kept to a minimum and "as long as the levels of control over the productive apparatus are in [their] hands, no [governmental] economic program can hope to succeed without their consent." [47]

So powerful are the structural forces shaping the misallocation of resources in capitalist society and actively preventing remedial federal action that those of its liberal spokesmen who are able to sense in some degree the magnitude of the gathering social crisis are themselves beginning to realize that to solve it within the limits of the existing system is not really possible. Thus, as one well-informed correspondent reported of the New Frontier: ". . . while [Kennedy] and his associates go on talking publicly about the progress they have made, privately they are beginning to fear that given the existing form of American society and the existing balance of political power, the evils they complain about simply cannot be remedied." [48]

One of the crises that had caused the President and his advisers most concern was inevitably the mounting tide of

---

[46] Huberman and Sweezy, "The Kennedy-Johnson Boom," in Gettleman and Mermelstein (eds.), *The Great Society Reader* (New York: Vintage Books, 1967). Cf. also the informative account by Hobart Rowen in *The Free Enterprisers: Kennedy, Johnson and the Business Establishment* (New York: Putnam, 1964).

[47] "They have the power to sabotage policies of which they disapprove . . . they can literally create a depression. In more orthodox terminology, their 'confidence' can be so badly shaken that buying is reduced to a hand-to-mouth basis and total demand shrinks to depression levels."—Paul M. Sweezy, *The Present as History* (New York: Monthly Review Press, 1953), p. 366.

[48] James Reston, *The New York Times*, October 26, 1963.

black revolt in the country—a direct consequence of the long-term social and economic oppression of black people, the colonial status of the black ghettos, and the regime of terror under which large sections of the black community have been compelled to live in the United States since reconstruction. The deep-rooted character of this oppression, symbolized by the failure of the ruling class to meet the most basic political and economic demands of the black movement, was starkly illuminated by the alacrity with which it was ready to squander men and resources in its murderous war to preserve the corporate frontier in Asia. Indeed, the basic priorities of America's imperialist and racist social order were unsparingly revealed in the comparative sums allocated, on the one hand, to the domestic "War on Poverty," and on the other, to the war against the peasantry in Vietnam. For every fifty-four dollars scraped together by the federal government (under the pressure of mass protest) to ease the plight of one exploited and oppressed black laborer in America, three hundred and fifty *thousand* dollars were made available to kill a yellow peasant in the deltas of Indochina. More money was being spent annually on ground ammunition alone for use in Vietnam than for the entire poverty program in the United States; and while Washington was willing to shed rivers of blood for its puppet dictatorship in Saigon, hardly an official white finger was raised to defend the lives and freedom of black Americans in the American South. This scale of priorities was itself an incitement to revolt, the index of a system depraved by the immensity of the effort necessary to maintain itself and its class privileges in an era in which it had lost the power to advance the struggle for human justice and liberty within its own institutional framework.

As the first-line official response to the ghetto uprisings resolved itself more and more clearly into the armed occupation of American cities, the symmetry of repression and rebellion on the national and international levels began to forge a unity of consciousness and purpose between the various forces struggling for self-determination and liberation. "We are living in an era of revolution," the American black leader Malcolm X had declared in the last year of his life, "and the revolt of the American Negro is part of the rebellion against the oppression and colonialism which has characterized this era. It is incorrect to classify the revolt of the Negro as simply a racial conflict of black against white, or as a purely American problem. Rather, we are today seeing a rebellion of the oppressed against the oppressor, the exploited against the exploiter." [49]

The more and more visible connection between the national and international structures of exploitation and oppression,[50] and the growing solidarity between the revolutionary forces challenging these structures, underscored both the general character and the historic import of the developing crisis. Rooted in the insoluble social and economic contradictions of the international capitalist system, the crisis found its expression *politically*, as a crisis of the democratic order itself. The increasing resort to militarism and repressive violence and the parallel expansion of the domestic apparatuses of authority and control, on the one hand, reflected the inability of the system to generate the sources of its own renewal while at the same time it posed an active challenge to the very concept of popular sovereignty, i.e., the legitimating principle of bourgeois rule and order.

The truly international foundations of this crisis, which manifested itself so intensely within the American national framework, were expressed in the fact that a major pressure against the constitutional system in the United States came from the exigencies of the war abroad. Thus, in order to carry out the intervention in Vietnam, for which there could be no popular sanction, the President had to present both

---

[49] *Malcolm X Speaks* (Beverly Hills, Calif.: Merit, 1965), p. 233.
[50] See, for example, the essays "Domestic Law and International Order" and "The Black Man's Stake in Vietnam," in Eldridge Cleaver, *Soul On Ice* (New York: McGraw-Hill, 1968).

Congress and the people with a *fait accompli* and launch the overt stage of U.S. aggression (the bombing of the North, the mass landing of U.S. troops in the South) "illegally," without a declaration of war.[51] He had, further, to contain a historically unprecedented resistance to the draft, which struck at the very basis of governmental authority. While the immediate impact of these events was to unsettle the political consensus which had governed and supported U.S. foreign policy since the Second World War, its implications as a reflection of basic forces and long-term trends were far more important.

Thus, historically, one of the main pressures leading toward fascism in the belated capitalist powers had been the incompatability of parliamentary or even constitutional rule with the requirements of a policy of military imperialism. Prior to the cold war, the liberal imperialist powers, and the United States in particular, had been able to carry out their interventions with only a minimal need for military mobilization. Consequently the potential conflicts between civil and military authority, between the popular sanctioning of policy required by democratic order and wars waged for predatory ends on behalf of a minute, if extremely powerful, section of society were effectively contained. With the strengthening of the socialist world movement and its renewed challenge in the wave of nationalist and Communist revolutions after the Second World War, however, the liberal powers, and especially the United States in its new preeminence, lost this margin of maneuver. In order to repress revolutions interna-

---

[51] Cf. *American Policy vis-à-vis Vietnam*, by the Lawyers Committee on American Policy towards Vietnam (New York: 1965). On the declining role of Congress, compare Fulbright, *op. cit.*, Chap. 2. It should be noted that very little that Johnson did with respect to deceiving the American people and Congress, violating the U.N. Charter, international law and U.S. statutes in the course of his actions in Vietnam could be called unprecedented. A glance at the Kennedy administration's performance in regard to the invasion of Cuba makes this eminently clear and emphasizes the trend character of this phenomenon.

tionally, to weaken and retard the development of the existing socialist states, and to sustain domestic demand amid the stagnationist tendencies of the increasingly monopolistic economic system, it became necessary to mobilize permanently on an immense and ever-expanding scale. In addition to causing powerful, new adverse economic pressures (a domestic inflationary spiral, a critical outflow of gold), this mobilization accelerated the corporatist-fascist trend within the economy,[52] bringing the most technologically advanced sectors within the province of a monopolistic complex of military-industrial interests.

At the same time, the growing desperation of the capitalist ruling classes before the prospect of the rising socialist challenge made them even more prone to intervene actively wherever revolution reared its head. The result was the frank embrace of the counterrevolutionary principle by Washington and the open articulation of a vast "counter-insurgency" program, linking the programs in "aid," "information" and "defense" to an expanding apparatus of subversion and intervention. At the heart of this network of institutions was the Central Intelligence Agency, a secretive body employing tens of thousands of agents and utilizing an astronomical, concealed budget to dominate and control the key organizations and agencies of social change both at home and abroad.[53]

---

[52] Cf. H. L. Nieburg, *In the Name of Science* (Chicago: Quadrangle Books, 1966), especially Chapter 10, "The Contract State."
[53] As a main instrument in maintaining the overseas empire, the CIA was administered at its highest levels by the most powerful, sophisticated and internationalist sector of the ruling class. Among the firms and foundations whose directors were instrumental in the creation of the CIA or active in its operations were the Ford and Rockefeller Foundations, the Rockefeller Brothers Fund, Inc. Standard Oil, Gulf Oil (a Mellon interest), Corning Glass, United Fruit and the Wall Street law firms of Sullivan and Cromwell, and Milbank, Hope, Hadley and Tweed, and this list is only meant to be suggestive.

Just as the militarization of a large area of the American economic system greatly increased the structural tendencies toward a fascist state, the counter-insurgency program and its expanding clandestine network, operating at all levels of political and cultural life, set up a powerful, parallel momentum toward totalitarian control. For the outlook developed and the techniques employed in maintaining an empire abroad could not be segregated from the approach to social conflict and the maintenance of the corporate empire at home, particularly when the social struggles were not themselves distinct.

Similarly, the liberal-racist ruling coalition, on which U.S. imperialist policy had depended throughout the century,[54] could not be dissolved to clear the way for the drastic reform of domestic racist institutions at a time when the pressure on the overseas empire was so great. The permanence of a fascist political base in the right wings of the Democratic and Republican parties was thus assured. Thus, too, the expansion of the domestic police forces and their arsenals of anti-"riot" weaponry, coupled with the resistance to structural reform, was only the domestic side of the intensified repression in answer to the demand for social change abroad.

These developments would tend to be less portentous if the economic expansion of the domestic system were itself assured. But the domestic economic system does not exist in a vacuum, and the tightening up of alternatives globally was

---

[54] This coalition in its present form dates from the post-Civil War compromise of 1877, when Northern industrial capital moved to save the plantation aristocracy from radical social reconstruction. No detailed study of the role of the coalition in U.S. imperialist expansion exists, but the prominence of upper-class Southerners in the military, the State Department and at the head of key Congressional committees dealing with military and foreign affairs is evidence of its importance. On the formation of the coalition, compare Barrington Moore, *op. cit.*, pp. 146–49; also C. Vann Woodward, *Reunion and Reaction* (Garden City, N.Y.: Anchor Books, 1956).

not accidentally matched with a narrowing margin of flexibility at home. Intensified competition from the revived capitalist powers of Western Europe and Japan for markets shrinking before the tremendous expansion of productive forces; intensified pressure from the industrial working classes pushing up wage levels and raising a political barrier to large-scale unemployment; spiraling inflation and mushrooming monetary crisis—all pointed to a period of increased instability for international capitalism, a consequent loss of options in dealing with the cumulative social crises, and hence a mounting pressure to abandon the democratic process and its forms.

Precisely because it expresses the deeper crisis of the social order and the moribund nature of the bourgeois epoch, the growing crisis of democratic power in the world capitalist system poses the central issues of the crises in both the national and international realms: on the one hand, the root injustices and irrationalities of a system in which social production and distribution remain beyond social control; on the other, the criminal character and military dangers of foreign policies of overseas expansion, armed repression and global counterrevolution on behalf of immensely powerful financial-corporate oligarchies.

By posing on the national level the central issues of the international conflict, by linking the international struggle for self-determination with the internal quest for social equality and social control, the crisis of democracy increasingly presents itself as the revolutionary crisis of the epoch. The movement for the sovereignty of the people within the imperial nation coincides with the struggle for self-determination in the international sphere. Just as domestically the demand for democratic power is a demand to overthrow the corporate ruling class and to make the productive apparatus responsive to social needs, so internationally the precondition of democratic sovereignty and inter-state coexistence is the dissolution of the government of the international corporations and financial institutions which have expropriated the sovereignty of nations in order to appropriate the wealth of the world.

The struggle which the Bolsheviks began more than half a century ago is still in its early stages—indeed, in a sense, is just beginning. The awakening of the consciousness of the peoples, particularly in the West, to the catastrophe of capitalism's continued rule and domination has been a slow and fitful process. But the contradiction between means and ends in the present era is reaching hitherto unimaginable proportions. More than ever before, for humanity to live under capitalism is to live on borrowed time. For the continuing world-wide oppression of class, nation and race, the incalculable waste and untold misery, the unending destruction and preparation for destruction and the permanent threat to democratic order that characterize the rule of capitalism in this, its most technically advanced, most "enlightened" and most materially wealthy era now threaten human survival itself. In the age of atomic weapons and intercontinental missiles, the predatory system of imperialist rivalry and global exploitation, of military intervention and counterrevolutionary war, faces mankind with the prospect of the ultimate barbarism.

Liberation is no longer, and can be no longer, merely a national concern. The dimension of the struggle, as Lenin and the Bolsheviks so clearly saw, is international: its road is the socialist revolution.

Bibliography

(Like the bibliography cited in the footnotes, the following list is meant to be selective. It does not represent a comprehensive account of works consulted in the writing of this book.)

Anderson, Perry, and Robin Blackburn. *Towards Socialism.* Ithaca: Cornell University Press, 1966.

Baran, Paul. *The Political Economy of Growth.* 2nd ed. New York: Monthly Review Press, 1962.

Baran, Paul, and Paul Sweezy. *Monopoly Capital.* New York: Monthly Review Press, 1966.

Boorstein, Edward. *The Economic Transformation of Cuba.* New York: Monthly Review Press, 1968.

Brady, Robert A. *Business as a System of Power.* New York: Columbia University Press, 1943.

Carr, E. H. *A History of Soviet Russia.* 7 volumes. New York: Macmillan, 1951–60.

Corey, Lewis. *The Decline of American Capitalism.* New York: Covici-Friede, 1934.

Deutscher, Isaac. *Stalin.* 2nd ed. New York: Oxford University Press, 1967.

Deutscher, Isaac. *The Prophet Armed.* New York: Vintage Books, 1965.

Deutscher, Isaac. *The Prophet Outcast.* New York: Vintage Books, 1965.

Deutscher, Isaac. *The Prophet Unarmed.* New York: Vintage Books, 1965.

Deutscher, Isaac. *The Unfinished Revolution.* New York: Oxford University Press, 1967.

Domhoff, G. William. *Who Rules America?* Englewood Cliffs, New Jersey: Prentice-Hall, 1967.

Fanon, Frantz. *The Wretched of the Earth.* New York: Grove Press, 1966.

Fitch, R., and M. Oppenheimer. *Ghana: End of an Illusion.* New York: Monthly Review Press, 1966.

Gerassi, John. *Venceremos: The Speeches and Writings of Che Guevara.* New York: Macmillan, 1968.

Gruber, Helmut. *International Communism in the Era of Lenin.* New York: Fawcett, 1967.

Hacker, Louis. *The Triumph of American Capitalism.* New York: McGraw-Hill, 1965.

Hobson, J. A. *Imperialism.* Ann Arbor: University of Michigan Press, 1965.

Lenin, V. I. *Collected Works.* 33 volumes. London: Lawrence and Wishart, 1960–1968.

Luxemburg, Rosa. *The Russian Revolution.* Ann Arbor: University of Michigan Press, 1961.

Magdoff, Harry. *Economic Aspects of U.S. Imperialism.* Pamphlet. New York: Monthly Review Press, 1966.

Malcolm X. *Malcolm X Speaks.* New York: Grove Press, 1965.

Mandel, Ernest. *Marxist Economic Theory.* New York: Monthly Review Press, 1968.

Mao Tse-tung. *Selected Works.* 4 volumes. Peking: 1965.

Marx, Karl, and Friedrich Engels. *Selected Works.* Moscow: Foreign Languages Publishing House, 1962.

Miliband, R., and J. Saville. *The Socialist Register 1964–1968.* 5 volumes. New York: Monthly Review Press, 1968.

Mills, C. Wright. *The Power Elite.* New York: Oxford University Press, 1956.

Moore, Barrington, Jr. *Social Origins of Dictatorship and Democracy.* Boston: Beacon Press, 1967.

Neumann, Franz. *Behemoth.* London: Gollancz, 1942.

Norman, E. H. *Japan's Emergence as a Modern State.* Vancouver, B.C.: Institute of Pacific Relations, 1940.

Oglesby, Carl. "Vietnamese Crucible," in *Containment and Change.* New York: Crowell Collier & Macmillan, 1967.

Perlo, Victor. *The Empire of High Finance.* New York: International Publishers, 1956.

Preobrazhensky, E. *The New Economics.* New York: Oxford University Press, 1965.

Sartre, Jean-Paul. *Search for a Method.* New York: Knopf, 1964.

Sweezy, Paul. *The Theory of Capitalist Development.* 2nd. ed. New York: Monthly Review Press, 1962.

Trotsky, Leon. *Permanent Revolution, and Results and Prospects.* New York: Pioneer, 1967.

Trotsky, Leon. *The History of the Russian Revolution.* New York: Macmillan, 1967.

Trotsky, Leon. *The Revolution Betrayed.* New York: Pioneer, 1965.

Van Alstyne, R. W. *The Rising American Empire.* Chicago: Quadrangle Books, 1965.

Williams, William A. *The Tragedy of American Diplomacy.* New York: Delta Books, 1962.

Index

Acheson, Dean, 233–4

Agency for International Development, 111 and *n*

Alliance for Progress, 111, 228–230, 246–8

Anti-Comintern Axis, 68, 79, 175

Arms, Western expenditure on, and prosperity, 85–7, 235, 250–1

Atomic bomb, initial test of, 73, and Western offensive, 74–5, 200; Russian possession of deters attack on China, 141

Badoglio regime, 74, 189

Baltic states, and cordon sanitaire, 66, and defense of Russia, 70, and absorption by Russia, 193 and *n*

Bandung Conference of 1955, 208

Baran, Paul, 107, 108 et seq.

Base-superstructure model, and Bolsheviks 17; and Mensheviks 21f; and German/Japanese development 48–49

Belated bourgeois revolution, 24–6; and Russia, 26, 97–8, 118–19; and chauvinistic nationalism, 42–5; and underdeveloped world, 48, 107–8; and Germany, 24–26, 48, 118–19; and Japan,

Belated bourgeois revolution (*continued*)
48; and China, 104–5, 162–4; and permanent revolution, 27–8, 101–6; 163–4; and fascism, 175–9; and imperialist conflict, 180–1

Bolshevik insurrection, 64

Bolshevik Marxists, 5–7, 17f, 21f, 29

Bolshevik Party, and Revolution in Russia 7, 104; and U.S. attitude to, 62; and aftermath of Civil War, 125–9; and socialism in one country, 130–3; and Soviet reality, 144–8

Bolshevik Peace Decree, 7; Woodrow Wilson's reaction to, 15

Bourgeois revolutions, failure of, in underdeveloped world, 95–6; 114–15; in Russia, 101–2, 199; in China 104–5; in Germany, 118–119; in Greece, 183–4; in Cuba, 245–7; in Latin America 246–8

Britain, bourgeois revolution and development of, 23–4, 48, 174; free trade empire and, 33; imperialism of, 44*n*, 91; anti-Communist intervention in Greece by, 72, 74, 183–4; in Vietnam,

DAVID HOROWITZ is the author of *Student: The Political Activities of the Berkeley Students*, a systematic appraisal of Marxism from the activist perspective of the New Left, as well as *The Free World Colossus* and *Marx and Modern Economics*. In addition, Mr. Horowitz wrote *Shakespeare: An Existential View*. He has also edited three collections of essays.

He was graduated from Columbia University and received an M.A. from the University of California at Berkeley. From 1963 to 1965, he was director of research for the Bertrand Russell Peace Foundation in London. Mr. Horowitz, a senior editor of *Ramparts,* now lives in Berkeley with his wife and their four children.

VINTAGE POLITICAL SCIENCE
AND SOCIAL CRITICISM

A free catalogue of VINTAGE BOOKS *will be sent at your request. Write to* Vintage Books, 457 Madison Avenue, New York, New York 10022.